Praise for *Learning to Breathe*

~

"Warner deftly describes her various treatments. She delves into painful family memories and recounts her panic attacks in detail. For those readers who have experienced this debilitating condition, or who have family members who have . . . insightful."

—*Publishers Weekly*

"Wise, searching, fearless, and bighearted, Priscilla Warner's search for inner peace will resonate with anyone who has ever been anxious or at sea—in other words, all of us. She is a comforting and stabilizing guide through her own life—and ours. This book is a gift."

—Dani Shapiro, author of *Devotion: A Memoir*

"The words leap off the page. Priscilla Warner's courageous story from panic to peace brims with insights that light the path to simply living a better life."

—Elisha Goldstein, Ph.D., author of *The Now Effect*

"A fascinating tale of courage, perseverance, and resolve. In lucid and entertaining prose—with several laugh-out-loud moments—Warner is a travel guide for the anxious and the wounded, leading us from a life of fear and burden to a perspective of freedom and wonder. Her story is a gift to anyone determined to find peace."

—Therese Borchard, author of *Beyond Blue: Surviving Depression & Anxiety and Making the Most of Bad Genes*

Also by Priscilla Warner

The Faith Club
by Ranya Idliby, Suzanne Oliver, and Priscilla Warner

Learning to Breathe

My Yearlong Quest
to Bring Calm to My Life

Priscilla Warner

Free Press

New York London Toronto Sydney New Delhi

Free Press
A Division of Simon & Schuster, Inc.
1230 Avenue of the Americas
New York, NY 10020

For information about special discounts for bulk purchases, please contact Simon
& Schuster Special Sales at 1-866-506-1949 or business@simonandschuster.com.

The Simon & Schuster Speakers Bureau can bring authors to your live event. For
more information or to book an event contact the Simon & Schuster Speakers
Bureau at 1-866-248-3049 or visit our website at www.simonspeakers.com.

Manufactured in the United States of America

5   7   9   10   8   6   4

Library of Congress Cataloging-in-Publication Data
Warner, Priscilla.
Learning to breathe: my yearlong quest to bring calm to my life /
Priscilla Warner.
p. cm.
Includes bibliographical references.
1. Warner, Priscilla—Health. 2. Panic attacks—Alternative treatment.
3. Anxiety disorders—Treatment. 4. Meditation. I. Title.
RC535.W37 2011

616.85'223—dc22   2011008429

ISBN 978-1-4391-8107-2
ISBN 978-1-4391-8109-6 (ebook)

NOTE TO READER

This book is an account of experiences I shared with many wonderful people. It's based on my recollections, as well as tape recordings I made of conversations and therapy sessions and careful notes I took during teaching sessions. In a few instances, the names and/or identifying characteristics of some people have been changed.

With Boundless Gratitude

to

Jimmy

Max and Jack

Riva and Paul

May all travelers find happiness
Everywhere they go,
And without any effort may they accomplish
Whatever they set out to do.

~

—Shantideva, *A Guide to the Bodhisattva's Way of Life*

Contents

❧

HOW TO LIVE

HOW TO LOVE

HOW TO DIE

How to Live

1

Takeoff

Slumped in my airplane seat, I could barely see enough of Tulsa, Oklahoma, to say goodbye to it in the early morning darkness. The plane took off and I was headed home to New York on the last leg of an intense three-year lecture tour. I opened a magazine . . . and there were the monks—yet again.

Dressed in crimson robes, their heads shaved, serene Tibetan men stared out at me from a photograph. These same men had been inadvertently haunting me for years, because they had found an inner peace that had eluded me for so long. While I'd been experiencing debilitating panic attacks and anxiety for decades, they had been meditating so effectively that their prefrontal brain lobes lit up on MRI scans, plumped up like perfectly ripe peaches.

That's not precisely the way the monks' brains were described in the medical studies I'd read about, but that's how I imagined them—happily pregnant with positive energy. Unlike my brain, which felt battered and bruised, swollen with anxiety, adrenaline, heartache, and hormones.

"I want the brain of a monk!" I decided right then and there.

I also wanted everything that went along with that brain—peace and tranquility, compassion and kindness, wisdom and patience. Was that too much to ask for?

And so my mission was born.

I became determined to get my prefrontal lobe to light up like the monks' lobes, to develop a brain that would run quietly and smoothly, instead of bouncing around in my skull like a Mexican jumping bean. Some people set up meth labs in their basements, but I wanted a Klonopin lab in my head, producing a natural version of the drug my therapist had prescribed for me several years earlier, to help me cope with chronic anxiety and panic.

I had already been searching for serenity on and off for forty years, during which I'd traveled to Turkey and toured the ancient caves of early Christian mystics, read Rumi's exquisite Sufi poetry, and learned about the mysteries of Kabbalah. I regularly drank herbal tea and lit incense in my bedroom. And I'd gotten my meridians massaged while my chakras were tended to by soft-spoken attendants at occasional spa splurges.

I would have loved to travel to Nepal to find inner peace, sitting at the feet of a monk on a mountaintop, but I panic at high altitudes. I didn't want to move to a monastery, but I figured there were dozens of things I could do in my own backyard that could make me positively monk-like. So I decided to try behaving like a monk while still shopping for dinner at my local suburban strip mall. And I decided to chronicle my adventures.

This full-scale brain renovation would take some time, planning, improvisation, and hard work. Still, I hoped, if I exercised my tired gray cells properly, on a sustained, regular basis, and fed my brain all sorts of good things like meditation, guided imagery, yoga, macrobiotic stuff, and Buddhist teachings, maybe it would change physically. I'd heard *neuroplasticity* thrown around in scientific reports, a term that means that the brain is supposedly able to transform itself at any age. Perhaps mine would be like Silly Putty—bendable and pliable and lots of fun to work with.

What did I have to lose? I shifted in my airplane seat, the monks still gazing up at me from the photograph.

On the outside, I was functioning just fine: I was a happily married mother of two terrific sons. I'd traveled to more than fifty cities around the country to promote a bestselling book I'd coauthored, called *The Faith Club*. But inside, the anxiety disorder I'd battled all my life had left me exhausted, out of shape, and devouring chocolate to boost my spirits and busted adrenal glands. My body and heart ached for my children, who had left the nest, and my mother, who was in her ninth year of Alzheimer's disease, confined to the advanced care unit of her nursing home. Twenty years earlier, my father had died from cancer; but he'd been just about my age when the tumor had started its deadly journey through his colon.

Clearly, I was facing my own mortality. Although I wanted to run like hell away from it.

In another rite of passage, a wonderful therapist I had seen for many years had died recently, and I had attended her memorial service. When I'd arrived at the Jewish funeral home, a woman with a shaved head, dressed in a simple dark outfit, had greeted me. Although her smile was kind, her presence initially threw me off. Was she Buddhist? Was she a nun? Did her brain light up on an MRI scan, too?

After greeting people at the entrance to the chapel with a calm that put everyone at ease, she conducted the proceedings with warmth, wit, and sensitivity, urging people to speak about our deceased friend. I took her appearance to be a message from my late shrink.

"Go for it," I imagined her saying. "Go find your inner monk."

I didn't know the difference between my dharma and my karma, but I was willing to learn. Perhaps I'd define other terms for myself, like *mindfulness, lovingkindness,* and maybe even *true happiness.* I'd try whatever techniques, treatments, and teachings I thought might move me along the road from panic to peace.

His Holiness, the Dalai Lama, believes human beings can change the negative emotions in their brains into positive ones.

And who was I to doubt the Dalai Lama?

Maybe my journey would resemble something like *Siddhartha* meets *Diary of a Mad Jewish Housewife.*

Forget "Physician, Heal Thyself," I decided as my plane landed in New York and my daydreaming turned into a reality.

My new mantra would be "Neurotic, heal thyself (and please stop complaining)."

2

Bowls Are Ringing

When you're ready to learn, your lessons find you in the oddest places. Like behind the Hertz car rental desk at San Francisco International Airport.

To celebrate the end of *The Faith Club* tour, I had flown out to California to visit my sister and some friends. A tall, friendly Hertz employee was finishing up my paperwork when he noticed a brightly colored necklace I was wearing. "You should go to this Tibetan store in Haight-Ashbury," he told me.

I was taken aback. How did this man know I yearned to be a serene Tibetan monk?

He gave me my car keys and an approximate address for Tibet Styles, which I scribbled down on my rental agreement. I was always up for a shopping adventure.

Three days later, I decided to follow the Hertz man's advice. My friend Judy drove me over to Haight-Ashbury, and we walked up and down the busy streets looking for Tibet Styles. A young man in a coffeehouse pointed us in the right direction. "Say hi to Dolma for me," he said. "She's an awesome lady."

Tucked into a block of tattoo parlors, record stores, and windows displaying groovy merchandise from the 1960s, Tibet Styles was a quiet haven, full of colorful jewelry, scarves, and woven wall hangings. We took our time examining necklaces made from silver and semiprecious stones, as we made our way to the back of the shop, where dozens of brass bowls were stacked up on a table.

I picked up a heavy copper bowl, and the suede-covered mallet beside it. "Push the mallet around the rim," Judy suggested with a smile. "See what happens."

I began rubbing the rim of the bowl with the mallet. But absolutely nothing happened. A small Tibetan woman about my age stepped out from behind the cash register. She wore a colorful, striped apron and her dark hair pulled back in a bun. "Not so fast," she said, taking the bowl out of my hand. "Like this." Gently, she rubbed the outer rim with the mallet. "You see? Very slowly."

The bowl began to hum, softly at first, and then loud enough to fill the small store with its sound, even above the chanting music on the CD that was playing in the background. The woman struck the bowl softly and it made a perfect, deep, complex "gongggg." Handing the bowl back to me, she said, "Now you try."

I rubbed the bowl with the mallet, producing nothing more than silence. The Tibetan woman left me to help a customer buying earrings. I picked up another bowl and pushed the mallet around the rim. Still no sound. Judy picked up a bowl, and of course it sang for her immediately.

The store owner came back as I picked up another bowl, dark bronze with a green patina. "Slowly, slowly!" She took the bowl out of my hands, rubbed the rim gently, and it sang in an instant.

I felt like a loser. Or whatever that word was in Tibetan.

I picked up one bowl after another, trying to make each one sing, to no avail. "Slowly, slowly. You're moving too fast," the woman kept saying. "Hold your palm flat. Don't touch the bowl with your fingers." She manipulated my hand to make every bowl sit firmly on my palm, but still I failed at Singing Bowl 101.

Finally she picked up a medium-sized, light brass bowl and handed it to me. "Try this."

I moved the mallet around the rim as slowly as I could, fearing that I was so neurotic and out of touch with my spiritual side that I wouldn't be able to clink a Tibetan bowl, let alone make it sing.

But then the bowl began speaking to me. It came alive in my hand, humming steadily. Then I struck it with the mallet. "Gongggg." Its powerful vibration moved up my arm, straight into my heart. I had found my bowl.

"You did it!" Judy exclaimed.

"Good," the Tibetan woman said, as if she knew I'd accomplish this all along. She moved back behind the cash register to help another customer.

I caressed my bowl lovingly. I was not a miserable failure. I could make a bowl sing. My karma wasn't so crummy after all.

The Tibetan woman came back. "Is that it?" she asked. "You'll take the bowl?"

"Is it the right one?" I asked.

"Yes, yes. That's it."

"The others are too hard for me?" My inner New Yorker was determined to turn bowl ringing into a competition.

"It's a good bowl, yours." The woman had spoken; the deal was done. I followed her over to the cash register, clutching my bowl. I made it sing again and smiled.

"I really need this," I blurted out. "I mean the bowl. I need some peace."

The woman calmly pulled out a shopping bag. "I want to learn how to meditate," I said. "Do you have any CDs that could help me?" The men chanting in the background music sounded as if they could impart some kind of peace.

"What's your name?" Judy asked the proprietor.

"My name's Dolma," the woman answered, turning back to me. "Do you like this music?"

I listened again, then shook my head. "No, thanks."

The chanters sounded too happy. I needed the equivalent of a Tibetan drill sergeant to put me through my paces. Whoever I brought home with me to soothe my troubled soul had their work cut out for them.

Dolma handed me a CD with a picture of the Gyuto Monks on the cover, then popped their disk into her player. The lowest, most guttural sounds I'd ever heard human beings make punched me in the gut. In a good way.

"I like this," I said, studying the portrait of the somber men clad in maroon robes, with shaved heads. My future drill sergeants stared out at me, looking like they meant business.

"This is good for you. Very strong. You need that." Dolma positioned herself squarely in front of me, taking hold of my shoulders. "You are a very calm person," she said.

Judy burst out laughing.

"No, she *is* very calm," Dolma insisted.

I knew exactly what she meant. Even though I'd suffered panic attacks for forty years, deep down inside, I knew I could be calm.

Judy had to leave for an appointment, so we said our goodbyes. But I had time to dawdle with Dolma.

And in her quiet, otherwise empty store Dolma had time to tend to me. She took my hands in hers and looked me straight in the eye. I never questioned what this stranger was doing. "You are full of compassion," Dolma said, standing still as a statue, in front of me.

"I don't know." I was embarrassed. "I'm not so compassionate. I'm just . . ."

"You *are* compassionate," Dolma repeated. "That's a *good* thing."

"I'm just . . ."

Dolma's grip on my hands tightened. Tears rolled down my

cheeks, slowly at first, then in a steady stream. But I didn't say a word and I didn't wipe away my tears, because I didn't want to take my hands away from Dolma's hands. She was holding on to mine so tightly.

"Oh, oh," she said. "It's okay. You have deep compassion for people. You feel their pain very strongly."

"I'm just trying to get through the day . . ." I sighed. "It's just hard."

"Why is it so hard?" she asked.

"I suffer from panic attacks. I have for many years. And my mother . . ." I paused.

"Your mother?"

"My mother has Alzheimer's. She's in a nursing home."

Dolma dropped my hands and scurried behind her counter to pick up a set of wooden beads. She closed her eyes, pushing the beads back and forth quickly along their cord, muttering prayers.

"It's okay," Dolma said. "Everything will be okay. It will be fine, you will be fine . . ." Her fingers flew faster than any fingers I'd ever seen. "And your mother? She will be fine."

I wanted to believe her.

Over and over again Dolma murmured to herself, or God, or the universe, with closed eyes. Occasionally she hummed. I stood dry-eyed, watching, fascinated, not understanding a word.

Dolma finished with her prayer beads, put them down, and stepped out from behind the counter, placing my hands in hers once more. Her hands were sturdy, slightly calloused but soft. The hands of a hardworking, hard-praying woman.

"Let it go," she said, standing before me, holding my hands tightly, staring into my eyes. "Let it go."

Let *what* go?

"Let it go," Dolma murmured. "Let all of your suffering drain out of you. Let your pain leave your body. Give it up. Let it go."

I looked deep into Dolma's dark eyes and held on to her strong hands as she began praying or chanting again, still holding my hands, nodding her head as she pulled on them gently.

I took a deep, jagged, uneven breath.

And then I let go.

Of pain and sadness, exhaustion and fear. Of disappointment and heartache. Of nursing homes and my mother's confused face, of my empty nest with my children gone, of my aging body's aches and pains. I let go of my yearning for youth, for happiness, for perfection, for a life with no suffering.

I let go of it all.

In a small, quiet store in San Francisco, I felt all of the suffering drain out of my fingertips, into Dolma's hands, and out into the world, into the great unknown.

And for just an instant, in the hands of a stranger, I experienced the tiniest hint of what it would feel like to be lighter.

3

Panicky Pris

Lightness was not something I had ever truly experienced before meeting Dolma. Panic was my comfort zone. And my nemesis.

I'd suffered my first panic attack when I was a fifteen-year-old waitress, working behind the grease-splattered, stainless steel serving counters of the Brown University cafeteria.

For a few weekends that fall, my friends and I had left the cocoon of the all-girls' high school we attended in Providence, Rhode Island, and set our sights on the boys at Brown. We worked in the dining halls until incoming students were hired to take over our jobs. Back then, Brown was an all-male school. As I dished out mystery meat in my aqua blue polyester uniform, I gawked at the opposite sex, pretending not to care what they thought of me.

Forty years ago, no one ever used the term *panic attack,* including me. No one talked about anxiety disorders or spilled their guts on national television. So I had no idea what was happening to me on that otherwise ordinary September day, when I showed up for work and then almost died. One minute I was dishing out faded green peas to masses of bored young men, and the next minute I was fading out, gasping for air. A bolt of electricity had shot up my arms, into my chest, locking my lungs in a vise. My heart pounded desperately. My whole body shook. I broke into a cold sweat. Stepping back from the counter, I tried to take a deep breath.

But I couldn't. I tried to swallow, but I couldn't do that, either. My tongue felt thick, and it was blocking my throat.

I panicked. I gulped. I gasped. I tried taking a deep, life-sustaining breath, but all I could inhale were little puffs of nothingness. I felt dizzy. The faces of the boys in line froze, but my thoughts raced as I gulped and gasped, thinking, What happens when your body gets no oxygen? Could I pass out? Keel over? Could I die?

Was I dying?

Mechanically, I tried to resume dishing out peas, but my hands shook noticeably.

"Calm down," I screamed to myself. But my body would not obey my commands.

I dropped my spoon, teetered away from my station, and staggered back to the kitchen, trying to breathe, over and over again, in giant spasms. My best friend Barbara appeared. I was shaking, holding on to countertops crowded with giant macaroni-and-cheese casseroles. I slumped to the floor, my back against the wall, my useless legs splayed out in front of me. "You look awful," Barbara observed.

"I can't breathe," I managed to whisper.

"Do you want me to call your house?" Barbara hauled me up and over to a desk, dialed my number, and Mrs. Quinn, the housekeeper my parents had recently hired, answered.

"I don't feel well," I said. Mrs. Quinn was not a warm, cuddly woman, but she arranged to meet me.

Barbara herded me out of the cafeteria and down to the street. I shuffled along the sidewalk, trying to take a deep breath, over and over again, shivering and shaking.

When Mrs. Quinn pulled up in her old gray Chevrolet at the appointed corner, Barbara opened the back door and nudged me onto the cracked vinyl seat. I returned home to curl up in my parents' big, empty bed, under the gaze of a giant, glassy-eyed swordfish my father had caught, stuffed, and hung on the wall.

When my parents came home, they called their doctor, who paid a house call and took my vital signs. He wrote me a prescription for a tranquilizer called Librium, remarking that I was "just a little bit nervous."

Just a little?

For the next forty years, panic attacks as dramatic as this one continued to ravage my body. Haunted by a story my parents used to tell me when I was a child, I often worried that one of these attacks might kill me. While other children drifted off to sleep listening to tales of dancing fairies or happy ducklings, for years my parents told me a story I've titled "The Night You Almost Died." Here's how my personal lullabye goes . . .

When I was sixteen months old, my father was on leave from the navy, and we were living in San Diego, California. I developed acute epiglottitis, a dangerous infection in my windpipe. When my fever shot up to 106, my parents took me to a pediatrician's office, where I turned purple and my eyes rolled back in my head. (My mother was an artist, with a flair for dramatic details.)

After watching me suffer one seizure after another, my father was too scared to drive me to the hospital. So he asked the pediatrician to take me with my mother and he followed behind in his car. My parents didn't go into details about the drive, but they did tell me the most important part of the story.

After getting to the hospital, my parents left me there and went home. And as I lay alone in my bed later that night, my airway closed up and I stopped breathing. Fortunately, a resident happened to wander into my room and found me in distress. He performed an emergency tracheotomy, which saved my life. My parents praised him every time they told me this story, which was often. "We were so scared!" they repeated, throughout my childhood. "We were so scared!"

And I became so nervous.

Done with waitressing at Brown, I took a job as a supermarket cashier on Saturdays. Back then, we had to type out the price of every single item, which made me anxious. My father owned the supermarket, which made me even more anxious. Desperate to prove that I deserved the job, I continually fought back panic, until one day I hyperventilated so badly that I had to abandon my register and go home. "You don't have to work there anymore," my father told me when I cried to him that night. He had no advice, however, about how to avoid panicking outside of supermarkets.

Which I did. A lot.

I hid my shameful condition from my father and everyone else in my life. For the next ten years, I carried a flask of vodka with me everywhere, taking a swig when I felt the telltale signs of an impending panic attack—a pounding heart, tingling hands, trouble breathing. The fiery liquid filled my chest cavity with warmth, and eventually calmed me down. I'd chosen vodka because I thought it was odorless. If I'd known it wasn't, I'd have panicked even more at the thought that people might know I was drinking.

When it came time to go to college, I became anxious about leaving my friends and family. I spent much of my time at the University of Pennsylvania sitting in the back of large lecture halls, so that I could bolt out the doors of the auditorium if I started to panic. When I was in smaller classes, I also took Valium, a new drug that an internist had prescribed, which I carried with me everywhere. My magic yellow pills were a lot easier to hide than my flask, and they didn't slosh around in my purse.

When I graduated from Penn, I began a job at an advertising agency in Boston as an art director. I enjoyed creating magazine ads and television commercials, but I was terrified of making presentations to our clients—which took me close to panic. Valium masked my fear well enough, but inside I felt like a fraud.

I met my husband, Jimmy, in a crowded bar, and we fell in love at first sight. That did wonders for my central nervous system. But when I tried to be adventurous and flew with Jimmy to France, I suffered a massive panic attack in our room at a lovely, small hotel after we'd eaten a magnificent dinner, drunk a rich red Burgundy, and consumed fabulous chocolates. My nervous system erupted in the middle of the night, my lungs convulsing in spasms. I was mortified. For the first time, I took a Valium in front of another person, pacing the room until the drug took hold.

We got married, and my husband loved me, neuroses and all. Five years later, I became pregnant, and I did not take a single Valium, although I'd developed high blood pressure in my eighth month and had to be sent to bed on phenobarbitol.

Happily, our first son, Max, was born healthy. But my fifty-eight-year-old father had been diagnosed with cancer. Seeing him through surgeries, radiation, and chemotherapy revved up my nerves, and the more he suffered, the more I panicked, whether I was in hospital waiting rooms or New York City taxicabs. When he died, I was heartbroken, and my panic attacks increased in frequency. I loved being a mother to my sweet son. But it wasn't until two years later that I felt emotionally ready to get pregnant again.

My second pregnancy was basically one long panic attack. My hormones surged, filling my body with terror. I begged my obstetrician to let me take Valium, but he refused. Our second son, Jack, arrived ten days early, as mellow as he could be.

In fact, all three men in our house are generally as mellow as monks. I seem to be anxious for all of them.

Jimmy's career took off and I became a corporate wife, accompanying him to various conferences. One afternoon, I set out in Manhattan to buy some appropriate clothes. Insecure about my ability to play the role I'd been thrust into, and famished since I'd skipped lunch to shop, I began to fall apart in a department store dressing room. I teetered unsteadily to my husband's skyscraper office building which was nearby, and tried to get into an elevator in the lobby.

Over and over again I pushed the button for the thirty-fifth floor, only to dash out of the small black box before the elevator doors closed. Finally I called my husband from a pay phone. "I'm down in your lobby," I croaked.

"Come on up," he said casually.

"I can't!" I burst into tears. "I can't get into the elevator!"

Prince Charming came down to the lobby and escorted me back up to his office, resuming his busy afternoon. I lay on his couch, a sad sack of anxiety with a bright new outfit in a shopping bag. A mass of insecurity whom, thank God, my husband still loved.

Panic attacks followed me everywhere over the next few years, even on vacation on Long Island, on a lovely summer day. "I bet you're the only person who ever popped a Valium on a beach," said my patient, but somewhat confused, husband, shaking his head.

My last panic attack before I set off to become a monk without a monastery took place on a street in Denver before a lecture for *The Faith Club*. One minute I was taking an afternoon stroll by myself, and the next minute my heart took off, galloping, and I started hyperventilating.

I sat down on a cold concrete stairwell and tried to talk myself out of a panic attack.

"Slow down!" I hissed.

I tried counting my breaths, but my frantic lungs ignored my commands, convulsing. I felt like I was going to throw up. I was shivering and shaking. And yet . . .

A still, small voice inside my brain spoke to me. "This is not your fault. You are not going crazy. You are not dying. You are not weak, or terrifyingly different from the rest of the world. You are a woman who has suffered hundreds of panic attacks. This is just one more."

It came to me that I was suffering from altitude sickness. I needed water and rest. I fished a Klonopin out of the depths of my purse, swallowed it, and staggered back to the friend's house where I was staying. I was a walking science experiment.

I drank several glasses of water, lay down, and called my internist to see if I should take some potassium, which he'd prescribed to counteract diuretics I was taking for high blood pressure. My body chemistry was out of whack.

As I rested up for that night's speaking engagement, I thought about how I would be surrounded by people of all faiths, eager to connect. I remembered what a woman at a book signing near Detroit had said to me: "The next time you fly over Michigan, I want you to look down at the ground below and remember how many people love you." Then she handed me her father's worn University of Michigan sweatshirt to treasure forever.

I'd been too moved to speak.

While pouring my heart out to thousands of people at our lectures, I hadn't always been able to receive the love flowing back my way. "I want to turn inward, I want to become a mystic," I'd begun to joke, without really knowing what a mystic was. It was finally time to find out.

I had managed to make several more trips across the country after my panic attack in Denver, and then the monks climbed on board with me on that fateful flight home from Tulsa. Somewhere in the skies over Oklahoma, that still, small voice inside my brain reappeared and told me that I would be okay. I flew home with my guardian monks meditating happily inside my magazine, and I landed in New York with a plan.

4

My Demons

⌒∞⌒

All religions and spiritual quests begin with the cry "Help!" according to William James. To help me meditate my way from panic to peace, a psychotherapist friend referred me to Tara Brach, a Buddhist meditation teacher and clinical psychologist whose audio lectures can be found online. Brach defines *courage* as "the willingness to stay with fear a little bit longer." Many people, says Brach, live in a "trance of fear," in which the mind is constantly anticipating what can go wrong. As Mark Twain wrote, "The worst things in life never actually happened." These people were talking my language.

Tara tells the story of a Tibetan meditation master who returns to his cave one day to discover that demons have taken it over. Bravely, he scares them away, but one powerful, stubborn demon refuses to leave. So the meditation master thrusts his head into the mouth of the demon.

Wow. That wasn't something I could do in this lifetime. Slay demons? I could barely shop for pantyhose in a department store. Buzzing fluorescent lights set my nervous system on fire and competed with the bees in my brain.

For years, I'd been battling my own demons, but I was no brave warrior. Every time panic struck, until that last attack in Denver,

I'd been scared that I was dying. But what scared me more than that was the possibility that I was going crazy—like many of my relatives.

My father was diagnosed as manic-depressive right around the time that I had my first panic attack. "It's a mild case," he reported to me, in a state of some optimism. Overwhelmed with the task of running a demanding family business, my father was also navigating a complicated marriage to my mother, who, according to him, was a "narcissist." Of course, my mother threw the word right back at him, claiming that he was the narcissist. If I'd known what that loaded word meant, I might have suggested they both take a good look in the mirror.

Our household, to put it kindly, was unconventional. Boundaries were constantly crossed, and borders violated, while my parents discussed their psychiatric diagnoses with me. Looking back, I should have charged them by the hour.

I sometimes fantasized about who my mother and father might have married if they'd never met. I often felt they could have been happier with other people, especially when they enlisted me as their confidante, enumerating their frustrations with each other and life in general.

Back then, I was fascinated with a popular TV show called *Queen for a Day,* on which unhappy housewives vied for prizes like new washing machines by recounting their sad stories to a studio audience, who voted for the most miserable contestant. These women were more fun to be with than my battling parents—and they got applause for their dramas.

"Not only am I psychic, but I also read tarot cards," my mother used to announce to people, making my skin crawl. She'd also tell me, "Nobody understands me. I'm different than everyone else." But I'd already figured that out.

My mother had grown up in Hollywood, California, a fact

she was proud of her whole life. She used to trick or treat at W. C. Fields's house and drink Coca-Colas at Schwab's. Her cousin won four Oscars for cinematography. Her father, who worked on the technical side of the film business, arranged for her to make a cameo appearance as a street urchin in a Bing Crosby movie.

Mom met my father on the steps of the library at UCLA, where they were both students. Dad had grown up in Massachusetts and gone to prep school, so perhaps the difference in their backgrounds seemed exciting to them at first. They became engaged three weeks after they met, and after they finished college, they got married and flew across the country to start their new life together.

My mother never got over leaving Hollywood. She dodged a bullet when she refused to move with my father to Fall River, Massachusetts, the dreary mill town where his family lived, and they settled in Providence, a college town where Brown University and the Rhode Island School of Design provided a measure of sophistication and stimulation. But Hollywood it wasn't.

Pictures of my mother in the 1950s show her in housewife garb, smiling for the camera, although I imagine her constantly plotting her escape from that life, if only in her mind. Wife of a successful businessman by day, she held dream analysis workshops in our basement every Friday night when I was a teenager. Strangers would parade through our front door and head downstairs, where a Jungian analyst oversaw their discussions. She took workshops on primal scream therapy and the Silva Mind Control course. She studied I Ching, attended past-life regression workshops, and hung around with diverse, unusual personalities, as if trying them on as alter egos, doing her best to be happy.

She hadn't married into a fun-loving family. The definition of a good time in my father's household was a four-hour Passover seder.

As a child, it seemed to me that my father was weighted down with worry, and that the whole world depended on him. He worked with his uncle Sam in the family supermarket business, toiling long hours to support many nonworking family members. Under enormous pressure, he always came home from work exhausted.

His twin brother, my uncle Nathan, seemed to drain him the most. A sensitive, troubled soul, Nathan had a terrible stutter. I sensed anger stifling his voice, and couldn't help but feel that he was a burden to my father. Literally shaking with anxiety, Uncle Nathan seemed to carry inside him all the pain festering in my father's family. We never saw any of my mother's relatives in far-off California, so I didn't worry much about their kind of crazy.

Dad and Uncle Nathan lived two entirely different lives. While my father worked for his uncle in Providence, Nathan was a bachelor and a poet living an hour away, socializing with other writers and artists. He wrote complex poems I couldn't understand and traveled to our house to attend family dinners that seemed to make him very nervous.

Uncle Nathan suffered on and off from what the adults in the family whispered were "nervous breakdowns." I had no idea what a breakdown was, but there was no hiding the fact that this man was nervous. Whenever I asked my mother what had happened to Nathan, she would describe how "the poor soul" suffered his first breakdown while he was in the navy. By my calculations, that meant I had a few years of sanity ahead of me. But there was another person in my father's family who did haunt me in real time.

Defying the Jewish tradition of never naming babies after living people, my father had named me after his favorite cousin, Priscilla, whose mother was mentally ill and institutionalized. I used to sit next to "the other Priscilla" at occasional family dinners, observing her every move, for clues about how we were alike.

Pretty, with a wide, open face, Priscilla spoke in a soft, fluttery voice and wore bohemian-style skirts and sandals; her light brown hair snaked down her back in a long braid. My father clearly adored her, but as I grew older, my parents began talking about Priscilla in the same hushed tones they had reserved for Nathan. Something had happened to her. She, like Nathan, had "broken down" and was hospitalized.

Terrified that the same thing might happen to me someday, I'd ask about Priscilla, but get stock answers. "Priscilla married a man, and it didn't work out, and they got divorced, and it was just downhill from there," my father said. According to him, the unwanted divorce triggered Priscilla's breakdown. Locked into his own strange dance with my mother, Dad seemed to equate an unhappy marriage with a descent into madness.

"Priscilla was always a little bit off," my mother recalled. "As a child, she used to climb onto her mother's dining room table and dance around naked." Okay. This anecdote gave me some comfort—I had no desire to strip down and perform for my family in our dining room, or anywhere else. But the letters I received periodically from my cousin Priscilla did fuel my own anxiety.

After college, I was basically holding my life together, even enjoying my job at a Boston ad agency, despite the fact that my boyfriend had broken up with me, my father's business had gone bankrupt, and I was battling my panic disorder without much success. At this precarious point in my life, Cousin Priscilla got my address from my mother and began a one-way correspondence with me. In carefully typed letters, Priscilla wrote:

> I wish I could write rightly to you at this time, but it is not feasible. My circumstances are confused and difficult; life right now is a question of sort of hobbling around and man-

aging to make the best of things. There simply is more to do than my nerves and health can cope with.

Yet I was the one seeing a psychiatrist for the first time, clutching a vial of tranquilizers as I rode the T in Boston, hyperventilating everywhere, telling absolutely no one how terrified I was.

"There seems to be no immediate possibility of a let-up as to the pressures that so distress me," Priscilla wrote. "I pray a lot and spend hours each day in bed this way . . . I would never have believed nerves and worry could so work a person up and wear them out. I sometimes get so exhausted from my mental state that I'm ready to go back to sleep before ever getting up."

Over the years, Priscilla became homeless, wandering the country and occasionally leaving packages by my mother's back door, full of items she'd picked out of garbage cans and copies of shrill letters she'd sent to the White House. My namesake was probably schizophrenic, my mother told me. Although she was clearly worse off than I was, I identified with her pain. Finally, in one poignant letter Priscilla released me from it:

There is no need to fret about me. I have the best of care and am managing as well as possible. The fault of things is in the circumstance, darn it, drat it, and what have you . . . there is still room for fun as long as I can discipline and control this monster project,,,,,,but it's awful hard,,,,,,and so, kind of count me out and put me in the shadows, at peace to rest with less, but sending my best thoughts and prayers.

I did try to put Priscilla in the shadows as I pulled my life together, but I saved all of her letters. I understood more about my uncle Nathan's wordless anger and pain when he finally came out of the closet at age sixty-five and lived openly with a man he loved. Still, he and Priscilla lingered in my thoughts and in my central nervous system. Long before vampires became romantic obsessions to teenagers all over America, I had my own two strange guardians, who both terrified and mesmerized me.

5

Be Still My Brain

❦

According to the National Institute of Mental Health, about six million Americans over the age of eighteen suffer from a panic disorder. But since I had never met another soul who suffered the way I did I was sure I was a freak.

The *Diagnostic and Statistical Manual of Mental Disorders* or *DSM*, the shrinks' bible, describes a panic attack clearly: pounding heart, palpitations, accelerated heart rate, sweating, trembling, shaking, the feeling of choking, chest pain or discomfort, nausea or abdominal distress, dizziness, lightheadedness, feelings of detachment from oneself or unreality, the fear of losing control or going crazy, fear of dying, numbness or tingling sensations, chills, and hot flushes.

Just seeing those words used to make me anxious. I'd experienced every symptom on the page. Someone had stolen my tenth-grade diary.

According to the National Alliance on Mental Illness, panic attacks can be set off by factors like chemical or hormone imbalances, drugs or alcohol, and stress or other "situational events," which are often mistaken for heart attacks, heart disease, or respiratory problems.

In other words, life can make you crazy.

The first time I ever saw the term *panic attack* in print was in a magazine article published more than twenty years ago, which linked my nemesis to another condition I had—mitral valve prolapse, a common heart murmur occurring in 5–20 percent of the population. The heart's mitral valve fails to close completely in between beats, and sometimes people with this condition feel their heart fluttering or skipping beats.

An internist I saw in my thirties dismissed the connection between mitral valve prolapse and panic attacks. A cardiologist I saw a few years later felt there might be a link and told me that 15 percent of people with MVP were once thought to have a panic disorder as well, but that statistics were actually "all over the place."

My panic had started before any real data on the disorder were available. Whatever statistics I could piece together were anecdotal, but all my life I'd been developing my own theories. I'd tried to be an unlicensed shrink, scientist, and nutritionist, carrying a flask instead of a diploma.

When I experienced panic just before my monthly periods and during my pregnancies, I figured hormones were at work. When I hyperventilated while playing tennis, I decided that short bursts of running were bad for me; sustained exercise like jogging calmed me down. When I suffered panic attacks shortly after devouring hot chocolate, I deduced that caffeine was the culprit. I stopped drinking coffee and Diet Coke, but could never kick my addiction to chocolate. When I woke up in the middle of the night with a pounding heart, just hours after consuming a bottle of white wine, I linked booze to panic and stopped drinking alcohol.

And when I met a psychotherapist named Dr. Jaeger ten years ago, she wrote me a prescription for a small daily dose of Klonopin, which changed my life.

Longer lasting than Valium, with fewer highs and lows associated with its use, Klonopin was the perfect drug for me. I never abused it and always appreciated it. I had always felt that my central nervous system operated faster than normal, but Klonopin set my inner clock back by just a second, which made all the difference.

Whenever I traveled for my book tour, I packed a little extra Klonopin, and not just for all of the flights I took to cities across the country. Getting up to speak in front of hundreds of people terrified me. When I didn't take the little pill, my heart pounded, my throat closed up, and I was sure I'd have a full-blown panic attack. That would have been mortifying.

"Just take it," my internist told me. "I have CEOs with ice running through their veins who take Klonopin when they speak in public."

Still I felt ashamed that I needed something to calm me down, until a friend told me about a study where the vital signs of actors about to go onstage were compared to those of astronauts ready to get shot into space: their heart rates were identical. "I use the adrenaline rush to fuel my performance onstage," this actress told me. "But if you don't like the feeling, you should make it go away."

As simply as that, my friend made me feel better. She didn't judge me or try to change me; she accepted me for who I was, panic and all.

If only I could do the same.

"Panic is a syndrome," my therapist, Dr. Jaeger, explained. "And any syndrome usually comes from a combination of factors—biological, sociological, and psychological. But you're going to have to understand panic attacks in *you*. Science gives us a lot of the raw information to work with, but how everything applies to you as an individual is a very specific thing, which you'll have to figure out for yourself."

If I could stay still long enough to do that. And that was my next step in becoming a monk—learning to sit still.

6

The Monk Who Knew Panic

On the day after I turned fifty-six, I headed up to Garrison, New York, to give myself a birthday present—the possibility of finding inner peace. I'd signed up for a beginners meditation course led by Yongey Mingyur Rinpoche, a Tibetan monk who had cured his panic disorder with meditation.

I was eager to meet the man who'd written that dread and fear had "followed him like hungry ghosts" when he was a child. On the other side of the globe, this monk had lived in that "trance of fear" I knew all too well.

But he'd broken through. And now I wanted some of what he was having.

As I drove north, on winding country roads, I passed landmarks that were familiar from the time when Jimmy and I had rented a house in the summertime twenty years earlier. Toward the end of my father's life, when he was terminally ill, my parents stayed with us there for long stretches of time. "Do you think you can stockpile memories?" I'd asked Jimmy.

"I don't know if life works that way," my husband answered. But he had helped make that time with my father as happy as possible. Max, then an adorable toddler, brought us all enormous joy. My parents were thrilled to be grandparents.

As I turned into the driveway of the retreat center, I realized that I was breaking my vow to seek enlightenment away from a cloistered life. Instead of becoming a monk in a minivan, I'd be moving into what had once been a monastery, if only for five days. I caught a glimpse of the Hudson River through lush green trees surrounding the property, and the distinctive stone complex of the U.S. Military Academy also came into view on the far shore.

My father had been a military history buff. We'd spent hours touring West Point together, sitting by the cannons overlooking the majestic banks of the Hudson. I parked my car and stared at the military academy, startled at the sudden revelation that I'd be spending five days across the river from my father.

Pulling myself together, I checked in and examined the retreat schedule. Silence would start after dinner every night, continuing through lunch the next day, giving us plenty of time to reflect on what we'd learn. For now I decided to explore the monastery's grounds and walked out the front door, across a huge lawn, to sit down on a bench high above the Hudson.

A handsome blond woman about my age approached me, dressed in khakis and a colorful scarf. A collection of silver charms dangled from a chain around her neck. "Is that West Point?" she asked.

I nodded my head. "Yes."

"It's so strange to be at this retreat, for this peaceful experience, with that other world so close by," she remarked. "My name's Anna," she said, with a lilting, unfamiliar accent. Anna Souza would become one of my most delightful companions on the quest for peace I was beginning.

Anna had spent years studying Buddhism and introducing Tibetan culture to the world as the director of Tibet House in New York City. She'd worked with the Dalai Lama decades earlier. Born in Mexico, she now lives in Colombia.

After eating dinner together in a crowded communal dining hall, Anna and I followed everyone attending the retreat to a large meditation hall. We removed our shoes and piled them neatly in the hallway outside. Then we selected chairs toward the back of the room. Other people claimed cushions on the floor closer to the front of the hall, where a large golden Buddha also sat.

I followed Anna's movements like a rookie baseball player following Babe Ruth, with a certain awe as she draped a beautiful square of paisley fabric over her shoulders. I hadn't packed a shawl. Or a notebook like the one Anna pulled out of her tote bag next. For five days I was reduced to scribbling down notes on the handouts we'd been given when we checked in.

Suddenly the crowd grew quiet. A group of tall men with shaved heads, dressed in crimson robes, entered from a side door. Behind these lamas, or "mother teachers" in Tibetan, walked Yongey Mingyur Rinpoche.

My hero.

Mingyur wasn't a large presence physically, but he was positively radiant. His head was shaved, he wore rimless glasses, and he, too, was dressed in crimson robes.

Mingyur sat down cross-legged on a platform covered with patterned fabrics and cushions, smiling as he adjusted his sitting position.

"Nice place, hunh?" His voice was high-pitched. "This is a five-star retreat!"

The crowd of about 120 people laughed. Some had come from as far away as Texas, Russia, France, Florida, and Washington state.

Mingyur took a sip from a silver thermos. "How is everybody today?" he asked. "Are you a ten? A seven? A zero?" He laughed. "Zero is good . . ."

He cracked himself up and his laughter was infectious.

"So . . ." Mingyur sipped from the thermos, then tilted his head to the side, thinking. "There are three ways to sip water," he said. "First way is to tighten your fingers . . ." He squeezed the thermos as if his fingers would break. *"I should drink this!"* he said, between clenched teeth. His hands shook, spilling water. "Too tight," he said simply, placing the thermos back down on the table.

"Second way to drink . . ." Mingyur slumped deep into his cushions, threw his head back, closed his eyes, and muttered "Oh, I should drink this, but . . . ohhhhh . . ." His head swung back and forth lazily, as he imitated a blissed-out surfer dude. "Maybe next day . . . next year . . . maybe next life . . . And the third way . . ." Mingyur sat up straight in his chair again. "You pick up the water, nicely balanced, and you take a sip . . ." He demonstrated. "You need effort, but you're relaxed."

"This is not the College of Meditation," Mingyur told us, "where you will finish with a degree. Don't worry too much about the result. Good meditation is okay; bad meditation is okay. Try to develop positive motivation. Just say 'I'm going to try my best to meditate.'"

He grinned. "In Tibet, we use this idea to help with meditation: meditate like an old cow pees. Not a steady, strong stream, or it's all gone, too fast! A little bit at a time is good." And then everyone in the room tried his or her best to meditate along with him.

I watched Anna, next to me, put her hands on her knees, close her eyes, and sit still. I copied her. I'd tried various forms of meditation over the years, starting in college with Dr. Herbert Benson's relaxation response technique, a method that involved being very conscious of my breath. That didn't work very well for a girl who hyperventilated. I'd tried reciting a made-up mantra, and also chanted "Om Mane Padme Om" to a tape my mother had once given me. But I'd never tried simply to sit still and meditate.

Actually, it wasn't that simple. My mind jumped around for a few minutes while I wondered what everybody else in the room was doing. And then Mingyur broke the silence. "How was that? Good?" He smiled. "We will learn how to keep our minds balanced," he promised.

I took his word for it. I loved this guy! He was so positive, so eager for others to feel what he was feeling. In his books, he had written that, through meditation, we are looking to increase our compassion, to awaken our hearts and minds. A deepened heart opens the door to compassion. Compassion is the essence of the teaching, or dharma. "We all have goodness," he said quietly. "We all have love, kindness, compassion. Try to recognize it within you."

That night, I slept restlessly in my spare little room, in my twin bed, with its starched sheets. I got up again and again to pee, shuffling barefoot down the dark corridor of the old monastery to the communal bathroom. I was peeing like crazy. Was it all the herbal tea I'd been drinking? Or was it Mingyur's message to meditate like an old cow pees?

The next morning, I felt more awake and aware, somehow. I found Anna in the dining room, where people were eating in silence. I selected oatmeal made from steel-cut oats, hard-boiled eggs in their shells, some blue, some gray, some buttery yellow, and cantaloupe slices from a serving table. I arranged them in a perfect still life on my plate. In that silent dining hall, the food looked more vibrant than I'd ever seen it.

I even liked the oatmeal. I'd always hated the stuff, but this bowl of steel-cut oats was a crunchy revelation. My whole life was changing, even my aversion to oatmeal. Maybe I'd be eating tofu instead of toffee before this retreat was over.

Anna and I walked into the meditation hall for that morning's teachings. Mingyur entered the room just as happy as he'd been the day before. "Now I'm going to teach you about monkey mind," he said, settling into his cushion. "What is monkey mind? It's when thoughts and emotions run around in your brain trying to make problems, like a monkey makes a mess in a grocery store. He takes a bite out of an apple, throws it away, peels a banana . . . messes up all the fruit.

"You have to give your monkey mind a job," Mingyur told us. "And the secret is that monkey mind actually loves having a job! The job you can give it is meditation."

In order to align our bodies, we could sit cross-legged on the floor or on a chair. Our hands could touch our knees, or we could place them one on top of the other lightly, in our laps. Our backs had to be straight and our shoulders open wide, so that energy could flow properly. Our eyes could be closed, although Mingyur suggested we keep them open, so that we could see things while learning not to focus on them but through them.

Who knew there would be so many rules? I was exhausted.

But then I heard something that spoke to me. "Be like a five- or six-year-old child in a museum," Mingyur said. "It's important to maintain awareness, but children don't see every little brushstroke when they look at paintings. They see things with an innocent kind of awareness. They feel joy, but they can't articulate it."

And then he gave us a wonderful suggestion.

"What you're aiming for," Mingyur said, "is the feeling you get when you come home from a long day of work, throw your coat off, and fall down on the couch. Or when you climb to the top of a mountain, sit down, and take in the view. A feeling of relief."

He asked us to sit, think of nothing, and relax. I followed his instructions.

But when we simply rest our minds, he told us, that's not meditation. That's relaxing.

Oy. I was so confused. I needed to relax but not relax. I needed to sit up straight but I loved to slouch. I needed to give my monkey mind a job but I wasn't sure that I could boss him around; he'd been swinging through the tangled vines in my brain freely for forty years.

As we all tried to meditate again, however, I felt a dullness, exhaustion, and lack of restlessness. Maybe this was actually the beginning of something good. Maybe I'd found a little ledge on my climb to the top of a mountain.

At lunch I sat with Eric Swanson, who wrote Yongey Mingyur Rinpoche's books with him. Eric referred to Mingyur as either "Mingyur" or "Rinpoche," the latter of which means "precious one" in Tibetan and signifies the fact that he is a reincarnated lama. Eric told me that Mingyur was as delightful in real life as he was when teaching his students. His brother was also a renowned teacher and their father had been an extraordinary meditation master.

After lunch I tried meditating in front of the golden Buddha statue by myself for almost an hour. I was determined at least to sit still, even if I were not meditating "correctly." But it still wasn't easy—or simple. My knees ached, so I piled two cushions together and sat on top of them. My back ached, so I moved to a padded mat. Then I went back to one cushion. Like Goldilocks, I kept trying to get things just right. As I sat, more people joined me until the hall was full.

Mingyur walked in, sat down, and taught us how to do "object meditation." To keep our minds focused, we meditated while staring at a vase of flowers on a table. I found this much easier than staring into space, where my mind floated around too much.

Mingyur shifted his weight on his cushion and said quietly, "When I was young, I had panic disorder."

Something in the center of my chest stirred.

"Bad story, good ending," said Mingyur, with a quick smile.

"My parents were very nice," he continued. "Beautiful Himalayan mountains, no iPhones or BlackBerrys. Yellow sunrise, with rocks, forests, big mountains, green fields . . ."

"Panic followed me like a shadow," Rinpoche said. "Panic about snowstorms, strangers. Winter winds were very strong." He paused. "We lived in a wooden and stone house, and I was always afraid it would fall down. I used to push on a pillar to keep it standing up. I would run to the caves nearby, to sit and meditate, even though I didn't really know how."

"And when I was thirteen," Rinpoche continued, "I went on a three-year retreat. Very hard. But I learned how to make panic the object of meditation."

He paused and took a sip of water. The hall was silent.

"Panic can become your boss," Rinpoche said. "Or you can make panic your friend. But you can't do it directly. You have to go step by step." I took notes as well as I could, but I had trouble paying attention. My palms were sweaty; my heart was racing. "Your body is like a house," Rinpoche said. "And panic is like a monkey, jumping all over the place."

My monkey mind was getting very close to wrecking my house. I felt like bolting out of the meditation hall, hearing that I had to make friends with my panic demon—even though it might be easier than slaying him.

Then Mingyur switched back to teaching object meditation. I stared at the green patterned shirt of a woman sitting directly in front of me and settled down a little bit. When the session was over, Mingyur left the meditation hall, and the audience filed out quietly. I stayed behind, slightly miserable and fuzzy-headed, still more monkey-minded than monk.

Yongey Mingyur Rinpoche had meditated his way through panic attacks. Of course he had. He came from a long line of enlightened Tibetan meditators. But I was an anxious woman, born to a family whose highest state of health was a healthy share of dysfunction, a clan of Russian Jews with dark, borscht-drinking demons.

I got up from my cushion and walked into the dining hall, where

I found Anna. "Just hearing Rinpoche talk about his panic attacks is making me panicky!" I said to her. "He's a monk, for God's sake! How's somebody like me supposed to get better?"

"It's natural that this would stir up feelings in you," Anna said. "Maybe you should ask for a private audience with Mingyur. You could approach one of the organizers and tell them your history."

I thanked Anna for her advice, went up to my room, and called Jimmy before our silent period began for the evening. "This is so painful," I said. "I'm about to have a panic attack at a retreat where I'm supposed to be getting rid of them! Why did I think coming here would be a good idea?"

Poor Jimmy was just trying to watch the Yankees. But he told me that I was strong, and that I would learn how to meditate.

I lay down on my bed, took some Klonopin, and tried to laugh. I'd been on a retreat for a single day and expected myself to be Deepak Chopra already?

I managed to fall asleep and, when I woke up the next morning, found a text message from Jimmy: "As we say when it gets tough in the world of bicycling: 'Enjoy the climb.'"

After eating breakfast alone in silence, I walked outdoors and discovered a chair underneath a tall oak tree. I sat down and began staring at a bush, just as we'd been taught to focus on flowers, inside the meditation hall.

And I meditated! People walked by, but I paid them no mind. I heard a train in the distance and birds singing overhead, but I didn't focus on them. I imagined I was surfing, barefoot, riding imaginary waves of calmness.

Meditating outdoors felt less intimidating than meditating in a room with a hundred strangers. I could imagine doing it all over the world, anywhere, anytime.

Buoyed by my success, I worked up the courage to ask Mingyur a question in that morning's session, after he'd told us how lucky we were to have problems to meditate on. "Poor monks in Himalayas!" he joked. "They have to come down from the mountains to the villages to find problems. But you have so many right here!"

"I suffer from panic attacks," I found myself saying, my voice a bit shaky. "And the problem with panic is that it builds on itself. So can you teach me how to break it down?"

Mingyur nodded. "Yes," he said. "Look at panic like shaving cream, with lots of little bubbles moving and shifting. We can talk about it more later."

That was it? He seemed to be holding back. Maybe my expectations for this retreat were too high. I started to get scared again, but worked up the courage, at the end of that morning's session, to get in line to ask one of the facilitators of the event if I could have a private audience with Mingyur, as Anna had advised me to do.

As soon as it was my turn to talk, I got terribly anxious. My whole body trembled; my voice shook. "I've been suffering from panic attacks for forty years," I managed to say to the facilitator. "I'm finding this retreat very painful. It's bringing up a lot of bad memories."

"Do you know what the first teaching of the Buddha is?" he asked gently.

"Yes." I'd done a bit of reading. The first teaching of the Buddha is that life is suffering.

"We all suffer," this man told me. "I've suffered, too."

After I received my appointment time, I went back to my room and read about the First Noble Truth of the Buddha: *Birth is suffering, aging is suffering, sickness is suffering, disassociation from the loved is suffering, not to get what one wants is suffering.* In other words, we all suffer.

"Did you get an audience with Rinpoche?" Anna asked brightly, when I met up with her later in the dining hall.

"I almost had a panic attack in front of one of the organizers," I said. "If I was in charge, I wouldn't let me anywhere near Mingyur. I probably came off like a psychopath."

Anna laughed. "I'm sure these people are used to students coming up to them with all kinds of intense feelings," she said. I did recall signing a psychiatric waiver along with a medical one when I registered.

And apparently I did not scare anyone off. After the next morning's teaching session, a list of names, including mine, was read. We were told to come to Mingyur's private quarters at an appointed time, at fifteen-minute intervals.

"I'm so nervous!" I told Anna at lunch. She rolled her eyes. "You've been wanting to meet him!"

"But now I'm scared!" I could barely touch my food.

Anna suggested that I use my ten minutes with Mingyur productively by making a list of questions beforehand to take to my meeting.

"I'm on a mission to transform myself from a neurotic Jew to a serene Tibetan monk," I blurted out to the facilitator I'd met earlier, outside Mingyur's living quarters.

"Why would you want to do that?" he asked, ushering me into an adjacent room. "You're not a monk, and you're not Tibetan. Why not just be the best neurotic Jew you can be?"

I was somewhat taken aback, but then I found myself face-to-face with Yongey Mingyur Rinpoche, who sat in a chair quietly, looking serious.

"I want to be just like you!" I said, taking a seat opposite him. "You're my hero!"

Fortunately Mingyur didn't run for the Himalayas. I told him about my history of panic attacks and that his courage and candor had moved me, and his style of teaching meditation suited me perfectly. He nodded his head.

I told him I had practiced yoga in the past, and planned to explore other methods of stress reduction in support of my meditation practice.

"Good," he said, simply.

Then I pulled out my questions.

Mingyur had taken part in a study conducted by neuroscientists at the University of Wisconsin and meditated inside an MRI machine. "Do you think meditation can cause physical changes in everyone's brain?" I asked.

Mingyur didn't hesitate. "Yes, definitely," he said. "But it takes more than meditation. Do you know the horse and rider?"

I shook my head no.

He explained the analogy. "The horse is your body. It needs yoga, exercise, proper foods, and diet. The rider is the brain. And what it needs is meditation."

"Will I ever be able to meditate on my panic?" I asked. "When I read in your book about the panic you felt as a boy, I cried."

Mingyur looked surprised and touched.

"Yes," he said. "Someday you can meditate on panic. When you're ready."

I felt a connection to a kindred spirit, but still I wanted to make sure that he was a card-carrying member of the Panic Attack Club. "Did you really have full-blown attacks?" I asked.

"Yes, yes," he said. "Panic attacks."

"Did you have physical sensations?"

"Yes."

We compared battle scars. Mingyur put his hands around his neck. "My throat, it closed."

I pointed to my chest. "Did your heart beat fast?"

"Yes," he said. "And I was shaking, and feeling like I was falling and falling. Down and down and down . . ."

"Were you afraid you were going to die?"

"Yes."

Yongey Mingyur Rinpoche was indeed a member of my tribe. He really did feel my pain. "Change your style of meditation all the time," he told me. "And remember that meditation won't always work with panic. Just accept that. Take a breath, do something physical. Exercise."

"Do you really not have panic attacks anymore?" I pressed him.

"I don't have panic," Mingyur said simply. "I do have some of the feelings, the symptoms. But I meditate on them. I work on them."

I thanked him profusely. And then I floated out of the room.

For the rest of the retreat, I believed that I could meditate, and began to get the hang of it. I learned to do walking meditation and to meditate while listening to music. I sat still and I lay down. I meditated outdoors and indoors, alone and with others. I vowed to meditate every day for the next year, for at least twenty minutes, and see how that might change my life. I felt remarkably calm as I drove home from the retreat.

But Mingyur had warned us not to worry if our emotions became strong as a result of our meditation practice, or if we began to see and hear things that seemed unusual. I would remember his words when my life began to shift in eerie, powerful ways.

7

Beginner's Luck

Back home from my first Buddhist retreat, I was eager to test my meditation skills, and so I started in right on my front porch, the afternoon that I arrived home. Sitting in a white wicker chair, I stared into the leaves of a large cherry tree in our front yard, doing the "object meditation" we'd been taught by Mingyur. But I couldn't tune out the birds chirping loudly all over my neighborhood.

Had they always been this vocal? They took over my thoughts, and I decided to switch to listening meditation. I became immersed in the birds' voices as they swelled into a huge chorus.

"Cool," I thought, remembering one of Mingyur's favorite words. With his approach to meditation, I could switch styles midstream, as long as I stayed engaged in "awareness." My brain buzzed along happily for twenty minutes, and my first meditation session in "the real world" was a success. The birds became a gospel chorus, singing joyfully to me.

On my second day home, I raced to the porch when I heard the sound of thunderstorms approaching. The sky cracked open, rain poured down all around me, and I stayed focused on my meditation practice.

In the next couple of weeks, I meditated wherever and whenever I felt like it, determined to meditate every day. I sat on a beach in the afternoon, staring at dozens of sailboats flickering across Long Island Sound. One evening, I meditated in our backyard, with crickets chirping all around me. In the morning, I sat in our sunny kitchen, meditating with our golden retriever Mickey at my feet. I kept my eyes open, which actually helped me to detach from the world around me.

I began to identify the feelings that a true state of meditation elicits. At first the signs are subtle. "I know it when I feel it," I told curious friends. "I feel intensely focused and relaxed at the same time. It's like when I get an eye exam and my optometrist slips all those different lenses over my eyes until, suddenly, everything comes into focus perfectly. I'm not straining or stressed. I'm just where I should be."

Jimmy and I drove up to Martha's Vineyard to visit our cousins, Linda and Jules. When we arrived, after watching seasick kids vomit on the ferry, I announced that I was going to meditate in their living room. Fifteen minutes into my practice, I heard Jimmy come into the room; I recognized his shuffle. Eyes straight ahead, focused on a tree outside the window, I could feel him watching me, but I was not annoyed or distracted; I was focused on being still.

He took a seat on a nearby couch. I meditated for a few more minutes, stretched my legs, and asked, "Were you watching me?"

Jimmy laughed.

"Meditation is not a spectator sport," I informed him. I explained that I could tune him out, but that it would be nice if he didn't stare.

"I didn't know there were rules for spouses," Jimmy said. And we laughed.

The next day, I drove to the beach to try walking meditation. But I was immediately distracted by the roar of the ocean, a sound I have always loved. I'll meditate on that, I thought. But I couldn't meditate while walking, hearing the roar of the ocean, feeling the wind, and thinking about what flavor pie I was going to buy later that afternoon.

I tried focusing on the impressions made by my footsteps, as the sand crunched underneath my sneakers. But hundreds of other footprints distracted me. Whose were they? Were they old or new? Big or little? Barefoot or wearing shoes?

Suddenly my BlackBerry found its way out of my pocket and into my hands. I always take it with me when I'm away from my kids. But neither one of them was looking for me; I shoved the BlackBerry back into my pocket.

The beach is my favorite place on earth, but meditating on the beach wasn't working out very well. So I turned away from the ocean and walked to a channel running parallel to the shoreline. It was much quieter away from the waves. I could hear the sound of my feet walking on the flat, packed sand. I focused on some bird tracks up ahead of me. The wind whipped my hair into my face.

Suddenly, I could meditate again.

I took off my shoes. Warm water lapped at my ankles. Farther out, the deeper water in the channel was moving quickly and forcefully. I sat down on the sand and watched the strong current, meditating on its movement.

The next day, I discovered that I could take short video clips with my little digital camera. I hiked over to the channel again, and took movies of the flowing water and swaying beach grasses. I was positively giddy with creative energy. Everything I saw, heard, and felt was a meditation. On my trek home, I was no longer distracted by crashing waves. I sat down on the beach and meditated to their sound and movement.

I returned home to New York and kept meditating every day. I had a hot flash in the middle of one sitting, but remembered Mingyur's words about everything being a source of meditation. Eventually the heat passed through me. I was a calm, menopausal monk.

I accompanied Jimmy on a business trip to San Francisco and paid another visit to Tibet Styles. "Do you remember me?" I asked Dolma, the owner. "I bought a singing bowl from you a few weeks ago."

"Of course!" She gave me a big hug.

"I've been meditating every day," I said. "And I feel better."

"That's good!" Dolma's eyes crinkled when she smiled.

"Remember when you held my hands?" I was sure Dolma had forgotten.

"Of course."

She held out her hands to me again. I placed mine in hers.

Dolma closed her eyes firmly, standing still as a statue. The store was silent. "You're much lighter," Dolma pronounced, opening her eyes.

I stood quietly. "You have let go of so much," she said.

"I've been trying," I murmured.

"We have to let go of suffering," Dolma told me. "We are always suffering."

Dolma offered to teach me a special meditation. She sat down on the floor of her empty store, her spine straight, eyes closed, hands cupped in her lap.

"Imagine your father on your right shoulder," Dolma told me. "Along with all of the men in your life. Then imagine your mother on your left shoulder, with all of the women in your life. Then place all of the world's pain and suffering on your front, and all of the world's living beings on your back."

Dolma seemed to do all this so effortlessly. But when I sat down on the floor next to her and tried to do the same meditation, my parents kept sliding off my shoulders.

I was lighter, but they were too heavy.

8

In Over My Head

After we returned home from San Francisco, I found that I particularly liked practicing meditation outdoors. I didn't mind the record amounts of rainfall in New York that summer, because I could meditate on my front porch. I photographed delicate cobwebs studded with raindrops, muddy puddles, and torrential downpours. I was mesmerized and comforted by water wherever I found it.

But I also felt myself becoming more emotional. Mingyur Rinpoche had warned us that this might happen. "After a couple of weeks of meditation, you might be very sad, very depressed, very agitated. This is normal."

Mingyur might have thought I was normal, but I had my doubts. And then a call I received from a doctor at my mother's nursing home didn't help matters. My mother had fallen, and although she had not injured herself badly, she was disoriented. When I drove up to visit her, she asked, "Where am I? Are you my mother? Are you taking me home?"

After I returned to New York, I stayed in bed the next day, pole-axed by guilt. Was my mother miserable in the nursing home? What house did she hope to return to? I'd sold the small, 170-year-old home she'd bought for herself not long after my father died, in a colorful neighborhood in Providence, near Brown University. She'd stuffed the place with beautiful antiques and strange objects she'd been hoarding for years. There was nowhere for me or my children to sit down when we came to visit, let alone a place to sleep. "Riva's house has everything in the world in it," Max had pronounced wisely when he was six, "except a husband."

Clutter covered every surface. Decapitated dolls were displayed next to bride and groom ornaments, some of which my mother had singed with fire. A life-sized Indian mannequin sat on her living room couch. Hundreds of pieces of her art hung on the walls. In this crazy environment, she pulled all-nighters and produced the best art of her life.

But she also developed Alzheimer's.

Her descent had been slow and steady. I hired a wonderful companion named Betty to take care of her, and my mother was able to live at home. But then she fell and began a series of stays in rehab facilities. Finally, Betty couldn't care for my mother by herself anymore, and I was forced to move her to a nursing home, a fact that haunted me, because, in her more lucid days, she had told me I'd be murdering her if I ever did that.

But my mother had changed dramatically over the last nine years. Once fiery and difficult, especially in the early stages of dementia, she was now docile, giggly, and compliant. Her angst seemed to have disappeared along with her familiar surroundings and belongings, some of which I'd auctioned off or discarded. I'd filled three storage units with what remained of her furniture and art.

I could've used three more to store away my guilt.

For all her eccentricities, I knew that my mother had lived a full life, and would want me to enjoy mine. I treasured the wonderful family I'd built with Jimmy. The fact that we had such a good marriage sometimes astonished me, since my parents' relationship had been more of a cautionary tale than a road map. And the life we'd established with our two healthy, happy sons brought me joy I could never have imagined. How had I managed to achieve this? "It's like I built a rocket ship out of toothpicks and flew it to the moon," I once told a friend.

But every so often, I fell back down to earth. Our son Jack would be flying off for his sophomore year at the University of Michigan in the fall. By mid-August, I already missed him. In many ways, Jack is the quiet anchor of our family, strong and steady, thoughtful and kind. He makes wise pronouncements, and puts life in perspective with a droll sense of humor that always delights me.

Max was getting ready to start his first job after graduating from college, at an advertising agency in New York City. He'd be moving into an apartment and expanding his already large circle of friends. His ability to connect with all kinds of people made me proud; his enthusiasm for life was infectious. I would have to trust that our relationship would remain close no matter how big his world became.

Letting go of my children was hard, but it was a gift I wanted to give them. Buddhists talked about letting go of attachments, which also meant that I had to let go of the people I loved. I wondered: How can you love someone and not become attached?

My mother was also spending more and more time in a world I couldn't enter. As she faded, she seemed like a boat that slips away from its mooring at night and vanishes out to sea.

Sharon Salzberg, in her exquisite memoir, *Faith*, writes, "A pain in our body, a heartache, an unjust treatment may seem inert, impermeable, unchanging. It may appear to be all that is, all that ever will be. But when we look closely, instead of solidity, we see porousness, fluidity, motion. We begin to see gaps between the moments of suffering. We see the small changes that are happening all the time in the texture, the intensity, the contours of our pain."

One late afternoon, I sat alone on the beach watching the waves spill onto the shore, and decided that maybe I could emulate Salzberg, one of the finest Buddhist teachers on the planet.

My manic-depressive father taught me to dream big.

I sat up straight, cross-legged, on the packed sand, looking out at the ocean. But then I heard my father's voice in the waves. "Look at all the problems that exist in the world," he said to me. "There are billions of heartaches forming out here, struggles people don't even know they'll face, waves that will knock them down."

I tried focusing on the water around me, dissolving into harmless little bubbles of foam.

But I sensed that a huge wave was building out in the ocean somewhere. That it would crash down on my mother one day. That another wave had my name on it. "Hang tough," I could hear my father say. I repeated that mantra. "Hang tough."

After our vacation ended, I drove one of our cars home alone and stopped off to see my mother. She was "happily demented," as a doctor had once described her to me.

Still, I was upset afterward as I sped through Connecticut, thinking of how my mother used to make this same drive by herself, in her station wagon bulging with art, toys, and junk, on her way to visit me and my family, when she'd been vibrant and alive.

I was a mess when I finally arrived home and sat down to meditate in our living room.

Alone, I thought to myself. My mother is alone. I tried meditating on the feeling of loneliness.

Big mistake.

Loneliness turned into sadness. Sadness turned to fear. Would I end up like my mother?

"Get a grip!" I said to myself. "Meditate!"

But I couldn't.

For the first time since I'd started this adventure, I wasn't able to sit still and calm down. I'd been so diligent about my practice. But now I was frustrated at my inability to focus. I walked upstairs to my bedroom, with Mickey trailing behind me. I lit a scented candle, sat on the floor, and tried to slow down my breathing. But I kept fidgeting and looking at the clock.

After twenty minutes, I headed out to the supermarket to buy groceries. Max called me from home, requesting a few items. While I was standing in line at the cash register, he called again. "Where are you?" he asked. "What's taking so long?"

"Excuse me?" I put my items onto the conveyor belt. Gone was every intention I ever had of being a mellow monk. I was suddenly one very angry mother.

"I'm starving!" Max said. "Why aren't you back already?"

I hung up the phone and paid for my groceries. It was pouring rain when I loaded them into my car, and I got soaked. I texted Max when I arrived home, to come help me with my bags.

"Here!" I threw them onto the floor of the garage. "I'm sorry I'm so late."

"What's your problem?" Max gathered up my purchases. "It's no big deal. I just wanted to see where you were."

"You were criticizing me!" I yelled. "And I was doing you a favor!"

Max carried the groceries up to the kitchen silently, not engaging me any further.

I burst into tears. "I'm all alone," I said to myself, trudging into a tiny bathroom in our basement. "I'm just like my mother." I slumped down on the floor and cried long and hard, picturing my mother lying on her bed, alone in the nursing home, her bulky diapers making her look like Humpty Dumpty.

Finally, even I couldn't cry anymore. Now what was I going to do?

Then I heard Max's giant basketball sneakers thumping down the stairs. He was looking for me and I was too embarrassed to let him see me like this, on the floor, red-eyed from weeping. How disturbing would that be?

But my stalwart, sweet son opened the door to the bathroom, saw my distraught face, and bent down to kiss the top of my head. "I'm sorry, Mom," he said. "What are you doing down here?"

"I'm so afraid I'm going to die all alone in a nursing home like my mother!" I wailed. Evidently, I could still cry some more.

Poor Max was paying quite a steep price for his groceries. "You're not alone, Mom," he said, patting the top of my head.

"We're all alone!" I cried yet again.

Yikes. In the midst of my grief about my mother and my fears for myself, I heard myself unloading on my son. I'd been so careful for more than twenty years not to do this. I had hated it when my own mother had done this to me. I'd snapped, but now I tried my best to snap out of it.

I pulled myself together. "I'm sorry, Max," I said.

"Come on upstairs." Max pulled me to my feet, and led me out of the bathroom and up to the kitchen.

"I'm sorry," I said again, while we unpacked groceries. "I shouldn't have spoken to you that way. I was just so upset about my mother."

"It's okay." Max opened up a container of yogurt and began making smoothies for all the lean, healthy men in my family.

I opened up a box of ginger snaps.

"It's not okay," I said. "I shouldn't have burdened you like that. But it's just so hard for me to see my mother deteriorating. I'm so afraid I'll end up like her."

"That's not going to happen," Max said. "You're not going to be alone. You have me, Dad, Jack, and all of your friends. And Mickey."

I did not point out that our beloved golden retriever was already thirteen years old and unlikely to be around when I hit my seventies. I'd hurt Max enough for one night.

I followed him upstairs to our den, where Jimmy and Jack were watching a Yankees game. I sat quietly on a couch, surrounded by the handsome men I loved, all drinking smoothies. "Are you okay, Mom?" Max asked after a while.

"I'm okay," I said.

"I think you need to do something joyful," he told me.

I perked up. "What do you mean?"

"I think you need to do something that makes you happy."

"What would that be?" I wondered.

"Why don't you come biking with me?" Jimmy asked brightly, looking up from the baseball game.

"No thanks," I said. "That's your thing."

"I can't tell you what to do," Max said. "You have to figure that out for yourself. Do something you've always wanted to do."

Jack came up with a suggestion: "Why don't you go to a play?"

That made me smile. The men in my family hate going to the theater. I'm always asking if they want to see a Broadway show and they're always turning me down politely.

"I go to the gym, work out, or play basketball when I need to relax," Max told me. "You'll find something that makes you happy."

The next day, I was sitting in the kitchen, my eyes still swollen from all the crying the day before, when my cell phone rang. A woman who'd lived with my family as a babysitter decades earlier was on the line. My mother had given Mamie my number a few years back, and she'd called a couple of times. But I hadn't seen her in forty years.

I decided to pick up the phone.

"What's happening, Pris?" Mamie asked immediately. "Are you all right?"

I began to cry. Again.

"Oh, child, what's the matter? How's Mom?" Mamie's voice was so kind.

"She's okay," I said. "I'm just . . . I'm just so tired. It's been nine years, Mamie. My mother has been sick for nine years."

"I know, doll, I know," Mamie said. "When can I see you? I need to see my girl."

"See me?" I paused. "Where do you live?"

"I'm in Queens," Mamie reminded me.

And that's how I found myself driving over the Whitestone Bridge, winding my way through the streets of Queens in search of my old babysitter's apartment house.

9

The Big House on the Hill

I called Mamie from the lobby of her building and she rushed downstairs to greet me. We hugged, rocking back and forth, stepping back to get a good look at each other, laughing.

Although she was now seventy, Mamie still had a slim, girlish figure and the same distinctive giggle I remembered from my childhood.

She took me up to her apartment, where her husband, Bill, greeted me warmly. "I remember your parents so fondly," he said. "They were 'good people,' as they say in Bensonhurst. They were classy and generous. So kind to me and Mamie."

Bill had met Mamie when he was a dashing young man in a navy uniform. I remembered their happy wedding. They'd raised three children since then, and suffered an enormous tragedy when their son Marty died at age thirty-two from congenital heart disease.

I met Mamie's beautiful grown daughters, Laura and Niyoka, while she fussed in her kitchen, arranging some chicken and a pretty salad on plates, despite my protests. "You must be hungry, girl. Come on. Just eat a little something."

She led me out onto a balcony, where we sat side by side in the sun, and I gratefully gobbled down Mamie's food. I was hungry, tired, and deeply touched by her kindness. "I'm so happy to be here," I said.

"You're happy?" Mamie giggled like a schoolgirl. "I have been waiting for this day for so long!" she said.

I felt embarrassed for my own silly emotional turmoil. I was crying over a mother who had lived a good, long life, and was slipping away slowly, without suffering any pain. "Let's talk about the good old days," I said. "How did you come to work for us, anyway?"

"God was good to me," Mamie said. "The day I met your parents, in that big house on the hill? That day changed my life."

"You were going to Zion Bible Institute." Mamie was a devout Christian and had taken me to her church with my brother and sister. It had all seemed so natural as my Jewish parents had sent me to a Hebrew day school until sixth grade, a Quaker school after that, and off to pray with Mamie at a Pentecostal church.

"I grew up the oldest of eleven children down in South Carolina," Mamie told me. "I washed all the children's clothing by hand. My father was a farmer. My mother believed in education, but she didn't want me to move up north. Her friends and neighbors persuaded her to let me go." She continued. "New York was tough, but I made enough money to buy my mother a washing machine. Thanks to me, she was the first one in her neighborhood to have a telephone."

Mamie attended a church in Park Slope, Brooklyn. One day, the minister looked out at the huge congregation and singled her out, a shy girl in a cream-colored suit. "Young lady, come on up here!" he said. "I can't deliver my message because God has another message for me to share with everyone today. He has an outstanding ministry for you."

Mamie recalled that moment vividly. She had been so nervous. The minister said, "You will help the poor, the unlearned, and you will teach and lecture the wealthy." He smiled at her. "I see you've talked to God about this plan," he said. "Haven't you?"

And Mamie had. She went on a mission, moving up to Rhode Island, where she had some family. She enrolled at Zion Bible Institute. One day she walked into their offices looking for a job. "The only ad they had up was for babysitting," she recalled. "And I didn't want that." But she was eighteen and needed to make some money. "I had a dream that week," Mamie said. "Of a mansion on a hill. And when I walked up to your parents' big old brick house for my interview, I remembered that dream."

My mother hired her on the spot. "She told me not to be afraid and not to worry about taking care of the house," Mamie said. "Your mother was uncomfortable with it. She was loving, and she didn't care about wealth or fancy cars, the fuss and the bother. She would get very nervous when she had to entertain your father's businesspeople."

Later in life, the family business went bankrupt, but Mamie wasn't around for that. My father fell into a depression. He ended up living by himself in a trailer park down in Florida, in an RV. But she remembered my father as a perfectionist in his big, beautiful house. "You weren't allowed to make a mess in your room," she said. "And you weren't allowed to boss me around."

"What was my parents' marriage like?" I asked.

"Your parents were very private people," Mamie said. "But because we were close, I knew when your mother was depressed. And I knew God was real when your father pulled me aside one day and asked for advice about his marriage."

"Wait a minute," I said. "My parents sought help from an eighteen-year-old?"

"I was twenty-three," Mamie said. "And I knew then that the promise of that minister in New York had been fulfilled. I'd been asked to counsel one of the wealthiest men in Providence. I prayed with your father, and it was a privilege."

"When was the last time you saw my mother?" I wondered.

"I went up to visit her after your father died," Mamie said. "In that crazy little house, with all her stuff everywhere. She had some strange things she collected! She was eating a can of beans. And she was finally happy."

"I found that house very disturbing," I said.

Mamie laughed. "I can see why."

"I've been trying to come to terms with my mother all my life," I told Mamie. "She was never very maternal. She always wanted me to be her mother."

Mamie put her arm around me. "God wakes me up every day with a melody," she said. "A song. The first thing I do is thank God for the new day, and for ushering me into that day. I thank God for all the people who healed me."

She looked me in the eye. "Your parents completed a job that my parents couldn't. My first opera was a gift from your parents. Your mother couldn't attend one night, and your father turned to me and said, 'Mamie, we're going to the opera!' He drove me up to Boston. I was as happy as a pig in the sunshine."

I smiled. "Your parents did the best they could," Mamie said. "Too bad you were too young to know that."

She walked me out to my car. We sat together in the front seat, saying our goodbyes. Mamie took my hands in hers. "Let's pray," she said. She thanked God for bringing us together, for all we'd shared in our lives, for my safe travel home. We told each other that we loved one another. I pulled out two pictures I had in my pocketbook, of Max and Jack. "These are my two sons," I told Mamie.

She gasped. "That's the boy!" she said, pointing to Max. "That's him! That's the boy in my dream!"

"What do you mean?" I looked down at Max's radiant smile.

"I had a dream last night," Mamie said, staring at the photo and shaking her head. "That's why I called you. I dreamed that I went back to your old house, back to the big mansion on the hill." She paused. "Do you have a dog?"

"Yes. Her name's Mickey."

"There was a yellow dog outside of the house," Mamie remembered. "I rang the bell, and a tall young man opened the door. He gave me a strong hug and he said, 'You must be Mamie.' We embraced and we cried together."

She looked down at the picture of Max in her hands, at the boy who had nursed me through my meltdown the night before. "This boy said to me, 'Mamie, we've been waiting for you. And we're so glad you're here.' I woke up this morning and I wondered, Who was that boy and what does he want?" Mamie recalled.

"And now we both know. He sent me to find you."

10

Joy Therapy

❧

"When I'm feeling blue," my friend Susie emailed me, "nothing cheers me up more than hearing Krishna Das chant." He "helps clean the dust off the mirror of my heart."

My heart was feeling pretty dusty, so when my dear friend Susie suggested that I attend a workshop of his in New Jersey, with Sharon Salzberg, the meditation teacher whose memoir *Faith* had made such a strong impression on me, I listened. Susie has done her homework when it comes to the important choices she makes in life. She's a yogi, a meditator, and a pediatric physical therapist who has quietly healed children and their parents for decades. Now she wrote me that Krishna Das, whose name means "Servant of Love" in Hindu, would also be "chanting kirtan," which meant that he'd be chanting the names of God. He travels around the world doing this, spreading joy, like a New Age Johnny Appleseed.

Two days later, I threw some protein bars and water bottles into my car, MapQuested the locale where KD, as Susie called him, would perform, kissed Jimmy goodbye, and set out for New Jersey.

I got totally lost and arrived at the venue two minutes before the kirtan was about to begin. The large hall was packed with people of all ages who sat on the floor and in chairs, dressed in muted yoga clothes and colorful Indian attire. I spotted a few psychedelic T-shirts and thought I smelled patchouli oil.

I paid for my ticket and found an empty chair at the back of the room, just as Krishna Das walked in with a couple of other musicians.

With a twinkle in his eyes, dressed in a plaid flannel shirt and jeans, KD looked a little like my handsome husband, if Jimmy had spent twenty years in India studying with a guru, wore glasses, and knew how to chant. He introduced himself, the other musicians, and then Sharon Salzberg.

Dressed casually in a black T-shirt and pants, Sharon had a wonderful, warm smile that lit up the room. She sat in a chair, her hands on her lap, while the musicians around her tuned up their instruments. She and Krishna Das seemed to know each other well.

They talked about how they'd gotten lost on their way to this event, just as I had. That was a revelation to me—even experienced Buddhists got lost, whether on their way to enlightenment or on the New Jersey Turnpike.

KD was very cool and I hoped that it came from some sort of cosmic energy he could pass along to me. He and Sharon certainly had a healthy amount of joy in their undusty hearts, which I hoped to absorb.

Sharon smiled as she quoted Krishna Das, who had quoted someone else. "The grace of God is coming down all the time, like rain, but we forget to cup our hands."

I cupped my hands. And the grace of God came pouring out of Krishna Das and Sharon Salzberg.

KD began playing an instrument that looked like an accordion in a box, which sat on the floor in front of him. It was a harmonium, a hand-pumped organ developed in France and brought to India by missionaries. He was one hip accordion player, and when a drum kicked in, accompanying his whiskey-smooth voice, my dusty, broken heart stirred.

KD's music is Indian, but his message is universal. His voice is sexy. There's just no other way to describe it. My heart was touched, my soul lifted, and I developed a tiny crush on this guy from Long Island who, I discovered online, was once named Jeffrey Kagel, and had become Krishna Das. I liked him. I really, really liked him.

After the first chant was over, my heart was feeling pretty damn good. Max would have been pleased, although mortified to see his mother swaying and grooving to the music. Krishna Das would sing a line with a few Indian words in it, and the audience would sing it right back to him. There didn't seem to be any rules, or any particular pressure to do something "right."

"The chants are the names of God," KD explained. "They have the power to move us more deeply than specific thoughts. What else can God be but that place in your heart of purity and love?"

He talked about sitting with his guru, waiting for something to happen. Finally he realized that nothing, in fact, was going to happen. "I kept looking and waiting, and I never imagined that real happiness could just be inside of me," KD said. "I was doing a practice in order to make myself feel like a different person after so many years of depression and hard work. But then I finally relaxed and didn't want to be somebody else."

Building a meditation practice is like loading explosives, he said. "You have to do both carefully or else . . . boom!"

I'd been unaware of how powerful the practice of meditation could be. I'd rushed to meditate on the heavy stuff—death, loneliness, grief—and I hadn't known I'd been working with explosives until I'd exploded in front of my son.

But now I was in the right place. I felt totally unself-conscious about chanting. I stood up and did a tiny bit of what could have passed as dancing. I was an aging hippie with wide hips, a house-wife masquerading as a hipster for a couple of hours.

The Buddha said that we suffer because of visiting forces like greed, anger, fear, and jealousy. Sharon said that she could be sitting in her kitchen, hear a knock at the door, and those forces would make their way inside. "Sometimes we think we can shut them out by barricading our homes, but that doesn't work," she said. "A lot of practices say 'Make friends with your fear,' but if that's too scary, maybe you can just offer fear a cup of tea."

I'd made the mistake of offering fear and sadness a full-course meal this past week when they'd visited me, I now realized. And poor Max. I'd served him up a whole lot of guilt.

Jimmy and I would be taking Jack back to Michigan for his sophomore year at college in a couple of weeks. I didn't want to pack fear and sadness in our suitcases. I wanted to set Jack up in his apartment with excitement and happiness, despite the fact that I knew how much I would miss him. "You're my Buddha," I told my kind, wise son on many occasions.

Sharon's voice was soothing as she prepared to teach us loving-kindness meditation. Whenever we drifted off we should forgive ourselves, she said. "Just keep coming back to the practice."

She taught us a series of phrases to whisper to ourselves. "May I be safe. May I be happy. May I be healthy. May I live with ease." Over and over again I wished for myself things I wasn't sure I was entitled to. Was I being selfish? Sharon Salzberg didn't seem to think so. And I certainly trusted her.

Next she asked us to think of a person who made us smile. I immediately thought of my husband. I followed Sharon's instructions and silently wished for Jimmy the same things I'd wished for myself—safety, happiness, health, and an ability to live with ease.

Then she told us to think of someone in the room, and I thought of a brave woman who'd shared details of her battle with cancer during a Q-and-A session. "May you be safe," I whispered to myself. "May you be happy, healthy, may you live with ease."

I felt a surge of heat enveloping my body. At first I thought it was just another hot flash, but it was so much more powerful than any hot flash I'd ever experienced. Maybe it had something to do with the lovingkindess that Sharon had planted inside me.

Finally Sharon asked us to open up our hearts to the entire world, to every living being, and to wish for them what we wished for ourselves. "If you go deeper and deeper into your own heart," she told us, "you'll be living in a world with less fear, isolation, and loneliness. When you're wide open, the world is a good place."

Or, as Krisha Das put it, "If you don't go on a spiritual quest, it's just beer and TV!"

I drove home in an altered state, and yet I didn't get lost. I kept grinning to myself as I listened to the Krishna Das CD I'd bought, chanting my way home on the New Jersey Turnpike.

In one interview with Krishna Das, he asserts that "some people have the karma to be big boats, to take a lot of people across a big body of water."

But he refers to himself modestly. "I'm a little paper origami thing."

To me, however, Krisha Das had been a giant ferryboat, calm, cool, and collected, running right on time, giving me the lift I needed. For at least one night, I'd transformed myself from a desperate housewife to a demi–Dalai Lama.

11

Getting Grounded

⚛

When I walked into Gina Colelli's waiting room, a big yellow Lab stood up from his spot on the floor, sniffed me a couple of times, and then plopped down again in a new location. Gina opened the door to her office and ushered me inside.

"I've been going to a therapist for half my life," I told her once I was seated on yet another therapist's couch. "But a friend raved about her experience with EMDR [eye movement desensitization and reprogramming] and another friend who's a therapist recommended you highly."

"Many patients do a lot of psychotherapy and then hit a wall," Gina said. "That's when they come here."

Had I hit a wall?

I'd been talking on to my therapist for a decade. Dr. Jaeger had helped me enormously, but she'd also approved of my plan to try EMDR, perhaps with the hope that I'd come back to her with some new material. Truth be told, my old stories were beginning to bore me, I felt my own act was wearing a bit thin.

Gina Colelli was a petite woman a few years younger than I am, whose short dark hair was streaked with gray. She seemed nice enough, but had a serious way about her. I glanced at a pillow on the couch next to me, with the word *Joy* written on it, and hoped for the best. I started speaking quickly, and filled in this stranger on my history of panic. That took up the entire session.

When I returned the next week, I was surprised to learn that we would not be doing EMDR yet. "I'm going to do something called Somatic Experience therapy with you first," Gina told me.

Had I failed at something already? Was I too messed up for EMDR?

Somatic Experience, Gina explained, had been developed by Peter Levine, a psychologist who studied stress and trauma for thirty-five years. As he describes in his book, *Waking the Tiger*, it frees trauma that has been frozen in our brain stems, the most ancient part of the brain, where our fight-or-flight response is located.

I sat frozen on Gina's couch as she explained the process. I was afraid of what this strange new therapy might unleash from my reptilian brain.

Where was my reptilian brain, anyway? I fiddled nervously with my hair.

"Somatic Experience is a very gentle method," Gina explained, "where less is more. We're not going to clear up everything in one session."

I smiled, a bit uneasily. "Aw, shucks."

"We all have a zone of tolerance," Gina said, pulling out a piece of paper. "In a healthy zone, we go up and down throughout the day." She drew a line moving up and down in symmetrical waves. "Most of us don't spike really high," she said. "And we don't go really low. In other words, we don't get hyperactivated and we don't collapse. We manage things."

Not me. I both spiked and collapsed.

"When you've been traumatized," Gina continued, "your zone of tolerance becomes more narrow. You spike up and down sharply." Her hand jerked as she drew a series of jagged movements. Just as I'd been agitated at the monastery by Mingyur talking about his panic, I got anxious at seeing that spiky pattern.

"I think my zone of tolerance is very narrow," I said, trying to sit still, in my meditation pose.

"We're going to widen your zone with Somatic Experience," Gina said confidently. "We're going to build a core inside of you that makes you feel you can handle things, no matter what."

That sounded like exactly what I needed.

"We're going to build that core together," Gina said. "And also discharge the traumatic sensations you've been living with."

And then we got down to business. "I'm going to do some grounding with you," Gina said. "Your only job is to notice and observe. That's it. You don't have to make something happen or take anything away. Just settle into your body, and notice what feels comfortable."

I closed my eyes and felt my legs relax.

"Become aware of how your body feels being supported by the couch," I heard Gina say. "And when you settle in, let me know what parts of your body are helping you to do that."

My feet felt grounded to the floor. My shoulders and hands felt calm. My jaw softened, along with my face. "My brain feels like it's settling down, like when I meditate," I reported.

"Excellent," Gina said. "So let's just play around with this a little bit. I want you to notice where you may be feeling uncomfortable in your body, and if you feel that, let me know."

I was feeling pretty good everywhere.

For now.

"Remember what we were talking about a few minutes ago?" Gina asked. "About the fight, flight, and freeze response?"

Yes.

"Remember how all your life you've been looking for a way to just feel centered?"

I had, indeed. But suddenly I felt anxious.

"Something's stirring . . ." I placed my hand over my heart.

"Okay." Gina sounded calm. I didn't feel so calm.

"Stay aware of where you're feeling comfortable in your body," she told me. "But also be aware of the stirring in your chest." I felt an urge to take a deep breath. Then another. I was scared.

But Gina's voice was still calm. "I just want you to notice that stirring," she said. "There's nothing you have to do. You have a comfortable place in your body that will hold you while you experience any unpleasant sensations. They'll move through your body and have a completion in your brain."

My throat was closing. "I'm trying to take a deep breath," I said. "But I can't."

"Just notice that," Gina said. "Are you still feeling grounded in the same places as before?"

I checked. My feet were still firmly attached to her floor. My legs were relaxed. But my lungs were getting ready to take off, galloping. My heart was already doing that. "I'm okay," I said, wishing it were so. "But if you weren't sitting here with me, I'd be very unhappy."

"That makes sense," Gina said. "And I'm not going to let things get out of control."

I believed her. But my body wasn't so sure. I took some jagged, shaky breaths.

"Your system is making an attempt to complete the flight response," Gina told me.

"I feel like running away," I reported. Suddenly, I made the connection—my body was trying to run away from my panic, but the panic was *in* my body. I had to use my mind to help my body's experience, the somatic experience.

"Follow the urge without doing it," Gina said. "Just follow that feeling of wanting to get up."

I waved my hands in the air, shrugged my shoulders, and scrunched up my face. I rocked back and forth on Gina's couch, itching to be active. To do something. Anything.

I was channeling Joe Cocker.

"If the feelings become uncomfortable, and you can't follow them, just go back to that place in your body where you feel grounded," Gina told me. "But try to follow the urge to get up and go. Do it very slowly, like you're moving through molasses. That's how the brain stem likes to get the message, and that will complete the response."

My feet felt rooted to the floor. I inhaled a tiny puff of air. And then I did that again. And again, stringing the little puffs together, until they became one long, deep, slow breath. Then another. And another.

I was teaching myself to breathe, at the age of fifty-six.

I paused. "I feel like something's gonna happen right here . . ." I pointed to the center of my chest.

"Does it feel the same as it did before?" Gina asked. "Or different?"

"A little different." I realized that the stirring was less intense.

"The body finds lots of ways to discharge," Gina assured me. "Like shaking or tingling, heating up, cooling down . . . But you can slow everything down by noticing where you feel grounded."

I felt my feet, glued to the floor. I continued to breathe, slowly and steadily.

"You're building your zone," Gina told me. "You're deepening and widening it."

I sighed.

"See that sigh?" Gina asked. "It's wonderful. It's the nervous system feeling a little release."

"I still feel something here . . ." I pointed to my heart.

Gina urged me to be aware of where I felt grounded, and

then to notice the stirring I felt in my chest. To go back and forth between those two places. To do what the founder of the method called "pendulating," between touching a fearful place and being grounded.

My hands and feet tingled like crazy. "That's wonderful!" Gina told me. "Your nervous system is discharging. Just allow it to do what it wants to do. It knows how to heal itself."

I took a deep, satisfying breath.

"You're doing very well," Gina said. Our session was almost over. "Shift away from noticing any disturbing sensations," she instructed me.

I stopped going back and forth between my chest and my grounded feet.

"Place all of your attention on a place in your body that feels comfortable. Just find a good place to land," Gina, my personal air traffic controller, told me.

I focused on my hands, folded in my lap. I imagined a bouquet of flowers there, opening up in slow motion. When Gina instructed me to do so, I opened my eyes.

I sighed again—a deep, glorious feeling. I felt like I did after an intense meditation session—fully relaxed and present.

"You did a really good job of grounding yourself," Gina told me. "And by going back and forth between being grounded and being uncomfortable, you were able to self-regulate."

"What did I do exactly?" I asked.

"When a tiger goes running after its prey," Gina explained, "and gets where he needs to go, all the hormones move through his body in a type of completion. Nothing gets frozen." She smiled. "And that's what you just did."

I'd never thought of myself as a tiger before. I'd always been more of a scaredy cat.

"When you followed the urge to get up from my couch and move, the cycle completed itself," Gina said. "When we're working in the oldest part of the brain, the instinctual reptilian brain, less is more. We need to take things slowly, like we did today. Everyone wants to do things quickly. But when you take it slow, the work is deeper, more solidified."

"Could I complete that cycle in real life?" I asked. "What if I'm in a subway car and it stops in between stations . . . I start to get a little panicky . . ."

"Sit and just ground yourself," Gina said. "Don't fight the panic, don't ignore it, but focus on where you feel grounded. I guarantee you that you could find a place—even just a tiny, little spot in your body—where you're grounded."

I tried to imagine that.

"You might say to the person sitting next to you, 'Can I talk to you? Because I suffer from panic attacks, and that would help me,'" Gina suggested. "Then you'd notice that somewhere in your body you felt calm. You could stay focused on that feeling."

"When I was a teenager," I said, "I used to carry a flask of vodka around with me. I'd take a swig to calm me down."

"That dulled your nervous system and suppressed it," Gina explained. "But it didn't complete a process. That's why alcohol ultimately doesn't work."

An old tiger can learn new tricks. The next time I stepped into a subway car, I took a seat and began meditating. The train hurtled underground, and I stared at the speckled black linoleum floor. When it pulled into my station, I got off the train, sat on a bench, and continued meditating on the subway platform. Nobody noticed me, but I wouldn't have noticed if they had noticed me. I'd started calming my inner lizard and making a giant leap in evolution.

12

Let the Games Begin

⁓⊗⁓

"When you first came to see me," Gina said at our next session, "because of your high level of anxiety, I needed to make sure you could get grounded, so that you could process disturbing memories."

And I thought Gina had seen me on a good day!

She pulled out a contraption hooked up to a tripod, placed it in front of me, and flipped a switch.

A panel of lights lit up and flashed in a continual loop a few feet away from my face, from left to right, then right to left . . .

Whoa. My reptilian brain was definitely a little spooked by these flashing lights. They reminded me of moving lights on an airport runway. I thought of Gina as a competent air traffic controller, but a scary crash in my head still seemed possible.

"I'd like to try some EMDR today," Gina said. "Keep your head steady and follow the lights with your eyes."

I practiced for a moment, watching the lights, not moving my head. Thankfully, I'd gotten my learner's permit in Somatic Experience before trying this eye movement desensitization and reprogramming. But still . . .

"I feel a little bit like Frankenstein," I said, laughing nervously. "I'm not sure what you're going to do with me."

Gina shut off the machine. "Let's get grounded," she said. "Settle in and notice what's happening in your body. Become aware of the sensations that let you know you're grounded."

I obeyed, closing my eyes. The backs of my calves relaxed against Gina's couch. The soles of my feet felt glued to the floor. I took a deep, satisfying breath. I could do this. I hoped.

"Think about a place, real or imagined, that feels 'delicious' to you," Gina suggested. "A place where you'd go to relax. A place of repose."

I tried to find a really good spot. A safe spot. I imagined myself at a beach in Narragansett, Rhode Island, where my family spent summers when I was seven and eight years old. "The sun is beating down," I said. "I'm sitting at a bathing pavilion, on a bench by the snack bar, holding a plate of french fries and tart, red ketchup. I can feel the hot, splintery deck under my feet. I can hear the waves beating against the shore. Everybody in my family is safe and secure . . ." I could picture it all vividly. "It was the last time my family felt intact," I heard myself say. "Before my father started having an affair . . ."

Warm tears raced down my cheeks. I opened my eyes.

"You seem upset," Gina said.

I was definitely in the wrong spot.

"We need a different one," Gina decided. "This is overlaid with other stuff. We want a more neutral space."

"Okay." I switched gears. "I like my front porch. Let's try that."

"What's the season?" Gina asked.

"Summer." I closed my eyes again. "Can I have my dog Mickey with me?"

"Sure," Gina said.

I pictured my golden retriever lying next to me on the porch floor.

"What time of day is it?" Gina asked.

"Late afternoon."

"What are you sitting on?"

"A white wicker couch with lots of pillows. Tall trees hide me from the street. I can't hear the phone out here. I don't have my BlackBerry with me . . ."

"You're off the grid," said Gina.

"Yup." I felt myself relax.

"So I want you to imagine yourself there, and notice how it feels in your body," she continued. "When you're in this private spot, on the porch, with your dog . . ."

I sank into Gina's couch.

"I'm going to turn on the machine again," she said. "Just follow the lights with your eyes. We'll do a short set, and I want you to hang out on the porch. Okay?"

The lights were strange, but I managed to keep my eyes focused on them, and it became easier to do that, even calming. "I feel a little weird," I said after a few minutes. My feet were tingling. "I'm going into a little trance now," I said quietly.

I liked these lights. I watched them, moving back and forth . . .

"I want you to think about something that's mildly annoying to you," Gina said. "The example I like to use is that you're in a supermarket with a full shopping cart. A woman behind you has only one item. You let her go in front of you, but she needs to pay with a check, she can't find a pen, you're waiting there . . ."

"Got it." I felt incredibly calm. But then I remembered that "I used to have panic attacks when I worked at a supermarket."

"How does your body feel when you think about that?" Gina asked.

"Hmmm . . . not so good." My chest was tightening.

Gina directed me back to the porch, and she shut off the lights until I calmed myself down and "drove" myself home.

"I'm back," I announced.

Gina turned on the flashing lights again, and I watched them. "Now go back to the checkout line at the supermarket," she instructed me. "And tell me how you feel."

"Actually, I feel better now." I smiled. "I could pick up a trashy magazine and just hang out."

"That's good," Gina said. "That means you can self-regulate by going back to the porch. You can take in positive information."

"What do the flashing lights do?"

"They bilaterally stimulate the left and right sides of the brain," Gina explained. "Emotional events are experienced on the right side, and when we metabolize them, they get moved to the left, where they're categorized and don't have a charge. We do that all day long. We move from an emotional state to a logical one, from subjective memory to objective, from a charge to no charge. But when we're traumatized, experiences don't get metabolized. They get frozen in time and space in the right side of our brain."

I laughed, my eyes still closed. "Thank you for that explanation, Gina, but I am completely zonked on this couch!" I said. "I haven't understood a word you said!"

Gina laughed. "You're going to have to come off the couch, though, so we can develop some of the targets we'll work on in future sessions."

"Make me!" I joked. But then I forced myself to focus.

"You told me about your tracheotomy, when you were very young," Gina said softly. "But we're not going to do that memory first."

I knew I wasn't tiger enough to handle that, yet.

"We don't want to touch early memories without clearing the older ones out first, and building your ego strength," Gina said.

"We'll start from the ages of four through twelve. Then we'll do twelve and up, and then younger." She paused to let me take that in. "So what are your most disturbing memories from the age of four through twelve?"

I thought for a minute, my eyes still closed. I gave Gina some nursery school and kindergarten memories.

"When I was in second grade, my mother used to wander into my room with a shoe box full of her father's letters, sit down on my bed, read them to me, and cry." I fidgeted. "Her father had died six weeks before I was born. My mother was so sad.

"Her mother visited us from California just once, when I was seven. It's the only memory I have of my grandmother. My mother was standing with me at the bottom of our stairs, screaming up at her frail, white-haired mother, above us on a landing: 'I hate you! I hate you! You're a witch! I hate you!'"

I started to cry. "When I got older, my father used to tell me his problems. I wanted to say, 'Tell this crap to your wife! Why are you telling it to me?' This was right around the time that I began having panic attacks."

"Tell me about your worst panic attack," Gina said.

I winced. "There are so many to choose from. Hundreds."

"I don't want the details now," Gina said. "What other disturbing memories do you have?"

"At what age?"

"Your most disturbing memories in your life."

I thought for a moment. "My father howling in pain when he was dying of cancer, in the bedroom next to mine, at a house we rented.

"Hyperventilating behind the cash register of my father's supermarket, over and over again, with a long line of people just watching me."

"I'm looking for the worst. Give me your top ten worst memories."

"My worst?" I paused. "I've had a pretty good life, Gina."

She didn't reply, so I continued.

"When my father was getting radiation treatments, he lived in his camper in the parking lot of the Lahey Clinic in Boston," I said. "My mother found out about his affair and checked herself into a mental hospital. She said she was going to kill herself. So I had a father with inoperable cancer and a mother in a mental hospital."

"I'm confused," Gina said. "Your mother checked herself into a mental hospital at the end of your father's life because of an affair he had years earlier?"

"Yes." I took a deep, jagged breath. "Then her roommate had slit her wrists and my mother realized this wasn't exactly Canyon Ranch, so she kept calling me to get her out of there. She couldn't get out. I had to find a psychiatrist . . ."

Gina interrupted me. "I want you to get grounded. Notice how you're getting activated. I'm being very direct with you for a reason. We're probably not going to get to EMDR today, because of all of the memory work we've done, so we'll just do Somatic Experience therapy. You'll be nice and grounded when you leave."

"I'm not feeling as good as I was before."

This session had not been what I'd hoped it would be. I felt scared. What if I'd backslid so far that I wouldn't be able to make my way back up and out of Gina's office? I was desperate for the same post-session high I'd experienced before.

"Notice how you're getting agitated," Gina said. "It's all right, but I bet that feels familiar to you. Getting anxious about something that's not going to happen or get completed."

She was right. I was back in the trance of fear I'd awakened from. "It's taking a while for my brain to calm down." My head felt fuzzy. I tried slowing myself down.

"It looks like you're getting grounded," Gina said.

But vivid memories kept surfacing and I felt anxious again. Gina instructed me to feel my body being supported by the couch. I closed my eyes and concentrated. I felt my feet glued to the floor. My body slowed itself down. I *could* put myself in the driver's seat of the terrifying roller coaster I'd been on for so long. I felt myself applying the brakes, gaining control of my panic.

"You're good at this," Gina told me.

"It's because I meditate," I said. "It's good preparation."

I sat there for a while, grounding myself, learning to breathe again.

"So how will we know that what we're doing here is working?" Gina asked eventually. "How will we measure that?"

I opened my eyes. "I'll be happy," I said simply. "And I'll own that happiness. I won't feel guilty for having a wonderful life and enjoying it. I'll be able to share my happiness with other people, to be able to say that I suffered from terrible panic attacks, but that I don't anymore. That I don't even describe myself as an anxious person. That I describe myself as a person who had a lot of pain, or the pain that everybody else in the world has. But that I've processed it. That I can be at peace."

"Excellent," Gina said.

And I believed, for a moment, that might all come true one day.

But once I returned home, I was drained from all the emotional turmoil stirred up in Gina's office and collapsed on the white wicker couch on my front porch, feeling drugged. It was an unseasonably warm fall day and I dozed, on and off, for three hours, with Mickey lying on the floor next to me. I felt no urge to eat, talk, or move. Was I exhausted or healed? I was too tired to figure that out.

In the meantime, I reflected on the wisdom of the Vietnamese Zen monk Thich Nhat Hanh. I'd seen him give a lecture in New York a few weeks earlier. "There is a tendency to want to go back to the past," he said. "Regret and sorrow are always there to draw us back."

And I thought of the Buddha, who said, "The past is already gone and the future not yet here. There is only one place for us to love and that is here and now."

13

The Art Sanctuary

Since high school, my refuge has always been any kind of an art studio. As a teenager I spent hours listening to Beatles albums while drawing or painting. No matter how anxious, bored, or worried I was, I felt better when my hands were moving, sending healing signals to my brain. My mother must have felt the same way. "People will disappoint you," she once told me. "But your work never will."

My mother was my first art teacher. As with her parenting, she didn't lay out a vision for me, but she gave me plenty of raw material to work with, buying me art supplies and taking me along with her to life drawing classes, museums, galleries, and her own art shows.

When I was eight, my mother enrolled me in children's art classes with an elderly Italian gentleman named Gino Conti, whose studio was a magical setting, filled with tribal art, masks, bleached horse skulls, and his own drawings and paintings. The courtyard behind his two-hundred-year-old studio, a former stable, contained gravestones, which we covered with newsprint, rubbing charcoal over them until the names of the deceased emerged. Somehow that didn't feel creepy at all.

Gino treated his young students as adults. We painted with real oil paint, on real canvas, just like the college kids at Rhode Island School of Design down the street. Every Saturday, I learned how to transport myself to another world, creating something from scratch that was all mine. Thanks to my mother and Gino, for the rest of my life, I was never bored.

When my mother was first diagnosed with Alzheimer's, I began the mammoth task of cleaning up her house, sorting through rooms full of art supplies, papers, and junk. I came across a stash of vintage beads and pendants in her basement, and channeling her creative energy, I signed up for an introductory jewelry-making class at my local high school, where I learned the fundamentals of beading.

And then I became obsessed. I bought beads, semiprecious stones, wire, clasps, and chains at various stores in lower Manhattan and on trips to Providence, which once had been the costume jewelry capital of the world. The more my mother faded, the more colorful the jewelry I produced became.

I sold my wares at local craft shows and stores. My hobby took over the spare bedroom in our house, which my family began to call "the bead room." I discovered a Tibetan store in Greenwich Village, where a woman named Karma sold me a spool of cord used to make Tibetan malas, or prayer beads. Inspired by the tribal beads and amulets I'd collected from all over the world, I started a new line of jewelry, making universal prayer beads with crosses, silver moons, stars, and tiny Buddhas.

But now that my meditation practice was going well, I was up for another way to soothe my soul, another creative adventure.

For years, I'd admired *thangka* paintings (pronounced "tahng-ka," Tibetan for painting). I was fascinated by the elaborate scenes in which the Buddha sat surrounded by deities, flowers, and creatures. "I want to draw the Buddha," I decided one day. I thought that might bring me some peace, joy, or even a touch of enlightenment.

When I googled "thangka painting," I discovered that a master painter from Tibet taught classes an hour away from me in New Haven, Connecticut. Lama Tsondru's intricate, colorful paintings were featured on his website.

On a Sunday afternoon I drove up to his house with nothing but a #2 pencil and high hopes. Plus a touch of guilt about leaving Jimmy behind, but only a touch, since the New York Giants were playing football that day, and I knew he'd be entertained and happy. If they won.

A young Tibetan woman ushered me into Lama Tsondru's front parlor, where a small group of friendly students of all ages was seated on the floor. Lama Tsondru, a slim man about my age, offered me green tea and cookies and sat down with me on a couch, opposite a colorful altar laden with fruits and flowers.

"Buddhism is like a room with many doors," Lama Tsondru said, sensing my uncertainty about being in an unfamiliar environment. "You can enter from any one of them—east, west, north, south—and you can leave through any door, also. The important thing is that you are in the room with us."

Clearly I was in the right room. This distinguished teacher's gentle manner put me at ease. The other students lent me a masonite clipboard, a blank piece of drawing paper, a protractor, and a mechanical pencil. Lama Tsondru clipped a photocopied drawing he'd made of the Buddha's face onto my board and told me to copy it, after I'd drawn a grid of very specific proportions.

Lama Tsondru handed me a flat plastic stick, marked with lines. "This is a *thigsed*," he said. "A Tibetan ruler." I would use it to measure my grid, copying his. Then I could begin the outline of the Buddha's round, graceful face. Every aspect of thangka painting is very precise. Though I am the queen of not being precise, I was eager to get started.

I sat cross-legged on the floor, making faint lines, constructing my grid. Every once in a while I had to shift my aching bones. The women in the room begin to chant softly. A young man pulled out nuts and dried fruit. A woman with a baby laid out cheese and crackers. I pulled a bar of dark Venezuelan chocolate out of my backpack and placed it on the table, happy to share my secret stash with these kind people.

By the end of my first session with Lama Tsondru, I had produced a perfectly drawn grid and a simple outline of the Buddha's round, symmetrical face. Tired and exhilarated, I returned the supplies I'd borrowed, and left after thanking my fellow students and Lama Tsondru for including me so graciously. I felt as if I had meditated more than my usual twenty minutes a day—blissed out.

On my second visit, I spent an entire hour just drawing the Buddha's nose and lips. I loved the feeling of being so meticulously present, focused on each tiny, feathery stroke of a pencil. I shut out everything else, including my chattering mind.

But when Lama Tsondru crouched down next to me and studied my Buddha's face, it was obvious that my measurements were off. One ear was longer than the other, one eyebrow wider than the other, and the Buddha's smile was crooked.

Still, I wasn't about to give up. "I really like this process," I said.

"The reason the Buddha is so hard to draw is because there are thirty-two excellent marks," Lama Tsondru told me, "and eighty lesser marks."

That was a lot to get right.

"The Buddha is the only one with a perfectly symmetrical face," he explained. "Because of his hard work, selflessness, and good motivation."

Thangka painting was established in India more than two thousand years ago, Lama Tsondru told me. Two kings of that era used to trade extravagant gifts, and when one king received a suit of diamond-covered armor, he commissioned a portrait of the Buddha in exchange. All of the artists in his kingdom were invited to a clear, still pond. The Buddha sat on its banks, and his perfect reflection appeared in the quiet waters, so that his likeness could be captured accurately.

The next week, I finished my Buddha's eyes. He stared out at me and I felt a rush of pleasure. But when Lama Tsondru approached and took measurements, it became clear that my Buddha's nose was too long. "I made him Jewish!" I said.

"Or French!" Lama Tsondru smiled.

Over the next few weeks, I drew the Buddha's face over and over again. His eyes grew less lopsided, his nose less crooked, his ears more symmetrical.

And I grew more calm when I was immersed in the drawing. Between that and my regular meditation practice, I was feeling productive and balanced. It amazed me that I could calm myself down so deeply with nothing but a pencil and paper. The power of deep creative engagement was thrilling.

I returned to Lama Tsondru's house one Sunday and spent some time drawing with his students. But I needed to leave early, because my husband and I had plans for the afternoon.

"He has attachment to you!" Lama Tsondru teased me.

"Speaking of attachments," I said, "I want to ask you a question." My mother's steady decline was on my mind. She'd slipped another notch, and I would be visiting her soon. "How can I let go of my attachment to her?" I wondered.

"How old is your mother?" Lama Tsondru asked.

She'd be celebrating her eighty-first birthday in two days, I said.

Lama Tsondru paused for a moment. "The Buddha says there are four stages of suffering—birth, coming of age, sickness, and death. But all are constant, like a river, always flowing. The nature of suffering never changes."

"My mother is not in much pain," I said. "But I am. And I don't know how to let go of that pain."

"Look to all the other mothers in the world who are suffering," Lama Tsondru told me. "Make yourself a bodhisattva, with compassion for others."

I felt a little embarrassed. There were so many other mothers suffering and even this kind man had suffered greatly. He had spent his childhood in a refugee camp in Darjeeling, India, with six thousand other children, after fleeing Tibet with his family. I was a fortunate woman who could not let go of my grief for what I perceived as my mother's misfortune.

But Lama Tsondru wasn't judging me. "If you open up your heart to others, the weight on your shoulders will lessen," he said. "You can visit with your mother. Hold her hand. Feed her food. Tell her a good story. Give her something nice. Anything."

Suddenly I remembered something. "I woke up this morning with a desire to draw flowers," I told Lama Tsondru.

Carefully, he drew a symmetrical flower resembling a water lily alongside my Buddha drawing.

"What kind of flower is that?" I asked.

"It's pema," he told me. "The lotus flower."

Thich Nhat Hanh describes the suffering we experience in life as mud, but also points out that a beautiful lotus flower can bloom only in that environment. "There cannot be a lotus flower without the mud," I heard him say.

That night as I meditated, an image of my mother as a lotus flower came to me. She is content, I realized. She is the lotus with roots in the mud that Thich Nhat Hanh described, floating happily through her last days.

I drove up to Providence and my mother was delighted to see me, although at times she thought that Betty and I were her cousins. She was thrilled with her birthday cake and gifts. I'd purchased her favorite licorice, a cactus garden, and a plant called "Chinese baby tears."

And then I gave her one more gift. A perfect birthday present.

"Are my parents alive?" my mother asked suddenly, looking up at me hopefully.

Lama Tsondru's words on becoming a compassionate bodhisattva popped into my head. Without any hesitation, I said, "Yes."

14

The Long Reach of Providence

I visited my mother as often as I could, depending on my schedule and emotional fortitude. Some visits were easier than others.

One day I peeked into the dining room of her nursing home and spotted her distinctive white thatch of hair. She sat slumped in a chair by the window, with her eyes closed. They flew open when I touched her arm, and she stared at me blankly.

"Hi there!" I said.

"Hello." She could have been talking to a census taker. Her eyes were watery and tired.

"I think we have a date!" I said, positively chirpy.

"A date?"

"I think I know you." I smiled. "Do you know who I am?"

"No," said my mother, her face six inches from mine. She looked like I'd woken her up from a dream. Or maybe I was the one who was dreaming.

"I think you *do* know me," I said. A flicker of worry crossed my mother's face. "We're related."

"We are?"

"I'm your daughter," I said. "I'm Priscilla."

Something behind her eyes clicked into place. She stared at me, smiling nervously. "It makes me feel wicked."

"Wicked?" Now I was confused.

"Because I didn't recognize you." Immediately, my mother tried to take some colorful beads off her neck, to give them to me. But I refused, smiling as brightly as I could.

"Let's go someplace quiet," I suggested. "Where we can talk."

She popped up from her chair like a marionette. "How did you do that?" I wondered aloud to her.

"I've been doing it all my life!" my mother responded, with a smile.

She wobbled for a moment, then took hold of her walker and began shuffling away from the table. She stopped to tell an elderly woman, "This is my daughter," eliciting no response.

I followed her across the dining room slowly, past dozens of silent elderly people. The television set was playing a religious video of some kind. A static orange sunset provided the backdrop for the words scrolling on the screen; a disembodied voice recited the Lord's Prayer.

And then I noticed the rabbi.

As my mother left the dining room, a man dressed head to toe in black, with a big hat and a long white beard, greeted her. "Hello, Riva!"

She stopped and looked at him, smiling sweetly. "This is my daughter," she said, motioning to me.

"How lucky you are!" the rabbi smiled. He had kind blue eyes, and a pale complexion.

"How long have you known my mother?" I asked.

"A long time. Right, Riva?" The rabbi looked directly at my mother, acknowledging her as a fully present human being. "I've been visiting Riva ever since she got here, maybe four years ago. I'm Rabbi Schafer."

Had I asked for a cleric to visit my mother? I couldn't remember. I'd signed a lot of papers on the day we'd brought her to the nursing home. My mother had called herself Buddhist for years. But I had a vague recollection that she'd authorized me to check the box marked "Jewish." Then this rabbi must have appeared.

And he wasn't going anywhere anytime soon.

I took my mother by the arm and led her down the hallway to her room. The rabbi accompanied us and watched as I helped her into a chair and sat down on her bed. He took a seat across from me.

"This is very difficult," I said, glancing at my mother.

"I'm sure," the rabbi replied.

"What are we doing?" my mother asked pleasantly.

"We're just visiting," the rabbi told her.

Trying to find common ground, I found myself dropping the one Hasidic name I knew. "My father used to have a close relationship with the Grande Rebbe in Boston," I said.

"Ah! The Bostoner!" Rabbi Schafer's eyes lit up.

"Is that what he was called? When my father's business was going bankrupt, he used to drive up to Boston every week to study Talmud and discuss ethics with the Rebbe."

After my father died, I had stored many of his belongings, I explained. I went through them slowly, and one day I found an envelope.

I glanced over at my mother, who may or may not have been following this tale.

"It was so worn out," I said. "It almost crumbled in my hands. I opened it and unfolded a piece of paper, with a diagram of a hand, and lots of writing I couldn't read. It wasn't Hebrew; maybe it was Aramaic."

"Was it handwritten?" the rabbi asked. "Or was it a photocopy?"

"I'm not sure," I answered.

"What you were holding was a *cameah*," Rabbi Schafer told me.

"A cameah?"

"An amulet. Your father must have been given a cameah by the Bostoner."

"Yes!" My father used to carry this envelope with him everywhere, I suddenly remembered. He used to keep it in his breast pocket. "When I put my father's cameah back into the envelope," I said, "I saw what was written on the back: DO NOT OPEN THIS."

I shuddered.

Later that day, I was standing with our son Jack in the kitchen, watching while he cut a mango with a little knife. It slipped, and he sliced his hand. I remembered the scene vividly. "It was bleeding a lot," I told the rabbi. "I thought he might need stitches, but then it stopped."

The rabbi listened quietly.

"Right after that," I continued, "I received a telephone call from the director of the camp where our older son was spending the summer. He told me that Max was fine, but that he had cut his hand, opening a care package with a box cutter."

I asked the director which hand Max had cut, but I already knew the answer. He'd cut his left hand, just like his younger brother, in exactly the same spot, right next to his thumb.

I shook my head. "I was stunned. That letter was something I was never supposed to open. It was like a warning from God."

The rabbi said nothing.

"What's your response to that story?" I asked.

"My response?" Rabbi Schafer said. "I'll tell you another story."

Then it was Riva's and my turn to sit quietly as Rabbi Schafer talked.

There once was a tzaddik—a wise man—who left Poland and went to live in Jerusalem, on a domed rooftop. Back then, people could walk from one rooftop to another, just like on the streets below.

This man had a neighbor who watched him from her window while he sat every day, studying Torah or praying. He was elderly, with no family. So she began to cook an extra portion of her meals and deliver it to him.

This woman had a daughter who was engaged to be married, but a week before her wedding, the bride-to-be suffered a nervous breakdown and her family was forced to put her in an insane asylum, which broke their hearts.

One day her mother realized that the man to whom she was delivering meals was a holy man. So she went up to see him, and explained her daughter's situation. He created a cameah, and sealed it in a leather pouch. "Put this around your daughter's neck and don't ever let her take it off," he told the woman. "When you take your daughter to the mikvah on the night before her wedding, remove it right before she dunks her head into the ritual bath, submerge her, and then put it back on immediately. And make sure she keeps it on at all other times."

The mother followed the wise man's instructions. She went to the insane asylum, slipped the cameah over her daughter's head, and suddenly the bride-to-be became healthy! Her mother checked her out of the asylum, and the family joyfully began wedding celebrations, which took place over seven days, as was the tradition of *shiva brachas,* or seven blessings. The couple received a blessing every night.

On the seventh night of their celebration, everything was going beautifully, and the bride was healthy and radiant. In the midst of all this happiness, one of the wedding guests, a miserable fellow, saw that the bride was wearing a cameah. "What's this?" he cried out, yanking the leather pouch off her neck.

He tore it open and saw what had been written inside—the name of one man.

And who was that man? Whose name had been powerful enough to heal the bride? The water carrier of Jerusalem, the man who hauled heavy buckets from the wells of the city through the streets, to its inhabitants. This humble man was the real tzaddik— the holiest of the holy men of Jerusalem.

A true tzaddik's identity, Rabbi Schafer explained, must always be kept hidden from the world. In fact, there are actually thirty-six hidden tzaddikim scattered around the globe. A tzaddik doesn't wear his righteousness on his sleeve or reveal his identity to any-one. He does his good deeds on earth anonymously.

In the story of the bride and the cameah, Rabbi Schafer explained, three lives had been ruined. The bride became insane again, and never recovered. The water carrier had to leave town, because his cover as a tzaddik was blown. And the wise man on the rooftop, who made the cameah in good faith, left also.

I thought about the story of the bride in the insane asylum for days. Had Rabbi Schafer sensed how fearful I'd been all my life of ending up like that bride? Would I ever meet a tzaddik on my road from panic to peace? Perhaps my father was speaking to me through Rabbi Schafer, and I needed to make my own cameah.

Or maybe I already was, with tools that included meditation, EMDR, chanting, and painting the Buddha.

15

Tinkering with My Tool Kit

When flight attendants on an airplane look tense, I get tense. When they pull out those little seats that unfold from the wall and strap themselves in, I take some Klonopin. And when the plane shakes violently, thirty thousand feet off the ground, I reach for the CD that Belleruth Naparstek recorded to help people like me who suffer from panic attacks.

A psychotherapist for more than thirty years, Belleruth Naparstek is an author and pioneer in the field of guided imagery, which she describes as "a deliberate day dream that sends appealing messages in an immersive, healing way, straight into the primitive channels of the brain."

On my extended book tour for *The Faith Club*, Belleruth's CDs had become my security blanket, which I carried with me to every city I visited, in my hot pink iPod nano. Whenever I was freaked out, strung out, or unable to sleep, Belleruth whispered to me,

"Gently allow yourself to turn your attention inward, focusing inside for just this next while . . . using the powerful alchemy of the breath . . . softly acknowledging the sore, weary places and the strong, solid places . . . no praise, no blame, just noticing what is so . . ."

Belleruth feels that guided imagery can heal people in ways that talk therapy and drugs can't. Often her therapy works for people who are not helped by psychotherapy. "Even macho marine grunts love this stuff," she's said. "But you don't have to be smart or disciplined or alert or old to benefit from guided imagery. It also works well on people who do not have the oomph to do mindfulness meditation."

Belleruth has plenty of oomph for those of us unable to achieve liftoff on our own. "She's like a gateway drug," I joked to the friend who first turned me on to her CDs. Right from the start, Belleruth took me to a blissed-out state I wanted to find over and over again on my own. Legally, of course.

She's recorded dozens of different guided imagery CDs, helping people deal with emotional and physical challenges of all kinds, from drug abuse to heart disease, from HIV to MS, from pain to weight loss, depression to diabetes. Belleruth has worked with mainstream health and pharmaceutical companies, hospitals, recovery clinics, and even the Pentagon, to distribute her guided imagery recordings—in many cases free of charge—to people who need them.

I emailed Belleruth and asked if I could thank her in person for all of the times she'd comforted me. I was delighted when she invited me to visit her on Martha's Vineyard while she closed her house down for the winter.

At this point in my meditation practice, I had begun to see real changes in myself. I was sleeping much better, for long stretches of time, sometimes even seven hours straight. I was dreaming and remembering my dreams, which I hadn't been able to do for years. Meditation was making me more present in all aspects of my life, even when I was asleep!

I'd never been much of an adventurer. I never liked taking long drives by myself, since I'd experienced so many panic attacks while driving. But lately I had been looking forward to exploring the world on my own. I relished the idea of an overnight road trip.

I drove up to Cape Cod, listening to Dustin O'Halloran's hypnotic, meditative piano solos, which I had come to love. I took the ferry across Vineyard Sound on a clear, crisp fall day, meditating to the sound of the engines churning, the cool breeze on my face, and the sun beaming down on me. On the island, I drove to some of my favorite spots, and I meditated again by the beach. Then I checked into a cozy hotel, and met Belleruth for breakfast the next day.

She was striking, a tall woman with a shock of white, curly hair. We settled into a booth and I stared at the powerful healer who lived inside my iPod. "I can't believe I'm meeting you after all these years of listening to you!" I gushed.

"Your voice is like magic!" I said. "So moving, so comforting!"

"I didn't try for any of this," Belleruth said modestly, sipping a cup of coffee. "I made the first few recordings, and was surprised that they sounded pretty good. The imagery's just an unobtrusive platform to help people get into themselves."

"Where does it come from?"

"Beats me!" Belleruth laughed. "I never know what I'm going to do. I have notes and sometimes I edit when I'm speaking . . . my favorite imagery is for the trauma recording . . . 'Enter your broken heart . . . '"

"I have to tell you," I said, "I cry like a baby when I get to a certain point in your sleep CD. Where you have me gather the people who love me in a circle . . ."

Belleruth grinned. "Opening tear ducts, and any other kind of facial leakage—runny nose, gunky throat—all that's an excellent indicator that the person is in an immersive state."

"I'm immersed, all right."

"But people don't even have to be particularly moved to reap the benefits," she said.

"For me, it's immediate," I confessed. "When I turn on my iPod, press play, and hear your voice . . . boom! I get tears in my eyes!"

"That's great!" Belleruth laughed. "You're a cheap date!"

I explained the mission I was on to change my brain and my life. "Do you think I'll be able to meditate my way from panic to peace?" I asked.

With no hesitation, Belleruth said, "Of course!"

"But I'll have plenty of anxious moments . . ."

"And you'll have tools that you can deploy to head off panic."

"I'll carry a tool kit around in my head?"

"Yes," said Belleruth. "You'll get better and better at recognizing the earliest stages of triggering and you'll head panic off at the pass. And maybe sometimes you won't, but most of the time you will. You won't think about it every day. You won't even know you're not thinking about it. Until one day you'll think Gee, I haven't worried about this for quite a while. That's how it works."

"I'll try to assemble that tool kit," I said.

Belleruth's guided imagery would always be one of my most important tools. Somatic Experience therapy was a shiny new addition to my kit, and I told Belleruth about my recent sessions with Gina.

"People who've suffered trauma are used to the disassociated state," Belleruth told me, "so they're good at body-based therapies like Somatic Experience and meditation."

I knew what she meant. Every panic attack I ever experienced had thrown me into a lonely state of mind where I'd felt disconnected from the universe. Meditation transported me to a different detached place, which felt healing instead of disturbing. I craved the twenty minutes a day I set aside to meditate. The thoughts I used to try to push out of my head now just floated on by, instead of streaking through my nervous system like destructive meteors.

I'd even bought a *zafu*, a comfortable meditation cushion filled with buckwheat, and had shown great restraint when shopping online, forgoing "intentional chocolates" exposed to the brain waves of meditating monks, a meditation timer that chimed like a Tibetan singing bowl, and yoga mats I could personalize with a photo of Mickey.

Belleruth and I stood up and walked over to the breakfast buffet, still talking about our Jewish backgrounds, my grief over my mother's Alzheimer's, and the challenges of parenting emotionally healthy children. "A supervisor of mine once said, 'The best you can aim for is to just give them a treatable neurosis!'" Belleruth said, laughing.

We sat back down in our booth to eat. "You never know who's going to heal completely," Belleruth said, "and who's going to heal a lot. But if they stay with it, people with panic can heal. It's a relatively simple condition—essentially a survival response. All that's required to reverse panic is to learn self-regulation of any sort. Breath work, guided imagery, meditation, whatever floats your boat."

"I'm getting pretty good at meditation," I told Belleruth. "But I don't follow any rules. I don't meditate at any particular time of day, or any particular place."

My latest meditation breakthrough had occurred on my commute home from New York City. I'd taken a train in which a fire had broken out and we all had to be evacuated in the Bronx. I was able to wait calmly for the right bus to arrive, stand for a half hour until I got a seat, and then meditate all the way home. I was one cool commuter.

"I like walking meditation," Belleruth said. "And this morning, I sat in my bed, with the shades up, and watched the sun come up over the ocean. Nothing beats that." She smiled. "If you're focusing your mind to the extent that other tangential things are excluded, if you're immersed in an experience, that's meditation."

According to Belleruth, you can peel potatoes and be meditating. If you step outside and feel the crisp air after a big storm passes through, that's also meditating. "It's really just gratitude," she said.

"Speaking of gratitude, how can I ever thank you?" I asked. "How can anyone ever thank the people who help them to heal?"

"I don't think it's necessary," Belleruth said, graciously. "Just enjoy whatever it is that you got."

"I did bring a present for you," I said, pulling out a long necklace of shimmering white pearls that I'd made for Belleruth, my mind-altering healer.

I raised my mug of tea and made a toast to her: "Who needs magic mushrooms?" I laughed. "I've got Belleruth Naparstek!"

16

Attuning to My Tribe

A neurologist in Denver, Dr. Robert Scaer, has written books (including *The Trauma Spectrum*) about the impact of sudden trauma on people, describing how helplessness and terror cause all sorts of changes in brain function, body chemistry, and many bodily systems. He's theorized that panic might be handed down in utero, from an anxious mother to her child. On Belleruth's recommendation, I emailed him and he suggested we talk the next day.

Unlike his name, Dr. Scaer's voice was friendly and calm. I thanked him for his time.

And then he healed me.

Not completely, of course, but in one telephone conversation, this physician caused a remarkable shift to take place inside me.

I filled him in on my background. My mother had lost her father suddenly just six weeks before I was born, and she'd talked about that loss repeatedly. Could she have passed panic on to me in utero?

Dr. Scaer agreed that she might have passed along some anxiety, but he felt that other factors were also at work.

"Your parents were unable to nurture you through your crises because they were traumatized by their *own* upbringings," Dr. Scaer told me.

I stopped taking notes. "How did you know *that?*" I asked.

"You told me about the history of mental illness."

So mental illness is a type of trauma.

"You mothered your own mother," Dr. Scaer said.

"And how did you know *that?*" I wondered.

"I recognize it because I mothered my own mother," Dr. Scaer said simply. "My mother was a victim of trauma herself, and that affected her ability to mother me."

I took that in, touched by his candor.

On my eighteenth birthday, I told Dr. Scaer, my mother had said to me, "I've been your mother for eighteen years. Now will you be my mine?"

"And how did you respond?" Dr. Scaer asked.

"I told her 'I sprang from your womb, so that's biologically impossible.'"

My response was a curiously composed one for an eighteen-year-old, but I'd been practicing it for years. My favorite Dr. Seuss character was always Horton, the serious, responsible elephant who was forced to sit on an egg and hatch it, while Maisie, a "lazy bird," abandoned her nest.

Guess who thought she was Horton?

Dr. Scaer was quiet for a minute, then said, "I survived a childhood with a lot of surgeries, without my parents in the hospital alongside me. I didn't know I was traumatized until I was sixty, when I got into all this stuff. But trauma stays with you."

"It's not like I saw combat in Vietnam, or survived an earthquake, or was raped . . . ," I said.

Although Gina had also mentioned the word *trauma* to me, I felt self-conscious about being called a trauma survivor. My sister had survived cancer and several of my close friends, and even their children, had battled life-threatening illnesses. Who was I to lay claim to such suffering?

But Dr. Scaer said, simply, "What you experienced was traumatic."

I let that sink in. Panic didn't feel like such a crazy reaction to trauma. As Belleruth had said, it's basically a survival response. And I seemed to be on the right path to put it to rest. "I'm hoping to find peace," I said to Dr. Scaer. "Do you think I can get there?"

"Why not?" Dr. Scaer said. "Trauma therapy is all about being in the present moment without intrusive thoughts. Achieving a space of emptiness, purity, and attunement with the body."

"I can only imagine what all the stress hormones my panic attacks have released over the years have done to my body," I said.

"I meditate twice a day for thirty minutes," Dr. Scaer said. "I exercise regularly, I've got hundreds of friends . . . and still I have issues with my heart."

"I have a lot of friends also," I said. "In all my years of panic, I never scared them off."

"We're meant to attune to our tribe," Dr. Scaer said. "Once healed, trauma provides survivors with an enormous capacity for empathy. Some of the people who accomplished the most in life had a lot of trauma in their history," he continued. "Like Mother Teresa, Gandhi . . ."

"I hope that when all this is over, I will be proud to be a sensitive person," I said. "All my life, I've been ashamed that I was so sensitive, that my wiring was so different . . ."

"That tracheotomy had to be horribly traumatizing," Dr. Scaer told me. "They slit your throat open without anesthesia. There would have been no time for that."

A little movie popped into my head, played once, and then disappeared.

No anesthesia?

I almost reached for some vodka.

17

Touching a Nerve

⊂≫⊃

Looking for more tools to add to my internal toolbox, I drove up to the Omega Institute in Rhinebeck, New York on the day before Halloween. I'd signed up for a Buddhist retreat called "Smiling at Fear," led by Pema Chödrön, the first American woman to be ordained as a Buddhist nun. The courage she displays in her books had led me to believe she could help me become less scared. But I'd talked my friend Anna into coming with me, just in case . . .

We drove up together, enjoying the brilliant fall foliage, and pulled into Omega, a sprawling complex of buildings, woods, meeting halls, and beautifully landscaped pathways. My room was situated in a cabin near the bookstore; Anna's was in another unit on the other side of the meditation hall. We unpacked our bags and took a walk before dinner, stopping by a cottage called "The Wellness Center."

"What do you offer that's really unique?" I asked a young girl behind the desk.

"Trager," she said. "It's the most relaxed feeling you can have while still being awake. I tend to dream and snore while I'm doing it." Then she sealed the deal. "It retrains your central nervous system to be calm."

The only appointment available all weekend started in ten

minutes. I'd miss dinner, but I could still make Pema's lecture that night.

"Do it!" Anna urged me. Then she left, promising to save me a seat in the meditation hall.

I filled out a medical form, checking off boxes that indicated "I'm fairly anxious and fairly low energy." I felt a twinge of guilt about how little exercise I had been getting lately. All the work I was doing to fix my brain seemed to have made my body more sluggish. I wasn't even doing any yoga, although I'd practiced it on my own for many years.

A pretty young woman with short curly hair came out and introduced herself as Lisa and led me to a small, dimly lit room, where I lay down on a padded massage table.

Lisa stood by my feet and held on to them, pausing before she did anything. I closed my eyes, and she began touching my feet. Her hands were incredibly soft; her touch even softer. She twisted my legs ever so slightly, bent my knees gently. I felt currents coursing up through my body, from my toes to my head.

"Can you describe what you're doing?" I asked. "It's not like massage . . ."

Lisa said politely that she preferred not to explain what she was doing, but that if I had a concern or question I should certainly let her know.

She continued working on my legs, and I felt something stir in my chest. But I let go of that thought. Soon I was breathing very slowly and very deeply. And then it happened, just like the girl at the front desk said it would. I began snoring while I was awake!

"It is so unfair . . . that I cannot experience this . . . every . . . single . . . day . . . of my . . . life," I murmured to Lisa. "What a cruel world this is." We laughed and I sank into a blissful state as she moved to the top of the table and began working on my arms.

She touched my left shoulder, and I suddenly had a body memory, for lack of a better word, of an experience I hadn't thought about in decades.

I had broken my collarbone when I was eleven. I fell off a horse while I was riding at a sleepover camp one summer. Suddenly I was back in the moment when I'd told the adults in charge how much it hurt and they told me not to tell my parents. They said I was a hypochondriac and didn't get me to a doctor.

Lisa's hands floated around my shoulder.

The pain had been brutal at first, I recalled, and then it diminished over time. For three weeks I rode horses, played sports, and didn't mention my ordeal in letters or phone calls home. Even after I returned from camp, I waited until a friend of my parents, who rode horses, came over to visit one night. "I have a bump on my collarbone," I said to this woman, pointing to the place where the bone jutted out, unhealed. She gasped and brought my mother over to take a look. They took me to a doctor, who reset it.

I must have been an expert at holding on to pain without complaint.

After Lisa stopped working on my body, I was completely relaxed, even peaceful. When I opened my eyes, her pretty face wobbled into focus, as if I were emerging from surgery, in an operating room, albeit a heavenly one. Lisa looked like an angel. "What did you do to me?" I asked.

"This is your birthright," she said. "This feeling of peace and wholeness and openness and potential. And it's available to us at any given moment. It's a matter of connecting your body to this universal life force."

I definitely wanted to find that umbilical cord.

"We're not finished," Lisa said when I tried to sit up. "I'd like you to turn over so that I can work on your back."

Oh . . . my . . . God. The second half of my treatment was as

wonderful as the first. I was speechless at the end, when Lisa finished. Which was, for me, truly a miracle.

I got up from the table and managed to walk out to the recep-
tion area, still stunned by the power of this seemingly simple process. I asked Lisa if she'd talk to me about what she'd done and she
demurred. "I'm not very eloquent," she said.

"Yes, you are," I told her. "Your hands are incredibly eloquent."

"Milton Trager invented this technique," Lisa said. "He was a
boxer in Miami who used to troll the beaches looking for people
to heal. Milton described his technique as 'creating peace in the
world, one person at a time.'" She handed me her card. "You'd better go, or you'll miss Pema."

"Pema who?" I joked.

We both laughed as I floated out the door.

Lisa's gentle rocking motions stayed with me as I followed a
well-lit path to the meditation hall, too blissed out to be afraid of
facing my fears.

18

Smiling at Fear

The next morning, Halloween day, I was awakened by the sound of a male voice moaning next to me in bed.

But I was alone.

In a sleepy haze, I checked my BlackBerry, to see if somehow I'd put my alarm setting on "moan." But, of course, I hadn't.

For the first time in months, I'd forgotten to meditate the night before. I'd been so zonked out by my Trager treatment that I'd gone straight to sleep after Pema's teaching session. I'd been meditating every day for at least twenty minutes, until yesterday. Were the meditation gods punishing me?

Or was somebody in another realm trying to reach me? Hundreds of workshops had been held at Omega over the years, many of them focusing on the afterlife. Maybe the psychic phone lines were jammed. Perhaps a spirit had dialed the wrong number, mistaking me for someone else. Or maybe my past lives were closing in on me.

I couldn't let myself panic while I was attending a retreat called "Smiling at Fear." Yet Pema Chödrön's book titles terrified me: *When Things Fall Apart, The Places That Scare You.*

"Strength doesn't come from running away from fear, armoring ourselves, or putting on a mask," Pema had told us the night before. "We can't try to run away from feelings or avoid them.

Strength comes from allowing ourselves to not grow a thick skin, to be willing to take a chance and not have anything to lose."

I certainly had nothing to lose by staying calm in the face of this strange voice in my room. Besides, it was too early to run for breakfast. So I picked up the notes I'd taken at last night's session and read them, shored up by Pema's insights. If I couldn't face my fears here, with Pema Chödrön holding my hand, where in the world could I?

It was time for me to become a warrior instead of a worrier. Time to exercise what Pema calls "tenderhearted bravery."

With my notebook in hand, I stepped out of my cabin, still slightly scared but determined. Closing the door, I discovered that I'd left my key in the lock all night. Anyone or any ghost could have walked right into my room. It turned out I'd been smiling at fear without even knowing it.

I met up with Anna for breakfast, observing the retreat's silence. We headed over to the meditation hall for another session with Pema, whose name, I remembered from drawing the Buddha, means lotus flower.

"No matter how wonderful you think the teachings are, you need to apply them on a day-to-day basis," she told us. "Sometimes you need to escalate yourself into a mess, and then you can learn from that."

Escalate myself into a mess? I was pretty good at that. I'd been doing it all my life. Wasn't that the definition of a panic attack?

A small woman with a strong face and a nearly shaved head, Pema dressed in the maroon robes of her order. She looked like she had it all together, but that hadn't happened overnight. "You don't discover courage right away," Pema told us. "You discover a tender, shaky vulnerability. It takes courage to be vulnerable. But when you live with a genuine heart, unarmored, you can trust the basic goodness of yourself and humanity."

My husband, Jimmy, the man to whom I'd handed my shaky self decades earlier, was the first person to set eyes on my "genuine heart." I had allowed myself to be truly vulnerable with him and had reaped the benefits, a loving relationship and friendship, two great-spirited sons, years of adventure and companionship.

Pema quoted her revered teacher, Chögyam Trungpa, who founded the first Tibetan Buddhist school in America, the Naropa Institute in Boulder, Colorado. Trungpa talked about discovering one's "genuine heart of sadness." When you do that, he said, "You can see the world without filters. You're much more able to see the blueness of an iris, the orangeness of fall leaves, the wetness of rain, the crunch of snow . . . the world is more accessible."

During question-and-answer periods, several people spoke in detail about their pain. Pema was compassionate but firm. Without being judgmental, she made the point that dwelling on one's own suffering or sadness was not productive. She gave me the perspective that I needed to stop dwelling on my own difficulties. She quoted Trungpa: "Pleasure is not a reward, and pain is not a punishment. They are just ordinary occurrences."

Pema didn't hold herself up as a brave, fearless warrior. Despite the fact that her words, as she put it, were "all over calendars," she admitted that she experienced fear, anger, resentment, and all of the other crippling emotions that her students had experienced. As Chögyam Trungpa taught her: "A rainbow is made of sunshine and tears mixed together."

"No feeling is ever final," Pema taught us. "Everything can fall apart. We all feel that what's happening now will last forever. But feeling your worst is the end of one thing and the beginning of something else."

"One hour of Pema is like a semester of college!" I whispered to Anna, who smiled and nodded in agreement.

"I can tell you this," Pema said. "It doesn't get any easier as you get older. Everything starts breaking down right about sixty-seven to sixty-eight, just as you're racing to seventy!" She smiled. She had us smiling in the face of all of our fears.

During a midday break, Anna and I took a walk around the meditation hall. We passed the Wellness Center, where I had received my Trager treatment the night before, and I told Anna how powerful it had been. But now I recalled more details around that time of my life when I'd broken my collarbone.

I was never an athlete, I told Anna. I was a girl who skipped gym class, hung out in the art room, and smoked Marlboros in high school. But for a short time, when I was ten and eleven, I competed in horse shows all across New England. My brief foray into the world of competitive riding began and ended abruptly, however. My father had decided that I should learn how to trot, canter, and gallop. A friend of his had two sons who competed at a high level, aiming for the Olympics. They rode giant horses and jumped six-foot-tall fences.

I rode a little pony and competed in shows where I jumped fences that were three feet high. I won ribbons and trophies, but it was spending time with my father that was the most important thing in the world to me. Every Sunday, my father used to drive me to the stables an hour away from our house and watch me perform. I liked this ritual, but the riding itself was often scary. During practice sessions, the couple who ran the stable used to stand in the middle of the riding rink with a giant bullwhip and crack it, so the pony I rode would start galloping. I'd hang on for dear life, terrified.

When my parents found out that I'd broken my collarbone, they decided abruptly that I would stop riding. I had no say in the matter, and I never rode a horse again. But when Anna and I returned to the meditation hall after our break, Pema announced that she was going to teach us a meditation practice called Windhorse. "This is a way of rousing your confidence when you're afraid," she said. "Or when there's the potential for you to be afraid."

Even though she was talking about a metaphysical horse, I felt a twinge of anxiety. Pema Chödrön was going to teach me how to get back onto a horse.

"You can practice this in the morning when you're not out of bed yet, or when you're scared, or panicking," she told us. "You can continue to do this again and again during the course of the day, and pull yourself out of a tailspin."

Windhorse meditation is not something that you have to manufacture, Pema explained. It's an awakening of a spark that's already inside you. "Feel where you are," she instructed us. "Be genuine, bored, or distressed. And then visualize the sun in your heart, however it works best for you. No matter what shape you're in, the sun is just there, shedding warmth and light, illuminating your own darkness. There's a much more expansive part of your being, far beyond your hopes and fears of how you want things to be," she assured us.

Everyone in the meditation hall prepared to practice Windhorse. I closed my eyes, visualizing an enormous, powerful sun filling my chest. I sat silently, feeling its warmth.

Then I opened my eyes suddenly, as Pema had instructed us to do. I visualized the sun shooting rays of light and warmth out into the universe. In Pema's words, I sent out "a tenderhearted wish to help the world in difficult times."

It felt fantastic. I was back in the saddle again.

At dinner that night, Anna handed me a present she'd bought at the bookstore—a large abalone shell and a huge stick of sage. "I think we should smudge your room before you go to sleep tonight," she said.

We walked to my little cabin together. Anna placed the abalone shell on a table, then lit the sage. "This is a traditional Native American way of cleaning out a space," she told me, smiling. "I'm going to ask all the spirits in this beautiful part of the world to come and protect you, so that you won't have any more strange voices moaning in your bed."

Anna lit a match, and then the stick of sage. But when she waved it around the four corners of my room, she set off a loud fire alarm. We screamed and giggled like schoolgirls. After a moment, the alarm stopped and my room was filled with a sharp, healing scent.

"Now, if anyone comes into your room tonight, you can just flash them a lovely smile, as we've been taught to do," Anna teased, bidding me good night. "Don't forget to smile at fear!"

I slept well that night, and woke up the next morning alone in my quiet bed, a tiny bit less afraid, and ready to rope and ride.

At our last teaching session, Pema didn't hold back. "Sometimes the S-H-I-T hits the F-A-N," she said. "And everything just falls apart.

"Suddenly you get ill, or someone dear to you becomes ill. Suddenly you're going to die very soon or someone very dear to you is dying or has died. Sometimes you return home and your house has burned down, or all of your possessions get stolen. Relationships end. Life falls apart in various ways."

"We spin out all sorts of storylines," Pema told us. "Drop the storyline and stay with the rawness of failure. Or the elation of success."

I'd been telling myself stories for so many years. But stories change. Plots twist and take unexpected turns. Maybe the story of my life with panic was something I could drop. Not suddenly, but my life story had already begun to unfurl before me in a new, exciting way.

Now that I could ride a horse again, anything seemed possible.

19

Hooked on Healing

After the retreat with Pema Chödrön, I made an appointment to see Adrienne R. Stone, a therapist who had trained with the late Milton Trager himself. I'd read about Milton's trailblazing career and developed a tiny crush on him, although in some photos he did look a bit like Ed Asner on a bad hair day. His craggy face radiated a strength and wisdom I wanted more of.

"How long was your trach tube in?" Adrienne asked, while taking my medical history.

"What?"

"After a tracheotomy, they usually leave the tube in place for a few days."

I stared at Adrienne, a petite woman with beautiful green eyes, long, curly brown hair, and a sweet face, as I tried to process this new information. Reflexively, I reached up and touched the round, white scar in the hollow of my throat.

"I have no idea," I said. "My parents never mentioned that."

My scar wasn't the only reminder of my near-death experience. High fevers and antibiotics had damaged the teeth forming in my gums at the time so that, when they'd emerged, they were misshapen and discolored. I'd been very self-conscious about them until I was allowed to get the front ones capped.

Adrienne guided me toward her padded massage table, where I lay on my back, and she stood, quietly, running her fingers across my temples lightly. She lifted my head, holding it as though weighing it, thoughtfully. Then she headed down to the other end of the table and began working on my feet and legs.

The room was silent, her movements deliberate but fluid. Adrienne's touch was gentle, and she seemed to be speaking to my tissue: whispering, guiding, suggesting, coaxing.

Every so often she'd stop for a moment and hold her hands in place, as though she needed to send a special message to that particular part of my body.

Adrienne touched my ribs, and my jaw suddenly relaxed. She held my rib cage, and my battle-scarred lungs felt safe in her hands.

"How do you feel?" she asked an hour later, at the end of our first session.

"You're a tiger tamer," I murmured. I stretched from head to toe, luxuriating in my relaxed state, feeling like a big cat stretching in the sunshine at the Bronx Zoo.

Holding my arm, Adrienne guided me back up to a seated position very slowly, teaching me how to stack every vertebra of my back carefully, one by one. Then she coaxed me to a standing position, getting me "back into gravity." I felt drugged.

She pushed my collarbones back gently, exposing the area around my throat, urging me to try standing more upright. I realized that I'd been protecting that part of my body. And as I gathered up my things and prepared to leave, Adrienne urged me to look in a mirror on her wall.

I gasped.

"What do you see?" she asked.

"Happiness and lightness," I replied, staring at my reflection.

But happiness and lightness come and go. The next week, I returned and told Adrienne, "I felt dead all weekend."

I think she flinched.

"I'm not used to being this relaxed," I explained. "That's why I felt dead."

"You might want to take a look at that word," Adrienne suggested.

I hopped onto her table and rubbed my hands together gleefully. I might not have described the results as well as I could have, but I did like the way she made me feel. "Let the games begin!" I said.

Adrienne stood at the head of the table, holding my head in her hands, just as she had the last time. Then she moved down to my feet and began softly manipulating my legs.

I felt a stirring in my chest. Had I felt this the last time?

Maybe. I tried to relax. I lay still while Adrienne moved up to the top of the table and began stroking my neck, rhythmically.

Boom! Electrical currents raced up and down my body. I wanted to scream. My heart was pounding. My throat began to close.

"I'm not feeling good," I managed to whisper.

Adrienne immediately took her hands off me. "What is it you're feeling?" she asked.

"I'm on the verge of a massive panic attack," I said, shaking. Every cell of my body was tingling. "If I was out in the real world and I felt like this? I'd gulp down some vodka. Quickly."

I started shivering.

"Maybe I'm dehydrated," I thought out loud.

Adrienne moved swiftly to pour me a glass of water. She handed it to me and I gulped it down. "Why don't you try lying on your side?" she suggested, her voice calm. She helped me to roll over.

I lay on my left side, curled up in a fetal position in her dimly lit room. I was quivering like a greyhound in a thunderstorm. Adrienne placed one hand on my back, another on my rib cage. She stood there silently, holding on to me. It felt like she knew what she was doing, and I began to calm down.

Slowly, Adrienne took her hands off me and guided me into a sitting position. My left collarbone, the one I'd broken decades earlier, ached.

"What did you do to me?" I asked as I got off the table and sat down next to Adrienne's desk. She had defused an imminent panic attack.

"I just stayed with you," she responded.

Nobody had done that so effectively before.

I composed myself and left Adrienne's office a bit wobbly. Unnerved, I thought about what had happened all week. I wasn't ready to abandon Trager therapy, but I wasn't sure if I was ready to place myself in Adrienne's hands again, so I had some questions for her at our next appointment.

"How do you decide what you're going to do?" I asked.

"I try to ground myself when I begin," Adrienne said. "I feel my feet on the floor, and just for a moment I go inside, so that I'm ready to give your body what I feel it needs. I want to receive what your body is telling me. Milton called this moment a hookup. It's the feeling you get when you look out the window at a brilliant blue sky, or see a newborn baby. It's a pure connection, where everything else falls away."

That sounded fine.

"But working with the body can be very unpredictable," Adrienne continued.

I laughed nervously. "You think?"

"More often than not, people do receive deep relaxation and peace with this work," she said. "But it's not a given."

I seemed to be able to turn any experience into an anxious one. "But I want this to work," I said. I wanted the good feelings I remembered from the first two sessions. "I want to feel calm," I told Adrienne.

"What would that feel like?" she asked me.

"I would like to feel a sense of connectedness to my body in a friendly way," I declared. "In a calm and peaceful way. In a confident way." I sighed. "My first session with you was so great, but I think there was probably a stirring in my chest even then."

"When we're quiet, we pay a lot more attention to what's going on inside us," Adrienne explained. "When you're busy, you might not notice that same feeling in your chest."

"What is your goal with Trager therapy?" I asked.

"Integration," Adrienne told me. "Working so that you can feel your entire body as a whole."

I wasn't so sure that I wanted to feel my whole body. When I became conscious of certain parts they seemed to want to run the show. But I knew I had to face my fear of them and let them become part of the family.

In the next few sessions, Adrienne helped me enormously. I was able to relax my body and mind, accepting whatever sensations passed through me without anticipation, judgment, or fear. It felt as though my body was meditating, letting any anxiety or panic flow through me without taking hold. After each session Adrienne gave me suggestions for walking and moving differently, exposing my chest and throat to the world.

"You're good at this," she told me. And, session by session, I got better.

In a book called *Moving Medicine*, by Jack Liskin, I learned that Milton Trager grew up in Chicago, dropped out of school after eighth grade, worked in factories, and hung around a theater on weekends, fascinated by acrobatics. In 1924, his family moved to Miami, where he performed gymnastics with his brother on the beach every Sunday. He also took up boxing, and one day offered to give his trainer, who was in pain, a rubdown. Trager healed him so successfully that he was inspired to work on his father back home, curing his sciatica after just four sessions.

Trager approached the parents of polio-stricken children on the beach, offering to work on them as well. When he was nineteen, he helped a child who had been paralyzed for four years learn how to walk, and Trager was hooked on healing. He moved out to Hollywood to become a stuntman, but instead found his calling as an extraordinary, perhaps revolutionary physical therapist.

And he never forgot the message he'd once read on a bulletin board: *"Take a deep breath."*

"That was the beginning of me," Trager said. By pausing to explore the most basic act of breathing, Trager discovered "an internal galaxy that he would continue to explore for the rest of his days," according to Jack Liskin. I vowed to become an explorer of my own internal galaxy, like Trager.

I'd already been shot into space. I'd become friends with my breath, and was getting more comfortable in my own body.

"Is this how normal human beings feel every day of their lives?" I asked Jimmy one afternoon.

He smiled. "Who says you're normal?"

But I did feel almost normal.

"When you cry, make it really count," Milton once told a woman who had been moved to tears by his therapy. Deep, heavy sobbing was therapeutic and refreshing in Trager's world. That made me feel less self-conscious about all the crying I'd done since I'd started meditating.

As my body grew stronger and more open, I learned to trust it a bit more. I didn't feel pressured to solve its mysteries through Trager therapy or Somatic Experience therapy, but both helped me learn to let go, and trust that my body could heal itself.

I also began to accept the unpredictability of my own internal galaxy.

Over the next few weeks, my sacrum, at the base of my spine, began to soften. I started standing up straighter, my chest more open. Around the house, I was careful to extend my back when I bent over. I moved my body as Adrienne had instructed me to do, and it began to realign itself.

I felt like a living, breathing illustration of a caveman, who slowly evolves into upright homo sapiens.

After a particularly wonderful session with Adrienne, my body felt tingly all over. "It feels like every cell is alive," I said. "Like my body is tapping out its own internal Morse code messages." I lay on Adrienne's table, beaming. "This feeling used to make me anxious," I remembered.

"And what does it make you feel now?" Adrienne asked.

"Alive," I answered, without hesitation.

"Alive is good," Adrienne said.

And, for the first time, every cell in my body seemed to agree.

How to Love

20

The Lovingkindness
Convention

A journey of a thousand miles begins with a single step, said Lao Tzu, the author of *The Tao Te Ching* or the *Book of the Way*. And sometimes that single step is almost the same step, taken again and again.

So, even though I'd been meditating every day as Mingyur had taught me, I had returned to the Garrison Institute, where I'd first studied with Mingyur Rinpoche, for a three-day meditation retreat with Sharon Salzberg and Sylvia Boorstein, two Buddhist teachers whose writings always inspire me. I'd come back to my spiritual roots—my new roots.

It was mid-November and, as I unpacked my suitcase in my little room, I could hear a woman on her cell phone planning Thanksgiving dinner. Her thoughts on food, transportation, and the guest list floated through the pipes of the old monastery's heating system. But silence was going to commence after dinner; I wouldn't be hearing any tantalizing cranberry sauce recipes after that.

I walked downstairs to the large meditation hall, sat facing the golden Buddha at the front of the room, and saved the cushion next to me for a friend who'd accompanied me. Closing my eyes, I meditated for a few minutes. When I opened them, a petite woman, Sylvia Boorstein, sat motionless on a chair facing me and the people who had filled the hall. Sylvia's salt-and-pepper hair was cropped close to her pretty face; her hands were cupped in her lap, her eyes closed.

Sharon Salzberg entered the room and sat down in a chair beside Sylvia, flashing her brilliant smile, which I remembered from the last time I had seen her, at the kirtan in New Jersey. Sharon radiated such kindness that she seemed like an old friend, someone who could comfort people in just the way they needed comforting.

A psychotherapist with the ability to cut to the chase, as well as a Jewish mother and grandmother, Sylvia introduced Sharon as "my friend, my colleague, and my teacher." She asked how many people had studied with the two of them before, and how many people had practiced meditation. Hands shot up and down in response to her questions.

"You all came to the right place," Sylvia told us, smiling. "We are always starting again, whether it's our hundred-and-third retreat or our first."

She told us that there is only one dharma (or practice) talk, and that it is about what we are doing, how we are doing it, and toward what end. "Life is complicated and challenging for everyone," Sylvia said. "There's a way of living it with joy, compassion, and goodwill." She began her teachings by telling us a Buddhist folk story.

After his enlightenment, the Buddha's demeanor radiated an aura of such confidence that someone asked him, "Are you a god?"

"No," the Buddha answered.

"Are you an ordinary man?" he was asked.

"No," he replied.

"What are you then?" someone wondered.

And the Buddha replied, "I am awake."

I could be awake, if being awake weren't so scary, I thought to myself. Still, I was certainly more awake and aware than six months before and had pierced through the trance of fear a number of times.

Sylvia has been married for fifty years to a psychologist, and has meditated for thirty of those years. Her husband once asked her what good all that meditation had done. "It made me kind," she told him. When he observed that she'd always been kind, even before meditating, she amended her observation: "It made me kind*er*."

Sylvia regularly leads a meditation group at Spirit Rock, a retreat center outside San Francisco. "When I'm meditating with people, I might think of someone I know who's having a hard time," she said, "and I'll mention that. Other voices will chime in: 'I'm thinking of my mother who's moving into assisted living,' or 'Our son just came home from college with severe depression.' Someone might have just gotten a cancer diagnosis, someone else might be pregnant with triplets. Not all challenges are dire.

"So many things cause pain and distress in the mind and body. It's stunning. I think, How can I possibly give a dharma talk?" Sylvia paused. "Life is difficult, and yet we want more of it. We're heroic, actually; we're incredibly resilient.

"Every day, one thousand dharma talks are being held on Upper Broadway," she said, meaning that we can learn from everyone around us and every situation we encounter. "But if I'm holed up in my own thoughts, I'll miss them."

I pictured myself outside Zabar's on the Upper West Side, becoming enlightened by the hundreds of people passing by me, along with a dose of Zabar's delicious chocolate babka.

Sharon began her teaching by explaining how meditation helps us to knit all the parts of ourselves together. "No matter what circumstances we're facing, we're looking for a state of balance," she said. "We acknowledge the universality of suffering but also look at joy, delight, happiness, and gratitude."

That night, I fell asleep like a peaceful nun in my single wooden bed, feeling content in my pursuit of understanding and peace. In a journey of a thousand steps, sometimes a girl simply needs to lie down.

Back in the meditation hall the next day, Sylvia advised us to look at the retreat as an extended Sabbath. "We're resting in the service of revelation," she said. "Life is challenging to humans because it's impermanent, and we can't grasp on to something that's impermanent."

She recalled driving up to her house in Sonoma, California, with her husband one day, to find that an enormous branch of a two-hundred-year-old tree had crashed to the ground, blocking their road. If their timing had been different, they could have been crushed. "It wouldn't have been the tree's fault," Sylvia told us. "It wouldn't have been our fault. It simply would have been time for the oak tree to drop that branch. Lots of things happen because they happen," she said. "We can't change them. And suffering, according to the Buddha, is that tension in the mind created by the thought that things should be different from the way they are."

Our ability to empathize with the pain of others comes from an early age, Sylvia said. "If we're born with good neurology, get fed a good diet, and live with people who look like they love us, we develop emotional attunement and can feel compassion for others."

Sylvia suggested that we meditate together now by looking for "a neutral, available, repetitive place to rest our attention." Then she urged us to focus on our breath and hold it lovingly.

I hesitated. My breath was hardly a neutral force. But I followed Sylvia's instructions and inhaled, saying silently, "May I meet this moment fully." I waited a beat and then let go of my breath. "May I meet it as a friend," I said to myself, exhaling.

I did that, over and over again, slowly.

My breath had never been a reliable friend, but more of a fair-weather one. I was still nervous that it could run away from me, but I kept meeting my breath gently and, when Sylvia rang a bell signifying the end of our meditation, I felt refreshed and calm, proud and relieved. I could breathe, thanks to Sylvia's comforting instructions.

Sharon took over the teaching next. And she taught about the breath, as well. "It's not elaborate," Sharon said. "The breath is so personal, and always available." She smiled. "In the middle of a contentious meeting, you don't have to pull out a cushion or incense. If you're breathing, you're meditating."

In the presence of these two kind, nurturing women, I felt safe and, for the second time that day, I had a positive experience while simply observing my breath coming and going, in and out of my body. For the first time in my life, I believed that I could make friends with my breath. Perhaps my panic could become a friend, too, or at least a nodding acquaintance.

When Sylvia suggested we use our breath for meditation yet again, I didn't tense up; I followed her instructions and took ten breaths, counting each one slowly, focusing on the beginning and end of each inhalation and exhalation. I managed to stay calm. "The breath comes and goes," Sylvia said, as my breath came and went. "We are breathed."

And, indeed, I was breathed.

"All beings want to be happy," Sharon said the next morning. "But very few know how to do that. We're so tormented and cause so much pain because of ignorance and confusion. We're all tremendously vulnerable, because life is shifting and changing all the time."

Sylvia spoke next. "Usually, when you can't feel compassion, you're in pain yourself," she said. "Only when you can get yourself out of that pain can you help others by showing compassion."

"Giving to others in that way rescues us from being caught up in the ideas and smallness of our own story," she said. "In the scripture, compassion is defined as the quivering of the heart in response to pain."

I loved that! After all my shaky heart had been through in the last forty years, I welcomed the idea that it could quiver in the very best way, not from my own selfish fear, but with compassion for others.

"If you're on a train or a plane," Sylvia continued, "and you look around at all the people, you don't know who's just been diagnosed with a tumor, whose mother is dying, whose partner has just proceeded with a divorce, whose son has just broken his sobriety, who's just been diagnosed with diabetes . . .

"Everyone has lost people they love," she said quietly, "along with wishes and hopes. Life is heartbreaking and uplifting. It's so hard to be a human being."

We broke for lunch, and I checked my BlackBerry. My mother's doctor had left me a voice mail, and I walked outside onto a terrace by the monastery in order to call her back.

It was a gorgeous fall day. I spent ten minutes explaining to yet another doctor why I did not want my mother taken off her anti-psychotic medication. Other people had tried to wean her off the same drug three times before, and she'd been miserable, confused, and delirious. I wanted my mother to be happy. I wanted to keep her from the pain of confusion as much as I possibly could.

I hung up and tried to calm myself down by walking around the grounds of the monastery. Then I ate some lunch and returned to the meditation hall, still a bit anxious.

"When the Buddha taught laypeople, he always began by talking about generosity," Sharon said, launching into an explanation of lovingkindness. "There are so many simple ways to be generous—small things like smiling at someone in an elevator, or listening to a stranger at a party."

"When you give," Sharon continued, "there's a sense of gladdening, moving toward simplicity, feeling your life whole, and that your ethics are based on integrity."

Gladdening? I was sick of worrying about my mother. That's all I could think about as I sat in front of Sharon. For ten years, I'd been a health advocate, financial advisor, and social worker, responsible for my mother's medical, monetary, and legal decisions. And I felt guilty for being resentful, especially with Sharon Salzberg and a giant Buddha sitting in front of me.

Sharon read my mind. "It's hard to have sympathy for others if we have an overwhelming sense of depletion," she said. "We're just exhausted. We don't have the resilience."

That did it. I started to cry. I took off my glasses, splattered with tears. I wiped them with my shirt, and they snapped in half. Here I was, midway into my journey to become calm and compassionate, and I was already tired of being compassionate to my own mother. I had snapped. I didn't want to continue living the way I had, with panic and fear, with grudging compassion. I had to change the way I viewed myself in the world. Without eyeglasses.

Sharon suggested that we try walking meditation, using the phrases "May I be happy" and "May I be peaceful" as we placed one foot in front of the other. People paced the meditation hall slowly, and then left to walk elsewhere. I approached Sharon.

"My mother has Alzheimer's," I said. "And I am so exhausted. Sometimes I wish that my mother would die," I found myself confessing to the queen of lovingkindness.

Sharon didn't flinch. She handed me a tissue, and said that she had friends going through what I was experiencing. She knew how hard it was. She'd visited a nursing home recently, where she'd seen how caregivers could comfort other caregivers. She was extraordinarily kind and I felt better about feeling crushed by guilt and responsibility.

I left the meditation hall to walk outside into the fall sunshine once more, back to my favorite bench overlooking the Hudson River. I heard the mournful sound of a train blowing its horn in the distance as an old, weathered train pulled into view, passing below the cliffs of West Point across the Hudson. The longest train I'd ever seen, it moved slowly and deliberately on its journey up the river.

"Move on with your life," I heard my father say. I felt a small shift, perhaps the beginning of the "gladdening" Sharon had spoken of.

Back in the meditation hall, my friend Elizabeth had placed some tissues and a bottle of water on my cushion. I smiled at her and whispered thanks.

Sylvia began teaching us once again about the impermanence of life. "If we are well parented and comfortable, we feel at ease," she said. "But a coming of age inevitably arrives. Life is finite. We lose everything and everyone that we love."

She urged us to look at life in a miraculous way. She spoke of the first time she had seen photos of Earth taken from outer space—of the green and blue planet we inhabit. "On this ball," Sylvia said, "we are all active participants in our lives. We are all interconnected. We are all suffering. Sometimes I think of this planet as a flying hospital."

Next Sharon told us of the Buddha's antidote to fear: the four simple phrases used to practice lovingkindness meditation, which she'd taught at the kirtan with Krishna Das months earlier. "Since they're words, they will be imperfect," Sharon told us. "We don't want to be imprisoned in them, but we do need a baseline." It was fine for us to shape and change the words as we saw fit.

I sat on my cushion, eyes closed. "May I be safe," I said to myself. "May I be happy, may I be healthy, may I live with ease."

Some of that seemed achievable.

I repeated the words over and over again to myself, and just as I was beginnng to feel a bit selfish, Sharon explained why it was important to wish ourselves well. "We need to be in tune with our own emotional states and reactions in order to develop sensitivity, which is the basis of empathy."

She urged us to think of a benefactor, or someone who made us smile, and to wish that person the same things we'd wished for ourselves. After that we chose someone we knew who was in pain. Finally we wished that all living beings around the world be safe, be happy, be healthy, and live with ease.

"You could spend the rest of your life wishing yourself well and it would be a perfect practice," Sylvia told us. "Because the only heart you can change is your own. The only mind you can change is your own." Quoting Chögyam Trungpa, she said, "Moments of grace are accidental. And meditation makes us accident prone."

At the end of that day's teachings, Sharon made a surprise announcement: her friend Krishna Das was coming to chant kirtan for us after dinner. My joy therapist was in the house!

That night I sang, chanting with Krishna Das, swaying to the music. My soul was lifted. The golden Buddha looked down upon us, and after the concert was over, my whole body was vibrating, like a Tibetan singing bowl.

With Sylvia, I had been breathed. With Krishna Das, I had been sung.

To come down from the high of the concert, I took a pad of paper and pencils into the communal lounge on my floor and carefully and methodically drew the face of the Buddha, as I had been taught by Lama Tsondru. Paying attention to every stroke of my pencil, I calmed down. And while flipping through some magazines and books stored in the lounge, I found a quote from Pema Chödrön:

> We really don't want to stay with the nakedness of our present experience. It goes against the grain to stay present. There are the times when only gentleness and a sense of humor can give us the strength to settle down.

21

Magical Repair

Meditating daily, I began to notice that I wasn't as reactive as I used to be when it came to my relationships with people. Jimmy noticed that I didn't snap at him anymore. In the thirty years that we'd known each other, I sometimes directed any anger I felt about life at the one person I thought wouldn't leave me—my husband. Without making a conscious effort, I now seemed to be able to let anger pass without taking my frustration out on poor Jimmy. "You're more present," he said to me when I asked if he'd noticed any difference in me since I'd begun meditating.

I also didn't jump to conclusions about other people's actions, words, or motives. A psychologist named Dr. Marsha Lucas recommends mindfulness meditation to her patients and writes, in an article, "When you practice mindfulness meditation, your brain gets better at making sense of incoming emotional information without jumping to conclusions, reacting out of old habits, or getting stuck in emotional dead-ends like worry or grudges. It does the right stuff with that information, helping you to wisely tell the difference between what's happening in the moment and what's your 'old stuff.'"

When I returned to work with Gina to process some of that

"old stuff," she noted that I looked different, that my face looked more relaxed.

"I think I'm ready to process my very first panic attack," I announced.

And then I promptly got a case of cold feet.

"What if I totally freak out?" I was worried about what this strange new therapy would unleash.

Gina assured me that she would help me through whatever I experienced. "Maybe it would be okay to say you're scared."

"What's the worst that could happen here?" I asked myself out loud. "I could go crazy. Do you think that's a possibility?"

"No," Gina said. "You're not psychotic."

"But panic is a mental illness, isn't it?" I asked.

"Yes," Gina said. "But it's not a psychosis."

She explained that, if I continued to try to analyze everything, I could just end up with a well-analyzed problem. "That's not the solution," Gina told me.

"So what is the solution?" I asked, and started to cry.

"What's making you cry?" Gina asked.

"My panic has been with me forever," I said. "I can't imagine letting go of it."

"Most people live lives of quiet desperation," Gina said. "But you're deciding that you don't have to."

"Why do I deserve happiness?" I asked.

"Why not?" Gina looked me in the eye. "Then there'd be one more happy person on the planet. Wouldn't that be lovely? If you ask people what they're looking for, they'll say they're looking for happiness."

I thought about happiness, tears streaming down my cheeks.

"If I become happy and healthy," I said, "then I will no longer be related to those people that I came from. I won't belong to the family that I grew up in."

I took that in.

"I think I've been suffering for a lot of people," I whispered. "I think that was always my job in the family. Give me your pain and I'll hold on to it for you. A broken collarbone? No problem. A panic disorder? Bring it on! I'm one of you guys, you people with all your pain. I'm not in a mental hospital. I don't want to go that far. But panic? That's my comfort zone. I'm good. Sign me up."

I took a deep, uneven breath. "I don't want to say goodbye to all those people in my family, to leave them in the dust," I managed to say. "On the other hand, I don't know how much time I have left. Why should I carry around their pain?"

"Good question," Gina said.

"I did not have a happy childhood," I heard myself say.

I was stunned.

"How did I not know this before?" I wondered.

In every picture ever taken of me as a child, I was solemn. While my brother and sister mugged for the camera, I looked deep in thought. I'd brought in several of those photos to show Gina weeks earlier.

"These sad pictures weren't just moments in my childhood," I realized now. "They *were* my childhood. Or a huge part of it. I was weighted down with so much pain for so long. I had my own, and then my parents gave me theirs."

It was time for me to leave. I'd been bawling on and off for almost an hour. I walked to my car, stuck some quarters in the meter, and sat down in the driver's seat, stunned.

I had an unhappy childhood, I told myself again. It seemed like such a cliché. But it was also real.

I'd tried to dress up my childhood over the years like a little Christmas tree, covering it with garlands and tinsel and ornaments, telling myself stories that masked certain memories. But now it stood before me, stripped bare.

It was what it was.

As Sylvia Boorstein once said, "We all have something."

My meditation practice had allowed me to see things more clearly. The Trager therapy had comforted me and made my body more open and receptive. Somatic Experience had grounded me and given me the courage to dig down deep, to discover the source of my panic.

And now I wasn't panicking. I was crying like there was no tomorrow, but I was not panicking.

Somewhere deep inside me, I had accepted something big.

I thought about all the problems my own parents had faced. My father had been manic-depressive and mental illness ran through his family like wildfire. My brother had described the weight and sadness in our background as Jewish Gothic. We'd joked about the heavy Russian food my grandmother cooked, but she'd also presided over a very heavy household. She'd been orphaned at a young age. Her husband had died suddenly at age fifty-nine. Her twin sons had led difficult lives. "I would never wish twins on anyone," she'd told me when I was pregnant and hoping for just that.

My mother had experienced no real connection to her own family and had been desperate for attention and love. When my father and his family couldn't provide that, she sought it from me.

Both of them had unloaded problems on me as though I was an adult. My friend Barbara had once recalled visiting me when my parents were fighting and my mother threw a glass of red wine in my father's face, then lay on our kitchen floor, sobbing.

For years, I'd pushed those kinds of scenes out of my head.

Still, even though my mother and father were not the best parents, they were not bad people.

I pulled myself together and ducked into a Greek coffee shop. Feeling calmer, I sat down in a tiny booth.

But then a call came through on my cell phone from Jimmy, and I burst into tears again.

"What's wrong?" Jimmy asked.

"I had a tough therapy session." I said, getting control of myself. "Do you think I had an unhappy childhood?"

"Yes," my husband of thirty years replied. "I think you did. Your parents had problems individually, and they also had problems as a couple. You didn't have the worst childhood in the world, and you didn't have the best."

My husband is a wise man.

I composed myself and took a deep breath.

"Why did you fall in love with me?" I asked.

"I don't know," Jimmy answered. "It's just not something that I can put into words."

I told Jimmy how much I loved him. I thanked him for loving me. We hung up and I managed to eat bites of my omelet, slowly.

I drove home and meditated, lying on the floor with Mickey pressed up against me. Jimmy and I watched mindless television that night.

The next morning, I went to see Dr. Jaeger, my dear, wise therapist of ten years, and she agreed with my revelation.

"Why did I never get this memo?" I wondered to her. "Why was I the last to know I had an unhappy childhood?"

"I think you did know," Dr. Jaeger said. "I think you always felt it. Children just sort of happened to your parents. They didn't give the process of parenting an enormous amount of thought. They were very self-involved."

I didn't argue with that.

"And everything that happened to them was such a drama," Dr. Jaeger said. "Your family stories are like something in a Broadway play, like Eugene O'Neill, or *Who's Afraid of Virginia Woolf?*"

"I was always terrified to see that play," I said. "I lived it."

It wasn't an accident that I had my first panic attack while I was dishing out peas to students at the Brown University cafeteria, I realized.

"When I watched all those boys parade by me, I must have seen the life I wanted to live right there in front of me," I told Dr. Jaeger. "I must have wanted a big, exciting life, but I was afraid to go out and get it all by myself. I wanted to *have* parents, not *be* the parent and I had to keep tamping down anxiety, to stop the fire from spreading. I was trapped."

"Being enraged at the people you need is a peculiar place to be," Dr. Jaeger said. "But what you experienced was all you knew. You needed to depend on your parents. So you did a combination of things. You tried to put your feelings out of your head, rationalize them, and distract yourself with all kinds of other stuff."

"I protected myself," I said.

"But the protection didn't work," Dr. Jaeger explained. "The panic attacks broke through."

Yes, they did. And all the vodka in the world couldn't stop them.

"The basic human instinct is to continue," my therapist told me. "And you went on to do what we call 'magical repair.'"

"What's that?" I asked.

"It's when people move beyond their unhappiness and manage to make themselves whole. They create very different lives from the ones they grew up with. Often they do it through their children. And that's what you've done. Magical repair."

I loved Jimmy, Max, and Jack for helping me to heal. And of course I loved my parents for doing the best they could. That night, however, while I was meditating, a nagging question I had asked myself for years resurfaced: Why would my parents leave a small child with a 106 degree fever and seizures all alone in a hospital? I would never do that. Was it hospital rules? Were they not allowed to spend the night?

Let go of that question, I told myself. They did the best they could.

I thought of Pema Chödrön's suggestion to "drop the storyline."

And suddenly I could. Because I replaced it with a revelation.

Somebody saved my life.

I looked up at the ceiling, and broke into a huge smile.

The resident who had been making his rounds in a hospital, in the middle of the night, fifty-five years ago, had been a smart, competent doctor.

He had slit my throat. And saved my life.

"I'm alive," I told myself.

"I'm alive, I'm alive, I'm alive, I'm alive . . ."

That became my mantra.

Enormous gratitude coursed through my veins.

I sent that gratitude out to my savior, the skilled resident, wherever he was now.

I hoped he had saved many lives.

I hoped he took joy in knowing that he saved mine.

I sent waves of love out to him, wherever he was.

And I thanked God that I was alive.

22

Reborn

After he had magically appeared at my mother's nursing home, I never saw Rabbi Schafer again. But I wanted to learn more about Jewish mysticism and meditation, so I bought a book called *Rabbi Nachman: Outpouring of the Soul.*

"King David was able to compose The Book of Psalms only because he was very strong in meditation," according to the author, Rabbi Aryeh Kaplan. "The main time King David would meditate was at night, under his bedcovers.

"Hidden from the sight of all others, [King David] would pour out his heart before God," saying, "'Every night I meditate in tears upon my bed.' (Psalms 6:7)"

I wasn't the only crybaby. I was in very good company. Regal company.

The Hebrew word for meditation, *hithbodeduth,* pops up regularly in more than one thousand years of Judaic writing. "A vast wealth of ancient literature describes how the prophets of Israel used meditation to reach their high spiritual states," wrote Kaplan. One technique involved repeating a divine name; another the recitation of a single prayer. For centuries, Jews have used mantras, controlled breathing, and even the silent scream to tap into a deep, restorative, sacred state.

Who knew?

Surely my father, through his relationship with "the Bostoner," must have known of the Baal Shem Tov, the founder of Hasidic Judaism. His great-grandson, Rabbi Nachman of Breslov, told his followers, "Give me your hearts and I will take you on a new path, which is really the old path upon which our fathers always walked."

And so I decided to walk the path my father had walked.

It was hardly the first time I'd explored my Jewish roots. I'd gone to a Hebrew day school, been married by an Orthodox rabbi, and both Max and Jack had been bar mitzvahed. My experience in *The Faith Club* had led me to read and research all sorts of historical and scriptural texts. But I knew very little about the more mystical side of Judaism.

After spending the last six months focused primarily on my brain, I was beginning to feel that my body was in trouble. I couldn't shake a stomach bug, and thoughts of my father's lost battle with colon cancer haunted me. I went to my doctor, who took tests that showed nothing abnormal, so I decided to do something symbolic. Something uplifting for my body. And the thought of going to a mikvah, the Jewish ritual bath, popped into my head.

Why not?

My friend Susie had raved about a mikvah in Los Angeles and invited me out. It was freezing in New York, so a warm West Coast dip sounded wonderful, but surely there was a good mikvah somewhere in New York City, with its pastrami sandwiches, sour pickles, and knishes the size of hockey pucks.

I googled "mikvah new york," and found one at the Upper East Side Chabad Center. (Described online as "spa-like, with marble and mosaic tiling, and lovely feminine touches such as candles and potpourri," it sounded like the mother of all mikvahs.) On the cold December morning I visited, the place was swarming with mothers, strollers, and toddlers. I told a man at the door that I wanted to speak to someone about their mikvah. He directed me up a flight of stairs, to an office where two women sat at a desk going through piles of children's photos. I assumed they were teachers in what was clearly a school. "Happy Chanukah!" they said, smiling.

The eight-day holiday was more than halfway over, and, with my children gone, I hadn't lit a single candle this year. But I didn't tell them that, worried that they'd disqualify me. Visions of spa-like amenities and magical holy waters danced in my head. "Happy Chanukah!" I replied.

The women introduced themselves, and the older of the two, Chanie, invited me into her husband's office so that we could talk privately. "He's the rabbi here," she said. "But he's gone for the day."

We sat down next to each other, and I described my panic-to-peace progress. I'd always been curious about the mikvah, I told her, and my father had studied with a rebbe . . . I tried to impress her with my Jewish credentials.

"And what about you?" I found myself asking. "What's your story?"

Chanie laughed. "Who am I?" She seemed used to answering questions about herself and the Hasidic movement from strangers who wandered in off the street. Chanie had grown up in Crown Heights, Brooklyn, in a large Lubavitcher community; her father was a journalist. Chanie and her husband had nine children. I studied her for a moment, a pretty woman dressed modestly, in long sleeves, with a flowered shawl draped over her shoulders, a very natural-looking wig in place.

"My stereotype is that Lubavitchers proselytize on street corners," I blurted out.

"Only to other Jews," Chanie said, smiling.

"But do Lubavitchers think other Jews are inferior?" I asked. "Or, for that matter, that other religions are inferior?"

"No," Chanie replied. "We're all learning. The Torah says that everybody is here for a reason. A lot of Jews search outside of their teachings, into Buddhism for example, because they don't know what's available in Judaism. But you were born with a Jewish soul, which will never be harmed, because it's a piece of God. If you identify with it, and nurture it, you will always have joy, because you'll be in touch with your essence, which can never be taken from you."

I'd fallen down the right rabbit hole. I could feel myself getting high on Chanie's brilliant spiritual tidbits, which she dispensed in rapid-fire succession.

"Why are human beings able to recuperate from tragedies?" she asked, rhetorically. "Because there's a part of them that can never be taken away. A Jewish soul is a little spark that never goes out. It can be covered over, like ash over a hot coal. But blow away the dust, put a fire or spark near it? And it's going to burst into a flame that will warm you from the inside out."

Forget hot flashes; this steady reliable flame sounded wonderful. "Does everybody have that little spark?" I asked, hopefully. "It's not just a Jewish thing, is it? I want an eternal spark, but not if the rest of the world can't have it." May others be happy, I heard Sharon Salzberg chant. May others have peace.

"Everybody was born into this world with a spark," Chanie said. "What I would ask you to do, however, is to put away all your intellectual barriers—to Judaism, to the fear of being exclusionary. A Jew loves every human being, every animal, every thread of grass, because everything comes from God."

That sounded good to me.

"A soul is like a flame that's in constant search," Chanie continued. "It will nag away until it finds expression. Have you ever seen a flame standing still? There's no such thing. It's constantly jumping off the wick."

"What's my soul looking for?" I wondered.

"It's always looking to connect," Chanie told me. "It's a flame, always moving upward. Turn it upside down, and it will shoot right back up again, toward the sky. Put two flames near each other and they will merge. A spark will leap into fire. And a flame can light a thousand other flames, but never take away from its own light."

I was smitten. Chanie was so spiritually alive. Plus she kept flashing her beautiful smile, even when she put things into perspective for me, firmly but politely.

"So how would I move from panic to peace?" I asked.

Chanie laughed. "My initial reaction—and please don't take this the wrong way—is that we think too much about our own needs."

I burst out laughing. "I totally agree!"

"But when you stop thinking about yourself, you start thinking about the world and why you're needed here. And that's where you see spiritual growth."

I wasn't going to argue with that.

"There are a few rules concerning the mikvah," Chanie said, pulling out a calendar.

I bristled a bit. Uh-oh, I thought.

"Actually," she explained, "I don't like the word *rules*. The Torah gives us six hundred and thirteen mitzvahs, which are ways to connect to God and the holiness inside us. We think of ourselves as very independent, and that God must be separate, maybe sitting up in the sky on a throne, watching over us, with a white beard. But there is really no reality outside of God. Everything is a detail of godliness. Every single thing. Who you meet, where you go, what you do . . . God re-creates the world every minute, in the form of energy, which is constantly buzzing around and bumping into itself."

I sat rapt, silent.

"In Kabbalistic literature," Chanie continued, "that energy is God's energy, which is why we don't believe in being stuck. Something can seem very static in your own life; you may feel that you can't move from point A to point B. But that's not the case. Things can be a certain way in one minute and entirely different in the next. We just have to tap into that energy."

For the first time, I understood the power of the spiritual journey my father had taken decades earlier, which no one else in our family had ever understood or validated. Talking to the Rebbe in Boston had made my father profoundly happy, I now realized. Sitting in this Lubavitcher rabbi's study, alongside his articulate, radiant wife, I realized that my father had not just gone to the Rebbe to discuss financial problems; he'd gone there to celebrate life.

And now my father had guided me to this moment. To the mikvah, to the mysterious ways of the Hasidim.

Delicately, Chanie asked about my last menstrual cycle and my marital relations with my husband, because precise guidelines are followed about sex and abstention before a mikvah. I'd decided that Christmas Eve would be a perfect time to dip myself into the holy waters, since I'd spent a very memorable, peaceful Christmas with my father the year before he died and always thought of him on Christmas Eve.

Chanie determined that, if I did not touch my husband between that afternoon and my mikvah, I could, by Jewish law, schedule it for that meaningful night.

"I can't touch him at all?" I asked.

"As little as possible," Chanie said, with a smile. She explained how the mikvah, with its very specific guidelines, intensified the spiritual and physical connections experienced by married couples when their bond was sanctified by God.

On our way downstairs to tour the mikvah, she laid out a few more rules. I was to wear white underwear and sleep on white sheets from now until Christmas Eve. When I arrived at sundown, I would shower and clean every inch of my body, in the beautiful bathroom and dressing area. The elegant details were every bit as luxurious as they'd been described online. And when Chanie and I entered the airy, tiled room housing the mikvah, I felt a sense of holiness and calm. The small, square pool, large enough for one person to float in its pale green waters, was pristine. Above it, on the ceiling, was a painting of a perfect blue sky and fluffy white clouds. "The mikvah is fed by pristine rainwater, untouched by human hands," Chanie told me. "That's why a woman has to be so pure in order to enter the waters."

She showed me the wells where the rainwater was trapped. Their Hebrew measurement, corresponding to the forty weeks a baby spent in the womb, had been prescribed in the Torah thousands of years ago.

I needed this.

But when I returned home and told Jimmy that I couldn't touch him for a week, his immediate reaction was "That's ridiculous!"

When I went back to the Chabad Center to see Chanie one more time before the mikvah, I told her that I had often begun to express affection toward my husband in the last week only to realize that I couldn't rest my hand on his shoulder while I watched him work on his computer, or kiss him hello when he walked in the door. "I never realized how significant those small, physical displays of affection are," I said, "until they were taken away. Even the tiniest gesture means something—the touch of a hand, ruffling someone's hair, a pat on the back . . ."

Chanie smiled. "If someone were to come into your home and take notes, as a scientific observer, about your relationship with your spouse, what would they say? 'She prepares dinner . . . he takes the clothes to the cleaners . . . she makes the bed . . .' But those are technicalities. Nobody can look into the soul of a relationship and see its true essence. They may catch a glimpse—a look in the eye, the way you smile at each other—but only someone experiencing that bond can feel its true depth.

"In the context of a Jewish marriage, the mikvah is not just a personal spiritual journey. There's something special about the bond between a husband and wife coming together and their physical interaction being a reflection of something sacred."

Chanie shifted in her chair and thought for a moment.

"I also love the fact that, with nine children and a very busy world, once a month I immerse myself in the rainwaters, and my life is suspended for a split second. I experience total *bitul*, or nullification. I tap into God's energy. For a second, I just disappear, like the moon vanishes for a moment before it's reborn and reconnects to the cosmos, to God. And when we disappear for just that second, it gives us the ability to not be caught up with everything that's bogging us down."

"Do you feel a lightness?" I asked.

"Totally," she answered. "I feel like I just handed it all over to God. I tap into him. I'm able to access his infinite energy."

"I feel like my father is saying to me, 'Dip yourself in the waters of the mikvah. Replenish yourself, and move on without me and your mother. Go forth, with a little bit of lightness,'" I said.

"That's beautiful." Chanie smiled. "So you're going to do all of your preparations—bathe, shower, comb your hair, remove nail polish and makeup. You'll come out of the dressing room in a robe, and an attendant will quickly glance at your fingers, toes, and your shoulders, for loose hairs. Next you'll step down into the water, splash yourself a little bit, and then submerge yourself totally, like a fish, without touching the floor. The attendant will say 'kosher' when you've covered yourself in the waters completely."

"Kosher?" I asked, smiling. Chanie had heard all the jokes.

"That will mean that it was all done according to Jewish law," she explained. "The water has totally covered you, like a baby in the womb. And just like a baby has no obstacles between itself and the water, and no intervening substances in the womb, there's nothing between you and the water, either. That's why you're not wearing anything—jewelry, makeup—nothing. After the first dip, you'll say a blessing, which is posted there for you to read. 'Blessed art thou, King of the Universe, who sanctified me through this mitzvah of immersion.'"

Chanie smiled. "I love that I can thank God for the ability to be sanctified, for something holy to take place, for me to connect to the infinite, to him."

She continued. "You're going to immerse yourself two more times. The attendant will pronounce you kosher, then leave the room, to give you some time alone. You can say any prayer that you'd like, for anyone or anything—your mother, father, your spouse, your children, yourself. This is not about physical cleanliness; it's spiritual."

And then she totally blew me away.

"I want to tell you one more thing about a menopausal woman experiencing the mikvah," she said. "If she has never done this before, what she's doing when she taps into these waters is she's tapping into God's energy, which is not limited to time. So she reaches back into her past and is able to transform things in her life on a DNA level—her own creation, her children's conceptions, everything that regularly, as human beings, we have no power to reach back and change. We can only change things as we move forward in life. But in God's world, and in the waters of the mikvah, past, present, and future merge. And only then can the past be rewritten."

I took all that in.

"I want to forgive my parents once and for all," I said. "They did the best they could. They didn't set out to do damage. They didn't give me everything I needed, but there would be no great literature if parents gave children everything they needed."

Chanie chuckled.

"I want to love my parents for who they were, for what they gave me, and for what lives inside of me," I said. "Then I want to move forward, heal myself, and do what I can to make the world a better place."

I kissed Chanie goodbye and drove home. I spent the next day reading and resting quietly.

That afternoon, I drove into the city just as the sun was beginning to set, turning the skyline pale orange and lavender. I felt my father's presence in the car, and then my mother's. They were a newly married couple, looking forward to their life together. In that moment, I saw them as happy.

I turned off the highway and parked my car, wondering if other women in my family, generations earlier, had done what I was about to do. I walked over to the mikvah's after-hours entrance, rang the bell as Chanie had instructed me, and was buzzed in.

Sarah, the mikvah attendant, showed me to the beautiful changing room and spotless bathroom suite, where I undressed, showered, and prepared myself emotionally—quietly and carefully—to be transformed.

I walked out into the room housing the mikvah, and stood still in my white robe, feeling the cool tiled floor through the paper slippers on my feet. Sarah inspected my hands, toes, neck, and shoulders, deeming me clean and ready to be sanctified. She held the back of my robe discreetly, and it slipped off my shoulders into her hands as I walked down a few steps into the warm, holy waters.

I submerged myself completely as Chanie had instructed me to do. I felt the heaviness of my body underwater, and then, as I broke the surface, coming up for air, a sudden, powerful lightness.

And when I heard Sarah call out "Kosher!" I looked up at the dome of the room, painted a perfect blue, with fluffy white clouds.

I stood still, up to my armpits in holy water.

I recited the prayer, posted by the side of the bath.

I immersed myself successfully two more times, and then Sarah left the room to give me some privacy.

I felt no barrier between myself and the waters.

I experienced total nullification.

I spoke to God.

I sensed my soul flickering, and felt gratitude.

Then I pulled myself together, left some heavy baggage on the floor of the mikvah, and climbed back up to shore and into a new beginning.

23

The Soul Doctor

A good mystical rabbi is hard to find.

After my transformative experience at the mikvah, I wanted to know more about Jewish mystical practices. Chanie suggested I talk with her brother, Rabbi Simon Jacobson, saying, "Simon is the brilliant one in the family. He's the one you have to meet."

That's how I came to be pacing a block in the East Village of Manhattan, over and over again, looking for the address Rabbi Jacobson had emailed me when he'd agreed to meet me that night, a few weeks after my mikvah. But all I saw was an abandoned brick synagogue, totally dark inside, its wrought iron gate locked with a padlock.

Finally I spotted a man in a long black overcoat, with a dark, bushy beard, rushing toward me, head down. Rabbi Jacobson introduced himself, apologizing for running late. I followed him as he unlocked the padlock, opened the iron gate, and then the door to the synagogue, which was not abandoned.

We walked into the sanctuary, filled with cozy, mismatched upholstered furniture. Rabbi Jacobson led me into a library, and we sat down at a long folding table.

I asked if he had any advice for me as I continued seeking peace on the other side of the ritual cleansing. "Would you like to be part of my journey?" I asked.

"I'm already part of your journey." Rabbi Jacobson smiled. "Because God is the one who creates the choreography of our trajectories, and we've intersected, even before we physically met. Our souls have already converged in some ways, which is an honor."

I was so touched that I began to cry. Quite a lot, actually. I wiped my eyes with my sleeve and apologized. Although I'd been crying for months now, I still hadn't learned to carry tissues.

"Mystics say that tears bathe the soul," Rabbi Jacobson said. "I see your tears as cleansing and healthy."

"But I don't want to cry all the time!" I said, laughing.

"You won't," the rabbi assured me. In a dark blue sweater and sport coat, with a yarmulke on his head, he could have been a college professor. Or a Jewish Santa, if Santa had a darker beard and was prone to soulful ruminations.

The night before, my son Max had developed food poisoning. He'd called himself an ambulance in the middle of the night and been taken to an emergency room. I'd spent the day at his apartment, making sure he was hydrated, feeding him soups and sodas. I was worried about him and said so. I was exhausted and apologized again to the rabbi for crying.

"You don't have to apologize," Rabbi Jacobson said. "To me, tears are a good thing. The Torah says that, when energy enters into us that our containers cannot hold, we erupt."

"That's exactly what it feels like," I managed to say, while erupting.

"May you only cry at times like this," Rabbi Jacobson said kindly. "People who cry in healthy ways are doing so because they sense a higher presence. And that's beyond us." He shrugged. "So we cry."

I nodded my head. Yes, we do.

"Every person should be able to cry from time to time," Rabbi Jacobson continued. "Isaac Luria, a great mystic of the sixteenth century, writes that in the days between Rosh Hashanah and Yom

Kippur, a soul that doesn't cry is a soul that's not complete. Vulnerable souls are not afraid to cry. It's only in this world, where they teach you to be tough and aggressive, that people believe crying is a sign of weakness. But it's not. So cry away!"

I laughed. "I don't want to waste my time with you."

"What's the first line of my book?" Rabbi Jacobson picked up my copy of *Toward a Meaningful Life*, and flipped to the first page, which asks, "Have you ever just burst into tears for no apparent reason?"

"On a deeper mystical level, the mystics say we cry because we're sensitive and we feel disconnected from the source," Rabbi Jacobson said. "So that dissonance makes us cry."

"I know that dissonance very well," I said. "It's like a vibration hovering around me."

I glanced around the room, lined with holy books. "You know, I went to a Hebrew day school."

"That usually screws up people's faith," Rabbi Jacobson said.

I laughed. "Why do you say that?"

"I went through the religious and school systems. They destroy the spirit. They're too mechanical and dogmatic, and there's a lack of sensitivity for the soul."

"You're a scoundrel," I blurted out.

"I would say I'm a rebel," Rabbi Jacobson replied. "I'm very anti-structure. I believe in disciplines, but I don't believe in man-made control."

"Is that a problem in your line of work?" I'd never heard a rabbi speak like this.

"No. I attract a pretty diverse group of people," he said. "There's a universality to my message that transcends religion and culture."

When he first started teaching many years ago, it was to an informal gathering of Jews and non-Jews, "an interesting mix," according to Rabbi Jacobson. Many would say their spirituality came from Zen Buddhism or LSD. "I come from a very traditional Jewish world," he said. "Before I even open my mouth I'm at a disadvantage, because I project a nonneutral image. I may remind people of an angry grandfather who schlepped them to synagogue on Yom Kippur, or an irrelevant Hebrew school teacher, or even something nice from their past, but I'm definitely not neutral."

I smiled. I'd stereotyped Rabbi Jacobson before I met him, assuming he'd be an Orthodox man in black who might judge a less religious Jew like me.

"I tried an experiment," Simon continued. "Instead of using any loaded words, I created my own language. Instead of *God* I used *The Essence,* or *Higher Reality.* If it was a particularly New Age group I might say 'Undefined Layers of Subconscious Energies.' Instead of *Torah* I used the word *blueprint.* Instead of *Mitzvah,* I used the word *Connections.* Instead of *Redemption* or *Messiah* I used *Destination.* And I was talking about this journey into the essence of reality, through these different connections, toward a destination and so on, and people thought 'Wow, this is really fascinating!'"

He chuckled. "After a few weeks, a guy came over to me and asked 'Are you talking about God?' and I said 'Yes! But shhhh! Don't spoil it for the others!'" Rabbi Jacobson shrugged. "To me we're all souls.

"One of the things that touches me deeply about Jewish mysticism is the two extremes," he said. "That you have the most mystical experiences in your mind, in an abstract, sublime world, and then you can bring everything down to a simple act, like being nice to a child. I find that many people are very spiritual but they're very elitist. They have a spiritual arrogance."

He continued. "I think spirituality can become selfish. You can be so consumed with your spiritual life that domestic life can seem trivial. I'm by nature a very fierce free spirit. I could have been a floater. But I got married and I have two children, because I realized that there's something beyond my spiritual inclinations."

Some Jewish mystics are so transported when they meditate that they need a guide by their side, to pull them back down to earth when they get seduced by a world beyond this one. I asked Rabbi Jacobson about that.

"The concept is called yearn and return," he explained. "Tension and resolution. The paradox of life is that if you're too much at peace in any situation, you're not in a good place. You have to be at peace with no peace."

"I was going to ask you how to find inner peace," I said. "But maybe that's not the right goal for me. Should I be unpeaceful?"

"There are two ways to be unpeaceful," Rabbi Jacobson told me. "Anxiety can be a cause of unpeacefulness. Or you can maintain a sense of healthy angst that keeps you motivated, alive, and not complacent. I think that's what you should strive for."

He pulled out a piece of paper and a pencil. "This is the key to life," he said, drawing a series of smooth waves, just as Gina had once done for me. "It's all about balance," Simon said. "You reach a high, there's a certain resolution, and then you go back down."

"How do you do that?" I asked.

"You need to have a mission, that keeps you grounded. And the rest grows from that."

"How do I find my mission?" I wondered.

"You probably know it already to a certain extent. It probably has to do with your writing. It would be nice if everyone came out of their mother's womb with instructions for their mission in life," Rabbi Jacobson said. "But it doesn't work that way. We're supposed to search for it."

"Is every soul's mission attainable?"

"Absolutely. It's always sitting and waiting for you. And there are signposts. You have a certain personality, certain opportunities, certain people you'll meet, and you'll travel to certain places. You'll see patterns start to emerge. And you'll use those patterns to chart your course, to make your mark on the world."

"Hopefully," I said.

"Does the panic still affect you?" Rabbi Jacobson asked.

I was touched by his interest. "Not so much," I found myself saying.

"Do you know why?"

"Everything I've been doing over the last eight months has helped me to desensitize the frightening physical aspects of panic," I said. "When I feel my heart racing, I find that it doesn't escalate. The panic has begun to dissipate physiologically; it doesn't have the same hold on me that it used to. I don't think about it so much."

"That's good that you've been able to heal," he said.

"I'm very grateful."

"When I was a teenager," said the rabbi, "I asked myself, Why am I here? There was no dysfunction in my family driving me. I was on a pure search. So I threw myself into books, realizing that knowledge is power."

He had studied Torah, but he also devoured novels, philosophy, and books on Jewish mysticism. "I started thinking about the world of the infinite and the invisible and realized that such a world is more real than this one," said my new favorite rabbi. "And then I saw that people wrote about that world, in biblical commentaries, the Zohar, Luria. But I saw it in other systems, too. I saw the parallels between Far Eastern mysticism and Jewish mysticism.

"Schools tell you the mechanics of things—eat kosher, keep shabbos, do this, do that," he said. "But they don't tell you about

the soul of it all, and as I began to delve into that soul, the resonance was like music to me. I said 'Ah! Now I get it!' And I realized
that I needed to forge my own path. I emerged as a spiritual human
being."

"You found your mission." I smiled.

"When I was a little child," Rabbi Jacobson said, "I had this
quirk. I would walk to school and if it was raining, I'd walk alongside the curb and watch the water running down to the sewers. I
would look for twigs, pebbles, or other things that were blocking
the flow, and I would push them out of the way. I felt like I was
achieving something. And that was my secret little activity; nobody
knew about it.

"Now," he continued, "when I think about my life, I realize that
I have a deep-rooted passion to help people get rid of the clutter
and let things flow. So my little childhood quirk is very connected
to who I am today. I really believe every one of us has what we need
in our lives, but there are so many things blocking our path that we
need someone to help push aside clutter.

"What I discovered most of all is the majesty of the soul. And
that has served me very well in helping people discover the majesty
of their own souls." Rabbi Jacobson smiled. "In a way, I'm a soul
doctor."

I laughed. "I think that's exactly right! But that's a hard job—
being a soul doctor."

"I know one thing for sure," Rabbi Jacobson said. "The environment for healing has to be accepting, trusting, and not judgmental. A soul is like a child. If a child feels frightened, it won't come
out of its hiding place. It's critical that the soul feel safe. This is
not a safe world we live in. Especially for those who grew up in
traumatic homes. A soul, like a child, needs to know that it's loved
unconditionally."

"Are you a Kabbalist?" I asked.

Simon shrugged. "You could call me a Kabbalist. The great Kabbalists always said, 'Those that know don't say; and those that say don't know.' So if I said I was a Kabbalist that would disqualify me."

"Are you a mystic?" My time with the soul doctor was coming to an end. People were filing into the synagogue for a lecture he was giving that night.

"Mysticism is the study of the soul," the rabbi said. "It was the mystics who said, 'We're not physical beings on a spiritual journey; we're spiritual beings on a physical journey.' People ask me where the soul goes after death, and I think of an imaginary dialogue between a refrigerator and the flow of electricity. The refrigerator asks the electricity, 'Where do you go when they pull out my plug?' And the electricity says, 'What arrogance! I go where I always go! Where do *you* go? They just invented you a hundred years ago—you're just a *box*. You learned to contain my energy for a little while, to refrigerate food, and now you think you're *it*? *You're* not where it's at! *I'm* where it's at! I go back to the unconfined place, unfettered by containers and boxes like you.'"

The rabbi folded his hands, and placed them on the table between us. "So the soul is where it's at," he concluded.

I had one last question. "I liked what you wrote in your book—that our birthdays should not be all about us. That it's a time to give back to the world. So what do you think I should do on my birthday?"

"When is it?" Simon asked.

"June twenty-fourth."

He shrugged. "It will come to you. Don't worry about it."

"I want to do something meaningful," I said.

"Some of the greatest things in life don't have to be so dramatic," the rabbi said. "Remember that. You can do something modest. When a mother cradles her child, fireworks don't explode. That's the secret of all life. Some of the most beautiful things happen below the radar. Not on Wall Street, not on television. Not with all the hoopla. It's in the quiet moments that our lives are shaped. In homes, in cribs, in bedrooms, in the little things," the soul doctor said to me sweetly. "That's where it all happens."

I walked out of Rabbi Jacobson's Meaningful Life Center calmer and happier, a humming refrigerator that had just tapped into an extraordinary, powerful energy source.

24

Breathing with a Twist

◦✺◦

Despite everything I'd done to heal my soul, my breath, and my brain, my body felt frozen. Still, I was doing my best to be kind to it:

I bathed it. And I fed it (too much, sometimes). I gave it a lot of rest. But I didn't give it enough exercise. I barely took it out for a walk.

Like my daily meditation for my mind, I needed a daily practice for my body, so that it would catch up with me and my brain, wherever we were along our thousand-steps journey.

One day, sitting in my favorite health food restaurant in New York City, Candle 79, I fed my body some fun along with some delicious tempeh, while my friend Meg and I laughed boisterously over lunch.

Someone tapped me on the shoulder. It was Alana, a young editor I worked with at the *Huffington Post*. She'd heard us laughing as she sat nearby, eating lunch with another woman and—could it be?—Deepak Chopra. The man who had popularized meditation and explained the mind-body connection was right there in the flesh and spirit.

But charismatic as he is, it wasn't Deepak I ended up falling for, but Alana's mother, Amy Elias Kornfeld, a radiant yogi with a beautiful, happy face and sparkling brown eyes.

After Deepak left the restaurant, I slipped into his seat, and Meg joined me as we laughed with Alana and Amy, digging into the desserts they'd ordered.

Amy seemed lit from within. I wanted some of what she had, so when I heard that she was a yoga instructor, I booked a private lesson with her for the following week, at her studio out on Long Island.

I'd practiced yoga for fifteen years, starting off with Bikram's hot yoga in the early 1990s. I'd done down dogs—with my golden, Mickey, watching—in my bedroom. I'd done yoga in hotel rooms from Boise to Boston on my book tour. I'd been to classes where women's artificially enhanced breasts stood up like silicone mountains. I'd taken classes where I was the oldest and slowest, as well as the youngest and most limber.

But I hadn't worn my black yoga pants in months, and as I drove over the Whitestone Bridge, I tried to ignore how tight they were. All the breath work I'd done came in handy as I sucked in my stomach, while digging into a bag of trail mix.

When I sat down opposite Amy on the floor of her cozy studio, whose walls were painted a warm chocolate brown, I felt safe. My sports bra was digging into my puffy flesh, but when Amy smiled, something inside me felt lighter. Not every yoga instructor can make a tired, middle-aged mama feel that way. It takes someone with soul, and Amy had that.

So I didn't mind when she pulled out a pen and paper and asked what I ate on a typical day. I answered somewhat honestly: I ate oatmeal, eggs, salads, and sandwiches. And a chocolate chip scone here and there. Amy smiled. "But they're whole wheat!" I said.

Amy talked about the principles of a macrobiotic diet and my heart sank. Was I going to have to eat gritty, brown, tasteless food if I wanted to look like the radiant woman in front of me? "We'll talk more about food as we go along," Amy said.

She turned on some Indian music and led me through a series of seated poses. When I stood up and tried staying in a lunge position for too long, my thighs burned, begging for mercy. "I need to rest," I said. "I'm so fat and out of shape."

"Why would you talk about yourself like that?" Amy asked.

"Because I'm fat and out of shape," I answered.

"But how is that going to make you feel better?" Amy asked.

She had a point. I wasn't getting any thinner by observing how fat I was. Amy urged me to look at myself in the mirror when I got home and say things like "You're beautiful and I love you." I cringed at the thought of doing that, but promised Amy that I would. I liked her, and I wanted to please her. I just prayed Jimmy wouldn't walk into our bathroom as I stared rapturously at my reflection in the mirror.

I watched Amy strike poses elegantly and smoothly, and I tried my best to follow her. I wanted to get to where she was, somehow, someday, and she started to take me there. "Breathe and feel a deeper connection to your muscles," Amy said. Slowly, she nudged me out of the numbness encasing my body. "It's all there," she promised. "Inside of you. Right now. Open up every possibility."

"That's beautiful!" she said as I stretched up tall. "Lift your heart. How do you feel?"

"Good!" I found myself saying.

"Good!" Amy echoed. "You look great!"

Although I wasn't so sure of that, I appreciated her vote of confidence. My body began to thaw, ever so slightly. At the end of our time together, Amy rewarded me for all my hard work by leading me through a magnificent, soothing meditation.

"Imagine a pool of water around you," she murmured, as I lay on my back, my chest open up to the sky.

I floated home, not minding the one-hour drive, and returned the next week, happily announcing that I had pretty much cut out sugar. "I only had one scone!" I reported.

Amy pulled out a sheet of paper and drew a circle, slashing it in half with her pen. "I look at my day as a big plate," she said. "Half my day is vegetables, wherever they happen—soup, baked squash, salad—and the rest is grains, protein, and fat. You can play with that."

"What about fruit?" I asked.

Amy suggested that I stick to fruits grown in temperate zones, eating them first thing in the morning or for dessert. "Apples, pears, prunes, apricots . . . And you can eat raisins, almonds, cashews . . ."

A gooey slice of pecan pie popped into my head.

"You want to keep your blood sugar level constant," I heard Amy say, "with beans and brown rice, seaweed."

"Seaweed?" I was back down to earth.

"It's delicious!" Amy said. "You toss it into a pan, heat it up, and it gets crispy, just like bacon! Sprinkle it on salads, or wherever you want."

I wasn't going to let a little seaweed get in the way of our friendship. And Amy wasn't pushing me too hard. "When you're fully in your body, you're going to know what to eat, when to meditate, when to do yoga," she said. "How often and for how long. Your body is the portal to the immortal."

I loved that. My body was an aging archway at the moment, but not yet a Roman ruin.

"I don't have upper body strength," I said.

"Your back is probably bigger than your front when you slouch like that," Amy observed. "You're concave, which doesn't allow you to take a really full, deep breath."

I tried sitting up straighter and pushing my collarbones back. Then I stood up, and Amy led me through a series of movements. "Fire up your toes . . . roll in your thighs . . . lift up your ribs . . . root yourself to the earth . . . bring your throat chakra up to the sky . . ." My body listened to Amy's instructions, as if she were inside me, pushing and prodding gently.

"Move your arms as though you're moving through thick honey or molasses," Amy suggested. I held my hands up high, and then pushed my arms out to my sides slowly. I bent my elbows, and moved them out in front of me. I repeated the movements over and over again, powerfully and deeply; I actually saw my biceps bulge.

At the end of our session, Amy helped me get into a "beautiful, loving twist," with my body on the floor, my head and chest resting on a bolster. "Restorative yoga positions aren't passive, lazy ways to avoid movement," Amy taught me. "They actually do something. They bypass the brain and send messages straight into the nervous system."

I stopped at a health food store on my way home and bought some seaweed. When I cooked it in a pan the next morning, it did taste crunchy, and a little bit like bacon. If I closed my eyes and imagined it slathered with mayonnaise and tucked into a BLT.

All week, I thought of the practice I'd done with Amy and wished I could do it on my own. But I couldn't replicate our session together, and complained about that when I saw her again.

"You want the McDonald's of yoga!" Amy laughed.

She was right. As usual, I wanted the quick fix. But I was in for some slow breathing instead.

I sat on the floor, spine straight, while Amy guided me through a series of deep, cleansing breaths. "Notice when the divine wants to pull the breath into your lungs," she said. "That's your inhale. And when it wants to push the breath out of your body? That's your exhale. You're being breathed by the divine."

Yes, I was.

"This is yoga," Amy said quietly. "Yoga is not about doing an incredible headstand, or what kind of jewelry you wear around your neck. It's about reflecting, tasting yourself in the moment, balancing your physical and mental states.

"We're not trying to get somewhere else. We're just embracing what life is right now, right here."

A hollow channel of energy runs up and down the body, like a river. Called the central *nadi,* the channel has two meridians running alongside it, intertwining and intersecting, forming the seven chakras, where our physiology connects with our consciousness. The first chakra is at the base of the tailbone. The second is in line with the pubic bone. The third is at the navel, the fourth at the heart, the fifth at the throat, the sixth at the "third eye," in the center of the forehead, just above the brow. And the seventh chakra "sits like a magical crown on top of your head," Amy said. "Like a thousand-petal lotus flower, connecting you to the universe."

My head was spinning, along with my chakras.

"Yoga was created to help us align ourselves," Amy said, "so that *prana,* an invisible form of energy, can flow freely through our bodies. Sometimes we have too much prana, and we have to burn it off with a fiery practice. On other days that same practice could exhaust us. We're different at every moment."

"Amen," I said, ready for a nap.

Amy urged me not to put too much pressure on myself. "My job is to touch everybody's life and shift it just a little bit. If you learn to breathe differently," Amy said, "to sit in your car and experience yourself differently, that's terrific. Bring yourself to a place of self-acceptance, honor, and self-nurturing."

I began moving again, with Amy guiding me. I stood and twisted and lunged as best as I could. Sometimes I used the wall as a prop.

Amy leaned into me, nudging my body into strong, rooted poses. I felt myself growing more powerful.

Finally I stood up, alone, and stretched to the sky.

Swooping down, I dived into a series of poses I used to dread— sun salutations, complete with lunges. "You're rooted to the reliability of the earth," Amy told me, as I tried my best to stay strong. "To the possibilities of the life outside of us. The universe, the sun, ocean, grass . . ." And I was. "Even when we're under stress we can find this kind of freedom," Amy assured me.

Overjoyed, I did another sun salutation. And then another. Slowly, but empowered.

"I felt a connection to the divine," I told Amy when I was done.

"I could see that," Amy said.

"Thank you for helping me to figure that out," I said. "I hated my body for not being able to feel graceful in those positions. But I can do them if I slow things way down."

I lay on the floor in savasana, or corpse pose, closing my eyes.

"It's said that we become the company we keep," Amy told me while I settled down. "So keep great company. That includes the thoughts we tell ourselves, our friends, the food that we eat, what we hold on to, what we let go of . . .

"Savasana is the hardest pose," Amy continued. "Great work is happening inside. The prana or energy knows where to travel and we're not in control of that."

"My body has scared me for so long," I said quietly. "It was panicky and unpredictable."

"Things change," Amy told me. "I know. I was so sick when I first started doing yoga. I couldn't get out of bed."

I turned my head to look at the pretty woman beside me, so vibrant and alive. "About thirteen years ago, after I stopped nursing my youngest son, I wanted to see how I could alter the shape of my body," Amy said, "so I got into major body building."

I couldn't imagine that. "The real deal?"

"The real deal." Amy smiled. "Like Arnold."

"I was getting ready to be in a major competition," she continued. "But I overdid it. My muscle enzymes went haywire. I was working them too hard, my immune system shut down, and I couldn't move. I got taken out of the gym in an ambulance."

"Oh, my God." I stared at the healthy woman beside me.

"I was really sick for three months," she told me. "But after lying on my back in bed for so long, doing nothing, and feeling like my life was over, I realized that there was something I could do. I could breathe." She smiled. "So I used my breath to bring me back. That's why I know that the breath is the answer. It's our body and breath working in unison that really makes the heart sing."

There was hope for me.

"I would lie down in my bed for hours," Amy continued, "putting myself into restorative positions that would let the breath move through me in different ways. Gradually, I got stronger. It didn't happen overnight. One day my husband drove me to the beach, but I was so exhausted that I couldn't get out of my car. I watched my friends doing yoga in the sand and vowed that I would be doing that again someday."

I continued visiting Amy's yoga studio over the next few weeks, until I knew that I could do the work on my own. Gradually, me, myself, and I (brain, breath, and body) got stronger, too.

My body did not transform itself into Scarlett Johansson's. But I became at peace with the way I looked and felt.

I developed a great recipe for chocolate chip cookies, using whole wheat flour, maple syrup, crushed walnuts, and organic chocolate. Like a mad scientist, I created healthy dishes in my test kitchen, with avocados, whole grains, and fresh greens.

I was preparing to offer up my body and brain to science.

25

This Is Your Brain on Love

Ꙍ

While researching the benefits of meditation, I developed a crush on the brain of a neuroscientist whose deepest beliefs came from a conversation he had with his mother about peas.

As a child, medical doctor and neuroscientist Andrew Newberg hated peas; his mother had a hard time getting him to eat them. But finally she came up with a solution. She told her four-year-old son that if he left peas on his dinner plate, they'd be lonely, because they couldn't be with their friends—the other peas he'd swallowed. "How would you feel if you lost some of your friends?" she asked.

"Suddenly," as Newberg writes in his book, *Born to Believe*, "I saw my plate in an entirely different light. Peas, I realized, had feelings—and friends!"

This, Dr. Newberg explains, was the beginning of his entirely new understanding of the world. He started to view all objects as animate beings with feelings and thoughts. He wouldn't leave his baseball glove out on the porch at night because it might get scared alone in the dark. When he played with his building blocks, he had to utilize every single one, every size and shape, for fear that unused blocks would feel hurt and left out.

"I began to believe that everything was somehow fundamentally connected," Newberg writes. "Whether it was the food I ate, or my family and friends. I felt that we all were bound to each other by some unseen mechanism or force."

As a researcher into consciousness at the University of Pennsylvania, Dr. Newberg has scanned the brains of Tibetan monks and Carmelite nuns, people who speak in tongues and atheists who meditate, in an effort to "neurobiologically measure what is happening to the brain" when people enter deep reflective, meditative states.

"We can demonstrate that transcendental, mystical and spiritual experiences have a real biological component," he writes. "Furthermore, the neurological changes that occur during meditation disrupt the normal processes of the brain—perceptually, emotionally and linguistically—in ways that make the experience indescribable, awe-inspiring, unifying, and indelibly real."

According to Newberg's research, monks and nuns display greater activity in their frontal lobes while in a deep meditative state. They are able to deliberately reduce activity in the parietal lobes, in particular, which is the part of the brain that keeps us conscious of our individuality. They describe themselves as entering a state of timelessness and spacelessness.

I wanted to enter that same state. And maybe a neuroscientist could chart my progress in getting there. Perhaps I could pose for a picture of my brain meditating, just like the monks who had inspired me. I worked up the courage to email Dr. Newberg and we set up a time to talk.

"What's your favorite type of meditation?" Dr. Newberg asked me.

"Lovingkindness," I replied. I figured a man who used to treat peas like friends would know about this practice.

And then my dream came true.

Dr. Newberg was doing studies on a variety of different meditation styles and their effects on the brain. He liked the idea of including lovingkindness meditation and asked me to refrain from doing that practice until he'd done a baseline scan of my brain. Then I would practice lovingkindness meditation for eight weeks, and he'd scan me one more time, noting any changes. I'd have a set of before-and-after pictures without having to lose weight or squeeze into a bathing suit.

I was thrilled.

We chose a date for me to travel to Penn, my alma mater, where Dr. Newberg conducts all of his research, and he told me to call him Andy. He also asked me to hold off from doing Somatic Experience or any other type of therapy that would affect my brain during this study. I was to stay on my current regimen of blood pressure medication and a small dose of Klonopin, without making any changes. I'd cut my dose of Klonopin in half in the last month, with my therapist's permission, a major step. Meditation had relaxed me to the point where I felt too tired on the dose I'd been taking for so many years. And I hadn't had a panic attack for a year, since I'd stumbled through the streets of Denver on my book tour.

But a few days before I was to be scanned, I began imagining myself deep in an MRI machine, alone with my brain. The hospital where Andy worked was a block from the dorms, classrooms, and quadrangles where I had suffered so many panic attacks as a terrified undergraduate. What if the MRI found something wrong with my brain? I'd done just enough reading to know that my amygdala—an almond-shaped gland in the primitive part of my brain—had been responsible for controlling my fight-or-flight response all these years. What if it had grown to freakish proportions as a result of all my panic? Even though that's not possible, to me it seemed a real possibility.

My imagination seemed not to have received the memo that brain, breath, and body were dropping out of our relationship with anxiety. To shut it down, I focused on the assignment Andy had given me: to find a fifteen- to twenty-minute lovingkindness meditation that was available on a CD, so that everyone participating in the study could meditate to the same instructions. I found a lovingkindness meditation that Sharon Salzberg had recorded, and contacted her for permission to use it for the study, which she graciously allowed.

All of my friends had been supportive of my panic-to-peace experiment, but when I thought of enlisting someone to accompany me down to Philadelphia, two friends in particular—Anne and Monica—came to mind. Both of them had battled illnesses bravely over the last few years and spent a lot of time in MRI machines. Their courage and grace inspired me, and they were excited to be part of my adventure. Anne would come down with me for the first scan, Monica for the second.

As we drove to Philadelphia, Anne gave me tips on how to relax while lying motionless, strapped onto a hard surface, crammed into a space the size of a coffin. Anne had been diagnosed with a large but benign brain tumor eight years earlier. She'd survived two grueling brain surgeries, dangerous infections, a seizure disorder, years of rehabilitative physical therapy, and several stays in the ICU and hospital. She had a lot more to teach me than how to relax during a brain scan. Her strength during everything she'd endured was humbling and awe-inspiring.

As soon as we drove over the Ben Franklin Bridge into Philadelphia, my brain got busy trying to locate and identify familiar landmarks. I had only been back to Philadelphia once since I'd graduated from Penn thirty-five years earlier. My memories of my time there were not happy. I'd been so afraid to leave home at the start of my freshman year, and I'd chosen Penn because of its excellent reputation, with no regard for how I would adapt to an urban environment at a large university. I was so anxious when my parents were about to leave me in my dorm room that my mother accepted my invitation to stay overnight with me, since my roommate hadn't shown up. I'd been the only freshman with her mom as her roommate, but my mother had actually come through for me that day, and she'd left the next afternoon, when my roommate did arrive.

On the night before the scan, my hands and feet tingled like crazy, just as they had in Gina's office, when I'd released so much nervous energy during Somatic Experience therapy. Yet my lungs and heart felt eerily calm, as though they'd been deactivated.

When Anne and I met Andy Newberg in the lobby of University Hospital the next morning, he looked younger than I expected, and he was as kind in person as he'd been on the phone, even though his schedule was jam-packed. He went through all of my paperwork with me in his office, checking again to make sure that I had no metal implanted anywhere in my body. I took off my watch and rings, handing them to Anne.

Andy led us into the basement where the huge MRI machine was located. My hands and feet were buzzing like crazy, but I tried to tune out every thought racing through my brain so that I could focus on the advice I'd been given. My friend Richard, no stranger to MRIs, had told me to make sure that I closed my eyes before I slipped into the machine, so that I would only see the backs of my eyelids, not the close confines I was actually in. So I did that. My sister Marcia had advised me to stare at beautiful tree branches that morning, and then picture them in my mind while my scans were being done; I did that as well.

I lay on a hard, plastic slab while a technician strapped me in loosely, covering me with a thin blanket and placing a cage-like contraption over my head, to hold it in place. "Are you okay?" Andy asked me through the headphones I was wearing. Surprisingly, I was.

I slid into the machine and Andy talked me through what was happening from an adjoining room, behind a huge glass window.

I had to lie very still for some adjustments and a baseline scan. Then I heard Sharon Salzberg's soothing voice in my ears, and I smiled, whispering her words to myself: "May I be safe, be happy, be healthy, live with ease . . ." I thought of Jimmy and sent him love. I sent love to someone I knew who was suffering. And then I sent it out into the universe, to all living beings.

Andy did a few more scans and I meditated to the beeping and clanging of the machine. I emerged relieved, thrilled, and proud of myself. "That was fantastic!" I said to Andy, smiling. "Thank you so much!"

I sat next to him while he pressed some buttons on a computer. A magnificent, lush flower popped onto the screen, blooming in black and white. But it wasn't a flower; it was my brain, moving in slow motion, in a delicate dance that Andy had choreographed and my brain had performed. It blossomed before my eyes, as Andy fast-forwarded the images. They were positively hypnotic.

"Where is my amygdala?" I asked.

Andy played with the scans. "Here it is," he said finally, pointing to something tiny that I couldn't see.

"Is it normal?" I bit my lip. Could the King Kong of amygdalas really be living in there somewhere?

Apparently not. My abnormal amygdala had been all in my head. And my brain, I gushed to Anne as we drove home to New York, had looked positively gorgeous. From now on, my brain and I were going to be happier with each other. I was transferring my crush on Andy's brain to my own.

Thinking back to the first week of practicing lovingkindness meditation after the scan, I hadn't slept well. I had felt stimulated instead of calm and centered, probably because I was sending so much love out into the world. And that exercise in lovingkindness had worked. I had transferred my attention away from my own pain, as Pema and Sharon had both said I would.

What a relief! It wasn't all about me!

After a week, I realized that, if I slowed down the practice, I could slow down my breath. There was no need to send all this love out into the universe by overnight FedEx. I could send the message slowly. My sleeping improved.

After two weeks, I sensed myself becoming more patient with people like my husband and kids. Even pushy people on the subway didn't stress me out.

After three weeks, I could rely on the meditation practice to calm me down. I loved meditating to Sharon's voice. When she instructed me to think of someone who'd been a teacher or an inspiration, I had so many people I loved to choose from. And when it was time to send lovingkindness to someone who was hurting, I knew many people who were in pain, either physical or emotional, whom I wanted to help.

One of my friends was struggling with her son's heroin addiction. Other friends struggled with financial problems, caring for aging parents, and their own health issues. I was able to be more present for them in our daily interactions, while sending secret packages of lovingkindness to them on the side, as well.

I felt I was achieving a healthy sense of detachment, which paradoxically allowed me to see the pain of others more clearly. I felt like I'd built a tiny observation deck outside myself. From there I could look at the world without factoring my own ego into the equation so frequently.

I celebrated my newly calm life by taking my friend Barbara to a Japanese tea ceremony class at the Urasenke Chanoyu Center in Manhattan. We spent two hours in the serene, spare space bowing to each other in our bare feet while trying not to giggle. We learned how to make, serve, and savor bright, bubbly green tea, along with one simple sugar wafer. Every turn of the cup was significant, every step we took purposeful. Learning how to fold a napkin properly was a meditation in itself, which took half an hour to teach. We marveled at how calm we felt when we left to return home.

Life seemed to slow down. Everything became a meditation, whether I was relishing a beautiful green salad or walking through Richard Serra's giant steel sculptures at the Dia Art Foundation's museum in Beacon, New York.

My mind no longer wandered to fearful places as often as it used to and I was able to summon more patience as a mother, giving my children space, allowing them to live their lives without worrying about them too much—and without letting them know I was worrying about them. Max and Jack were aware that I was meditating daily and off on a spiritual adventure, but they were living their own lives in Manhattan and Michigan, and I began to trust and appreciate that they were doing so with maturity and grace.

One of the most interesting parts of Sharon's guided meditation was when she asked me to conjure up someone I barely knew and wish that person happiness, safety, health, and well-being. I thought of an older blond woman behind the cash register at my local supermarket, our mailman, a friendly doorman I knew from Dr. Jaeger's building in New York, and work colleagues I hadn't seen in ages. I'd even managed to send lovingkindness toward a neighbor who left angry notes on our doorstep and rants on our phone machine when Mickey wandered over to his lawn to pee.

I grew quieter and, I hoped, kinder.

Nonetheless, my progress was not always smooth. One day Jimmy walked into the bedroom while I was meditating, with my headphones on, to Sharon's voice. He turned on the television, and when I was done meditating, I told him that I thought it was inconsiderate of him to do that. I started off speaking softly and matter-of-factly, but when he got defensive, I grew angry. We spoke harshly to each other, and I left the room.

That spat was symptomatic of an underlying worry of mine. I thought that maybe Jimmy and I had become out of sync, that our busy lives were pulling us in different directions now that the kids were grown and out of the house. I was meditating and leading a quiet, sedentary life. Jimmy was working hard and playing hard, cycling with a passion and often riding forty or fifty miles in a day with a group of people I hardly knew. His already lean frame was getting skinnier, while the scale never budged whenever I stepped on it. I'd begin to call us "Mr. and Mrs. Spratt," laughing at the notion that I ate no lean while he ate no cupcakes. But inside I did feel sometimes estranged from the person I had loved so completely for so long.

I had thought earlier that maybe Jimmy needed to do some lovingkindness meditation alongside me, but a longtime friend had disagreed. "Just because you're doing it doesn't mean he has to," she said, nicely.

Maybe she was right. Maybe one Krishna Das groupie in a household was enough. Jimmy had thought that the Gyuto Monks' CD sounded like bullfrogs. Meditation isn't everyone's cup of tea.

But lovingkindness, I was beginning to feel, was essential. I wanted my spouse of three decades to show me the love.

First, however, I had to show it to him.

So after I'd left the room, I returned and tried talking calmly to Jimmy. I pointed out that he started every day by going off into the den with Mickey and the *New York Times*, instead of staying with me, in the bedroom, where I usually read or wrote.

"You could come in and read with me and Mickey," he pointed out, reasonably, and I saw his point.

As a result, we started being kinder to each other in small ways. I remembered what the mikvah had taught me—that a little gesture can mean a great deal. I discovered that basic lovingkindness is something two people who have known each other for thirty years might need to rediscover.

Jimmy invited me on his daily walk with Mickey. When he'd asked me to come in the past, I had declined, especially when it was cold outside, but now I said yes, and we walked down to a park by the water, with Mickey panting between us, more heavily than she used to. I watched her a bit sadly; our puppy was aging. "Slow down," I said to Jimmy. "Mickey is fourteen years old."

"She's thirteen," Jimmy said, and pointed out that my usual critique of him—that he was a pessimist—was clearly not accurate. I had aged Mickey before her time. I wasn't living in the moment. And so I tried to.

Eight weeks after my first MRI, I returned to Philadelphia, with my friend Monica. This time my hands and feet weren't tingling, although that night I got up every two hours with performance anxiety, worried about my upcoming scan. The chocolate-covered pretzels I'd discovered at the Reading Terminal Market in downtown Philadelphia that day hadn't helped my sleeping.

Early the next morning, Monica and I rushed over to the hospital to meet Andy. My heart was beating fast as I hopped into the MRI machine. But I slowed it down, along with my breathing. I found myself audibly sighing by the end of the practice. I had brought so many people into that narrow little chamber with me. With Sharon's voice in my ears, my heart swelled with love for all of them. Every person who had helped me to develop confidence and compassion. Every person who had assured me that I could find peace. Every person who had listened to me and taught me and healed me and believed in me.

I was positively radiant when I got out of the machine. "Hallelujah!" I said to Monica. "That was so great!"

I barely noticed that we had a flat tire when we got into my car to drive home. Calmly, I found a service station on my BlackBerry and managed to drive there. A sweet cabdriver named Muhammad helped me patch the tire and fill it with air.

Monica remarked on how calm I was. "Do you think you could have been helped by meditation back when you were an undergraduate here?" she asked me.

I thought for a moment, but couldn't imagine meditating back then. I couldn't have calmed down on my own—my body was just too wired. Maybe a good, strong yoga practice would have helped, but things had happened for me when they were supposed to happen. Better late than never.

Andy had told us that in his studies he includes all types of meditation because everyone has different needs and different brains at various times in their lives. It would be several months before he would share the results of my brain scan with me, but in the meantime, as I continued my meditation practice, I grinned whenever I thought of the gorgeous images he'd shown me—of my own happy, flowering brain.

Thich Nhat Hanh teaches that we all have the seeds of peace and compassion within us and, with meditation practice, we can help these seeds grow, sprout, and bring forth flowers. It seemed that all my meditation was helping to make my garden grow.

26

A Good Friend

When my mother used to come to our house, she slept in the spare bedroom that we now call the Bead Room. Once she was no longer able to visit, the room became a bit of a dumping ground, piled high with books, clothes, magazines, art supplies, my jewelry-making materials, and boxes full of things I'd taken from her house after it was sold. I'd been unable to part with these belongings but too sad to sort through them.

Eventually I did that, throwing away trash bags full of my mother's bills and papers, giving away her clothes. While I was opening one of the last boxes of my mother's belongings, I discovered a pile of CDs, and when I went through them, I met some old friends of mine.

The Gyuto Monks—the same men who had spoken to me so powerfully in Dolma's store in San Francisco—had apparently spoken to my mother over the years as well. I smiled when I slipped their CD into my computer and listened to them chanting. Their voices were as distinctive as they were when I first heard them.

One day I decided to smudge the Bead Room. I lit the thick stick of sage Anna had used in my cabin at Pema Chödrön's retreat. As I paced back and forth, I watched the smoke curl up into the walls of the space where my mother had deteriorated so steadily. I lay on the bed and breathed in the scent of healing.

I was lying on that same bed a few nights later when the phone rang.

"Is this Priscilla Warner?"

I didn't recognize the woman on the other end of the line. She sounder older than me.

"I'm not sure if this is the right Priscilla," she continued, tentatively. "But are you Riva Leviten's daughter?"

I paused. This woman didn't sound like a telemarketer or anyone from my mother's nursing home. "Yes," I said.

"My book group is reading *The Faith Club*," she said. "You wrote that you grew up in Providence, that your mother was an artist from California . . ." She sounded far away. "Well, this is so strange, but . . . I think your mother was my best friend in college."

I took that in. "You went to UCLA?"

"Yes," the woman said. "I'm calling from California."

"How did you find my phone number?" I wondered.

"I looked it up online."

Quickly, I did the math. This woman had to be at least eighty. And she knew how to track me down on a computer? And then she told me her name—Louise Goodfriend.

I sat up in bed. "How do you spell that?" I asked.

"Just like it sounds," Louise told me.

Energy shifted. Clouds parted. A brilliant bolt of sunshine broke through.

Just when I had resigned myself to the fact that my mother was ending her days on earth by moving further and further away from me, just when I'd let go of understanding who she was through dynamic conversations, of knowing her in the perfect way I imagined daughters knew their mothers, just when I'd accepted things as they were . . . things changed.

"What was my mother like?" I asked Louise.

"Oh, she was wonderful." I could feel Louise smiling. We were both silent for a moment.

"I was crazy about her," Louise continued. "I'm just . . . I'm stunned. I thought there was a chance you were Riva's daughter." She paused. "Is Riva alive?"

"Yes," I said. "She has Alzheimer's."

"You wrote about that," Louise said.

"When was the last time you spoke to my mother?" I wondered.

"Maybe ten years ago? I read in the paper that her brother had died. I called the funeral home and left my phone number." Louise paused. "I hadn't heard from her in so long. But then Riva called and we chatted. We exchanged a few cards after that, but we never really connected again. I felt so bad."

"That's okay." I didn't tell Louise that my mother's relationships with people had waxed and waned. That many friends had disappeared from her life mysteriously.

"It seemed like my mother deliberately left her whole life behind in California," I said. "From what I could piece together, she didn't have a lot of fond memories."

"Maybe," Louise said. "But you know how some people just connect? Your mother and I shared all of our thoughts and dreams. She was wonderful." I could hear the love in Louise's voice. "She was different."

"In what way?"

"She thought very deeply," Louise said. "She was certainly very bright. Very creative in her thinking. And very outspoken."

"Wow." I used my mother's favorite word.

"Riva had such a wonderful sense of humor," Louise continued.

I was so glad to hear that. My father was funny and a great story-teller. My brother had spent years doing stand-up comedy in New York. What had saved my family was our collective sense of humor.

It was gratifying to learn that Riva had developed hers at an early age.

"Did you know my father?" I asked.

"Oh, yes," Louise said.

"My parents didn't have the best marriage," I said.

"I knew that," Louise responded.

"Why do you think my mother and father got married?" I asked.

"Your father was very good-looking, and very charming," Louise said. "Your mother was, too, despite her problems."

"Problems?"

"Well," Louise paused. She sounded refined, intelligent, and as if she didn't want to hurt me. "Riva had difficulty adjusting to life," she said, softly.

My heart sank. "Those feelings weren't bad enough that they controlled her," Louise continued. "She was strong enough to rise above them, but they were there." She sighed. "I wouldn't call her mentally ill, but she just wasn't the happiest person all the time. She definitely had emotional problems."

I took that in, quietly.

"You didn't see that growing up?" Louise asked.

Of course I had, but I'd tried to push those thoughts away and make things better.

"I don't know . . . maybe it was because she was an artist," Louise continued. "But she was just kind of troubled. I don't know how else to put it. I don't mean to sound harsh. But there was something . . . unsettled about her."

"Did you know her mother?" I asked.

"I didn't," Louise said. "But I know that Riva had a very difficult relationship with her. That her mother had a lot of emotional problems. She was unstable."

In the toughest times of their marriage, my father used to say that my mother was going crazy, just like her own mother had. My mother would get angry.

"I think you either control mental illness or it controls you," Louise said, thoughtfully. "I felt Riva controlled it, but it was there."

Mental illness was there. On my mother's side of the family as well as my father's.

I'd been surrounded.

All of the people in my mother's family were virtual strangers to me. I'd labeled her relatives "the black-and-white people," since I'd only caught glimpses of them in the tiny, deckle-edged photographs she kept in a tin box on the bottom shelf of a bookcase. They'd been among the last items I discovered when I cleaned out her house. My mother had buried her family in her basement.

Louise and I sat on the phone, silent for a few moments.

"My mother died of Alzheimer's," Louise said. "So I know what you're going through."

"It's agonizing," I told her. "Particularly because my mother was in some ways always unknowable. I'm trying to come to terms with that, and I can't believe you're giving me all this information, now."

"I don't know what to say," Louise said, kindly. "Hang in there."

"I'll be fine," I said. "I'm really happy that you called, but it's just kind of crazy."

"It's surreal." Louise said. "I wish I could talk to Riva."

"I could record a message from you!" I suddenly realized.

"That would be great!" Louise spoke slowly and clearly, as I held my cheap little tape recorder up to the phone, capturing the love in her voice while she left a message for my mother.

We said goodbye and promised to stay in touch. I gave Louise a link to www.rivaleviten.com, the website I'd built for my mother's artwork. I said she could visit Riva there, watch videos of her, and browse through old photographs.

I drove up to Providence two days later, and tried to see the city through my mother's eyes. To imagine how she felt when she'd first come to this quiet New England town, after leaving her life in California, to join a husband she was in love with but barely knew. I parked my car across the street from the Victorian apartment house where they had first lived, and took a picture of it. My mother used to take pleasure in the fact that the curtains she'd sewn had remained in the windows for years. Now they were gone.

I drove to the nursing home and held the tape recorder up to my mother's ear.

"Riva, I hope you remember me. This is Louise. It was Louise Kaffesieder and now it's Louise Goodfriend."

My mother smiled. Her eyes sparkled.

"And you remember probably what close friends we were in college?"

Riva nodded. She seemed to know who this was.

"How we told each other our most intimate thoughts and our secrets?"

My mother giggled.

"I love you so much and I hope you remember me. And maybe we can talk again soon . . ." Louise's voice trailed off. *"Take care."*

"Do you remember Louise?" I asked.

"Oh yes," my mother said. "It's such an unusual name. Kaffe . . ."

"Kaffesieder," I said. "She really loved you, Mom."

The moment was gone. My mother looked at me, confused. "I don't remember her."

I thought of Sylvia Boorstein as my heart quivered in response to pain, just as she'd said it would. Compassion took hold of me

"I love you too, Mom," I said, meaning every word.

27

Finding the Golden Buddha

⌒⨯⌒

"Welcome to the realm of ten thousand joys and ten thousand sorrows."

As soon as Jack Kornfield spoke those words, I knew I'd made the right decision signing up for yet another retreat, this one about Buddhism and Western psychology. Jack had trained to be a monk in the monasteries of Thailand, India, and Burma, and had cofounded meditation centers on both the east and west coasts. He was teaching the workshop all weekend with Tara Brach, whose audio dharmas had inspired me. Both of them were trained clinical psychologists, as well as practicing Buddhists.

"You're going to add more shrinks to the mix?" Jimmy had asked me as I left the house that morning.

"The more the merrier!" I'd responded, only half joking.

Addressing hundreds of people in the Grand Ballroom of the Sheraton hotel in midtown Manhattan, Jack wore a cream-colored vest and pants. His kind face, gentle demeanor, and soft voice made him seem like a Buddhist Mr. Rogers. He appeared to be the perfect therapist.

Tara, a beautiful woman with an equally empathetic, intelligent presence, began her presentation by telling a story about a huge, plaster Buddha statue that had been discovered in Southeast

Asia. When it began to develop cracks in its surface, a monk shined a flashlight into the cracks and caught a glimpse of gold glittering from deep inside the sculpture. Slowly and carefully, workers removed pieces of what turned out to be a giant plaster shell that had encased the entire statue. Underneath all that plaster was a magnificent golden Buddha.

A golden Buddha exists inside each and every one of us, Tara said. We sometimes forget that, but the path of true healing lies in our ability to gain access to that gold. Certainly, I'd been doing some renovation on my own plaster, getting past any struts to some core, elemental truth.

Jack spoke about Buddhist psychology, which he called "the science of the mind." Our culture focuses on mental illness instead of mental health, said Jack. But meditation can help us release our fears and cultivate emotional well-being. We're not limited to our biography, Jack explained. We can shift our identity. We can systematically train ourselves with mindfulness, lovingkindness, and forgiveness, and by paying attention to the body's messages. We can make measurable changes to our whole central nervous system, and shift our inner landscapes from unhealthy states to healthy ones, from suffering to well-being.

Instead of grasping, we can learn to let go, Jack told us. Instead of feeling aversion, we can cultivate love. Instead of living in delusion, we can live with clarity and wisdom.

The *DSM*, the reference guide for all psychopathology, lists thirty-five forms of depressive and bipolar disorders. Jack wondered: "What if we were to diagnose and encourage thirty-five positive forms of emotional and mental happiness?" In Buddhist psychology, twenty-five different kinds of rapture exist. According to Jack, "There's tingling rapture, thrilling rapture, cold rapture, rapture that moves the body, rapture with luminosity . . ."

There are twenty-five different kinds of joy in Buddhist psychology, and twenty-five different kinds of light—from the light of fire-flies to the sun or moon shining on our faces.

Human beings and our minds are vigilant. "I read somewhere that we wake up ten times a night to scan ourselves and make sure everything is all right," Tara told us. This vigilance is part of our natural instincts. "If our ancestors had relaxed on a rock, sunning themselves, chanting mantras, they wouldn't have survived!" she said, to laughter from the crowd. "But in our competitive culture, there are very few places for an easy belonging."

She read a poem to us, which listed a host of challenges most human beings would find daunting.

"If you can start the day without caffeine or pep pills . . . If you can be cheerful ignoring aches and pains . . . take criticism without resent-ment . . . conquer tension without medical help . . . relax without liquor . . . and sleep without the aid of drugs . . . Then you are probably a dog!"

The audience erupted in laughter at that truth.

Some of us enter planet earth with a spacesuit of sorts, much like the plaster cast that surrounded the beautiful golden Buddha, said Tara. We lose valuable life moments when we're inside that spacesuit, cut off from the aliveness, the passion, and even the lone-liness of our lives. We have to find a way to feel better, and each of us develops strategies for doing that.

"When we're caught in a trance," Tara asked softly, "how do we come home?"

We can train ourselves to wake up to a homecoming of sorts, "to the mystery of our lives, to a lucidity or awakeness."

She told the story of an Alzheimer's patient, a psychoana-lyst who was speaking to a group of people when his mind sud-denly went blank. Instead of panicking, he paused, put his palms together, and named what he was noticing. "Confused . . . anx-ious . . . heart pounding . . . embarrassed . . ." That helped him to settle down.

"He hit a stuck place that we all do, sometimes," Tara explained. "He allowed himself to be where he was in that moment. He found a space that could hold what was going on for him, and a shift took place."

"No one has ever taught us this way," someone in the audience said to the man with Alzheimer's.

I recalled a visit I had just paid to my mother. I'd walked into her room while she was dozing, and caught her in a reflective, calm mood. "What can I do for you?" I'd asked.

"Just be yourself," she answered, smiling.

"Is there something you need?"

"Need?" She paused, thinking. "It'll work," she said. "Everything will work out."

"Really?" I asked. "How do you know that?"

"Because . . ." She searched for words. "That's what . . . faith is."

"You have faith?" I asked.

"I have faith."

"In what?" I wondered.

"Everything."

"That's nice." I looked at my mother, lying alone in a nursing home. "How did you get that?" I asked.

"I just waited," she told me. My mother's golden Buddha came shining through the cracks of her old self.

"There's an alchemy to healing," Tara said. "When you know and trust that you are your own ocean, you're not afraid of the waves."

Apparently, my mother was swimming in her own ocean. She'd gotten to a place where she was no longer afraid. Even as her body and brain were failing, she still had faith.

Tara spoke of forgiveness. "As long as there's blame, there's no healing," she said. "Everybody thinks forgiveness is a good idea, until they have something to forgive."

When we are hurt, our bodies and hearts develop armor. We want to hurt others to distract us from our own vulnerability. If we forgive someone, there's a fear that they will never know how much we've suffered. "We can get hooked on suffering," Tara said.

I knew just what she meant.

28

Breathing Breakthrough

I hadn't seen Gina for two months when I walked into her office. "You look fabulous!" she told me. "You're radiating so much light and happiness and love!"

And then things went dark for a while, because we finally began doing sessions of EMDR, or eye movement desensitization and reprocessing. I allowed my eyes to follow the panel of flashing lights on Gina's tripod while I pictured myself in specific situations she and I selected. Memories I had suppressed for years swam up to the surface of my mind and clobbered me. There was no way I could stop them from coming, but Gina had prepared me, waiting until I was strong enough to process them.

I was still meditating every day, and craving that quiet healing time. With Dr. Jaeger's okay, I had cut my Klonopin dose in half once again, to almost nothing. I was beginning to tell the difference between excitement and fear. The physical symptoms that used to haunt me—a galloping heart, tightness in my lungs, fierce, erratic breathing—seemed to have been deactivated.

But I had some final connections to make between the panic I'd experienced all my life and what had prompted it. With Gina's help, watching her "magic machine," as I came to call her flashing lights, I made a connection that I had never made before.

My father's business went bankrupt just as I was launching my own career. When I put those two events together for the first time in my life, my chest tightened, over and over again, on Gina's couch. I had trouble breathing.

My father lost the family business—a chain of thirty supermarkets—very suddenly, all by himself, or so it had seemed. He'd gone to work for his father and uncle right out of college. The profit margin in the supermarket business was tiny, the competition fierce. There was no room for error.

But my father made some serious mistakes. When his uncle retired and he took over the business, my father made a deal to expand the number of stores and overextended himself. The business went into Chapter 11 just as I was rising through the ranks in advertising. Rhode Island is a tiny state. The story of his failure was all over the newspapers and television.

"I was like a plane trying to take off," I told Gina, as our first EMDR session ended. "Every time I tried to ascend, I hit turbulence, and guilt. But I was doomed to succeed."

For days after I left Gina's office, intense memories about my father's bankruptcy kept floating up into my consciousness, and I couldn't stop them. An ironclad safe, full of family secrets and miserable memories, had been cracked open.

I went back for another appointment and we examined more of the safe's contents.

Desperate to stay afloat, my father had injected millions of his own dollars into a bankrupt business that devoured it all, I told Gina. When the money in our family disappeared, so did the emotional safety net it provided. Cracks and fissures appeared in our foundation, igniting tension between us, increasing the frequency of my panic attacks. The money had masked a lot of the pain and sorrow in my family. Now it was on full display.

My father never recovered from the bankruptcy. Fighting to overcome a deep depression, he took my mother down to the Florida panhandle, where he wanted to start a new life, but she hated it there. So she moved back up north, and he lived in his camper, in a trailer park, without a telephone, trying to put together an oyster business.

"There was no way to reach him, except by calling a man who lived nearby," I told Gina. "I could have used a father. I really missed him. He was my only parent in so many ways."

And meanwhile, I was doomed to succeed in my personal life.

"Your mother and I could never have had the kind of marriage you and Jimmy have," my father once told me, when he and my mother were fighting, after he'd come up north to be diagnosed with cancer and, ultimately, to die.

After I left Gina's office, painful memories kept coming, slowly and surely, swimming up to the surface of my consciousness like the huge marlin, swordfish, and giant bluefin tuna my father used to catch on his beloved boat.

I went back for another EMDR session and told Gina about all the memories that were haunting me.

"They kick your butt," Gina said. "Your brain will go wherever it needs to go in order to heal. With this therapy, you don't receive any new information, but you put things together in ways that you haven't before. And that's part of the healing process."

Gina suggested I choose a memory for us to work on from as early a time as possible. "Go where the charge is," she said.

So where was that? I thought for a minute.

And then I knew just where to go.

Not long after I suffered my first panic attack as a teenager, the phone rang at our house very early one morning, waking everyone up. A state trooper from somewhere down south was on the line.

My father took the call from behind the closed doors of my parents' bedroom. I stood outside in the hallway, trying to listen in on
the conversation, to no avail. My father got dressed and dashed out
of the house. "Uncle Nathan is sick," he told me and my siblings. "I
have to go get him."

He flew south to a VA hospital, where his brother had been
brought after state troopers found him pulled off I-95 somewhere.
I imagined him slumped over the steering wheel of his car, miserable and incoherent. My father flew his brother back north, and
admitted him to a psychiatric hospital.

When Dad finally arrived home, he was too exhausted and
strung out to talk. He walked into his bedroom, shut the door,
and wept. I could hear the sounds of his crying all the way down
the hall, as I stood on a back stairway and eavesdropped. It was the
first time I ever heard my father cry.

In the years to come, I often suffered panic attacks when I
was driving. Piecing together what little I knew about Nathan's
"breakdown" on I-95, I deduced that a person could go from being
relatively functional to a quivering mess in a matter of minutes.
I actually thought you could be driving down the highway, feel a
nervous breakdown coming on, pull over to the side of the road,
and fall apart. I worried that I could go crazy in just that way.

As I thought of this in Gina's office, watching her flashing lights,
I felt my chest tighten, and my throat begin to close. But I was able
to stay with those feelings until they passed, and they led me to
more deeply buried memories.

My father's partner in the family business was his uncle Sam,
who tortured and tormented him every minute of his life, I told
Gina. Sam was an abusive tyrant and my father had to do his
bidding.

I hadn't thought about my uncle Sam in decades, but he was

such a destructive force in my family that he came back to me vividly, like a giant, powerful animal.

Uncle Sam never married; he hung out with mobsters and hookers. His best friend was a man whose claim to fame was that he'd been shot in the stomach and walked a mile to the hospital, to avoid calling the cops. Sam had once boasted about sticking a man's head down a toilet until he got him to do what he wanted.

"There was no way my father could stand up to a man as evil as Uncle Sam," I told Gina. "He destroyed any chance my father ever had of leading a happy life."

Sam set up a special telephone at our house called "the private line," so that he could reach my father at any hour of the day and night. He once caught my sister chatting on that line. "If I ever catch you doing that again, I will come over there personally and cut your arm off," he screamed at her.

Suddenly I remembered where my second panic attack had occurred. For some reason, Sam liked me, so I had to spend time with him. He'd taken me and my friend Barbara to an Italian restaurant, I told Gina. In the middle of dinner, I felt my throat suddenly close up; my heart started pounding. So I got up from the table, locked myself in a ladies' bathroom stall hyperventilating, popped a Librium, then waited for it to take hold. When I returned to the dinner table, I didn't say a word. Sam would not have understood or respected a weakling prone to panic.

The only person who had ever stood up to Sam, oddly enough, was my mother. After he'd suffered a stroke, Sam lived with a caretaker in an apartment near our house. And he continued to torment my father. One night my mother drove over to Sam's apartment, took every framed photo of her children off his dressers and walls, and left with them. "You're a devil," she told Sam. "And you will never lay eyes on my children again."

For the first time in his life, Sam was speechless. And when my mother returned home, she discovered that a portrait of Sam's brother—my father's father—which had been hanging in our front hallway for more than a decade, had jumped off the wall and fallen to the floor. Finally, someone had stood up to Sam, and apparently my father was not the only one who was thrilled.

This memory made me feel dizzy and nauseated. I allowed those feelings to pass through me gradually and then I processed more disturbing memories, until I began to feel better—alive and resilient. I was ready to leave the pain of my family behind.

I drove home from Gina's office and pulled up to my house, where three cherry trees in our front yard were covered in thick, pink blossoms, announcing the arrival of spring.

I set my backpack down in the front yard, lay flat on my back underneath the largest of the three trees, on the damp green grass, and stared up at the swollen pink flowers. Every branch was exploding with blossoms, swaying softly in the wind, sending pink petals onto the grass around me, onto my face, chest, and legs.

Outside the home where Jimmy and I had constructed a wonderful life together, I meditated. And for the first time since I'd begun my year of meditation, I knew that everything was going to be all right.

Gina had seen the lightness that I now knew was inside of me. I could go out into the world radiating that light.

I sat up, filled my lungs with air, and sighed.

It felt fantastic.

"Do you know what *sigh* stands for?" Gina had asked me once.

I'd shaken my head, no.

"Sitting in God's hands," Gina had said.

I took another deep, glorious, breath and let it go, sighing.

Sitting in God's hands.

I savored the feeling of air passing through me.

I took another deep breath, and let it go, just as smoothly. Then another. And another.

"There's no end to the happiness I can feel," I said, releasing my breath, and so much else, over and over and over again, sitting in God's hands.

How to Die

29

Learning to Die Happy

Relieved and exhilarated after my EMDR sessions with Gina, I left behind pain I'd felt for decades, and moved forward. I felt strong enough to face what I knew was coming for my mother, for me, and for everyone I loved, and decided to consult an expert on death and dying.

I signed up to see Robert Thurman, Columbia professor and expert on Buddhism, give a series of lectures at Tibet House in New York City. Surrounded by a collection of exquisite antiquities, Thurman, who's a decade older than I am, announced to the people assembled, "It's time to die!"

As the daughter of a woman who attended dream analysis workshops the way some women attended PTA meetings, I was intrigued, but still somewhat of a rookie when it came to facing death. Twenty years earlier, the hardest thing for me to accept about my father's death had been its finality. I couldn't believe that I would never be able to touch his hand again, or look into his pale blue eyes. After his funeral, my family returned to the apartment my parents had rented, and I hid out in his closet. At first I was planning just to peek inside. But when I removed one of my father's favorite cowboy shirts from a hanger, held it to my face, and smelled him, I wept, closing the closet door and sinking to the floor. I hadn't wanted my father to leave the planet. He was only sixty years old.

I sat on the floor of my father's closet for so long that I could hear people asking, "Where's Priscilla?" Eventually I emerged with the cowboy shirt, which now hangs in a closet at my house.

I'd come to Bob Thurman's lecture series with my friend Patty, who wasn't afraid to study death and dying; I hoped her bravery would rub off on me.

Tall and handsome in a ruddy way, with a shock of blondish gray hair, Bob Thurman wore faded blue jeans and fiddled with a set of wooden and silver Tibetan prayer beads while he spoke, twisting them around his wrist, tucking them into his pocket, throwing around ideas like "Life is the subtle energy continuum of our souls."

Thurman's lecture series was called "How to Die Happy— Increasing Chances of Rebirth in a Good Neighborhood." I should have known from the title that he'd be funny and irreverent, profound and profane. The text he was teaching was his own translation of *The Tibetan Book of the Dead*.

The Tibetan theory on the afterlife is derived from centuries of empirical scientific inquiry by Tibetans who studied the mind. Bob called these wise men "psychonauts," or "astronauts of the inner life, traveling in the mind space." The debate about life, death, and the afterlife is not religious but scientific, according to Thurman.

Wow. I felt like I'd stepped into one of my mother's past-life regression workshops from the 1960s. For as long as I could remember, she had referred to her eventual death as "the day I drop my body." Bob was speaking her language.

Before any being is conceived, Thurman explained, the soul, or spiritual gene, spends time in the Bardo, or in-between state of death and rebirth. But it craves a physical body, so it travels around looking for parents. After flying through realms populated with deities and demons, against the backdrop of dramatic landscapes and fiery elements, it's eager to be reborn.

Thurman put his audience into the mind of an unborn soul. "Imagine that you're cruising up and down the avenue," he told us, "nine times more intelligent than in real life. You see all these couples getting it on in apartments . . . You zoom over and get into it with them! If you're going to be male, you're attracted to the female; if you're going to be female, you've got your eye on the male."

According to Thurman, you merge with the couple you've chosen, just as their two seeds meet. "The mother is red, the father is white, and you're blue," Bob told us. "It's very patriotic!"

And also, apparently, exhausting. "You pass out," Bob said, "and the zygote is created."

The meeting of the red, white, and blue drops marks the creation of the heart chakra. According to Buddhists, when we die we can eject our souls from our bodies, by shooting pure energy up through the crowns of our heads, out of our uppermost chakra, in a process known as soul transmission and ejection. We have to be taught to do this, but it is possible.

The experience of dying is laid out in detail in *The Tibetan Book of the Dead*. "A trusted, beloved relative or friend" should read from the text to the dying person, Thurman said. "You want to die quietly, so that you can slowly withdraw from the body."

Suddenly I remembered that my mother had read to my father from *The Tibetan Book of the Dead* as he spent his last week at a nursing home. I had not been present at the time of my father's death. In fact, I had called Jimmy from the home on my final visit, pleading for advice.

"I don't want to leave my father," I told him. "But I don't want to be here when he dies."

"Do whatever feels right to you," Jimmy advised me. I'd nursed my father through his valiant battle with cancer for more than two years. His last weeks on earth had been excruciatingly painful for him and me. I needed to see Jimmy and Max and hold them in my arms, and I knew that my father would understand. Exhausted and brokenhearted, I was terrified to actually see his life end.

So I left my father's bedside and returned home to the new family I'd made with his help and blessings. But first I told my father how much I loved him. I promised him that I would tell his grandchildren all about him. He sat in a chair, motionless, his eyes dull and milky from recent strokes. Although he hadn't moved in days, when I thanked him for loving me, he extended his arms out to me and moaned, trying to speak.

I hugged him, absorbing his life energy for the last time, pressing my head to his chest to hear his heart beating. And then I left his room, dissolving into tears only when I was out the door. My mother and sister remained behind. For days, my mother read to him and, finally, just before he died, my sister told him that his mother was waiting for him in heaven, that she'd baked his favorite orange coconut cake, which was ready. One tear fell from my father's eye and ran down his cheek as he took his last rattling breath.

For a long time, my siblings and I used to joke about that tear. It was easier to make fun of my parents' relationship than to understand it. "Dad must have been saying, "Enough already with the Tibetan Buddhist thing!'" we told ourselves, laughing. He was Jewish, plain and simple. He hadn't embraced the New Age the way my mother had.

But as Thurman read aloud to us now from *The Tibetan Book of the Dead*, I sat in the front row and reevaluated that teardrop falling from my father's eye. Maybe it had been the beginning of some sort of soul transmission. Maybe my father had been enormously touched and comforted by the text my mother read to him.

Inspired even, to continue on the afterlife journey Thurman was laying out for us now.

"Hey, noble one!" he read from the text, addressing the unborn soul. "You nomad—now the time has come for you to seek the way . . ."

I was going to learn how to die, twenty years after I'd run away from death.

"You experience reality, stark and final," Thurman said. "You lose consciousness, or organized thought through the senses. It seems like you're losing yourself. People are afraid of being nothing if they let go. That's why we cling to control of what's around us."

And that's why we run away from rooms where people we love are dying.

But apparently I'd been dying every night without knowing it. When we go to sleep, we "give up the guarding of our own environment," Bob explained. Sleep is the time when our cells "are immersed in the deepest level of the universe, so we wake up restored, to face the horrible mess the next day."

My soul left my body in the middle of the night—that's why I'd been afraid to surrender to sleep during the worst years of my panic. I used to whisper a Jewish prayer, the Shema, every night in bed, praying that I'd wake up the next morning.

When Jack was four, he had been afraid of dying. Every night, I comforted him by reading a book called *The Mountains of Tibet*, by Mordicai Gerstein, about an old woodcutter from Tibet who had died and ascended to the heavens. He looked down on galaxy upon galaxy, finally selecting one where he'd like to be reborn. Next he chose the blue and green planet called Earth. He picked a country to live in, and a set of parents. Finally he chose to be reborn as a girl, since he'd already experienced life as a boy.

"Don't forget to ask for another life!" Jack used to plead with Jimmy and me when we put him to bed at night. He made us promise to be reborn, along with him, night after night. He had a master plan for the family. "Tell Max to ask for another life, too!" he urged us.

Eventually Jack grew out of his nighttime fears. I hadn't thought about his childhood concerns until I met Bob Thurman, whom I dubbed "the merry prankster of death."

At the next teaching session, Thurman prepared us for a meditation upon our own deaths, which he described as "inexpressibly far-out!" And when he led us through the meditation, I did "drop my body" for several minutes. I passed through all the stages Bob described to us, into a clear light. I felt my body fall away, like something an astronaut might drop into the weightless void of outer space. At one point, I got scared. What if I was truly gone? I had to open my eyes and tell myself, "You're at Tibet House; Patty is sitting beside you; Bob Thurman is teaching you how to die, *but you don't have to do it unless you want to!*"

"HOLY SHIT!" I wrote in my journal when I came to.

"The Dalai Lama does this practice seven times a day," Thurman told us. "To remind himself of his ability to go back and forth between these stages."

Seven times a day. No wonder he's the Dalai Lama.

While I still recalled some of my "psychonaut adventure," as I thought of it, I scribbled down—to the best of my memory—where I'd gone, with Thurman leading the way.

We'd done a rehearsal for our own death in stages that involved a lake, a giant Buddha, gods with emerald eyes, smoke, bright light, moonlight, a candle flame, a pure drop of clear light, a melting of my body, a luminescence, people I knew and didn't know watching me across a body of water, light radiating from me and next to me . . . and not in that exact order.

Jimmy had almost come with me to that night's teachings. Maybe it was better that he hadn't, I thought when we were done.

Bob guided us through our father's phallus, into our mother's womb, and then into our present bodies. I felt I was melting, glowing, nothing, everything, nowhere, everywhere.

"Tonight might have been a bit much for Jimmy's first initiation into Buddhist studies," I told Patty, laughing as we left Tibet House.

But Jimmy did come back with us the next week, for the last of Bob's lectures. A national treasure, Bob talked about designing a way for people to die peacefully, about providing training programs for people doing hospice work and for patients classified as terminal. I wished my father had been able to experience a comforting rehearsal of his own death at a relatively young age. It gave me some solace to think that my mother had guided him through it at the end.

"Why tinker around the edges of this precious life we have? Everybody has to grow up," Thurman said, when speaking of the challenges facing mankind. He advised us to "choose our womb wisely." As we imagined ourselves cruising down Fifth Avenue in New York, looking for a family to be born into, "Have some restraint," Bob suggested. "Check out the décor of the house. Is there a Buddha on the mantel?" he grinned. "Check out the titles of the books in the library. And do they have children?" Bob chuckled. "Maybe you want to wait until they've worked out all their neuroses on their first child!"

Tibetan women who want to have a child construct a beautiful shrine in their home, to attract an enlightened being into their lives. Making a short list of all the qualities you're looking for in parents could be a good idea, Bob told us. It works for people shopping for an apartment in New York City.

"The world is made of infinite, pure bliss, free of suffering," Bob said. "What the Buddha discovered is that this is nirvana. That he had always been in nirvana. We are in it right now. People tormenting each other is intolerable, because we are tormenting ourselves."

Bob's definition of karma is straightforward. "It's not fate," he said. "Karma is just action. Cause and effect." Everything we do creates tendencies. If we're stingy, mean, and nasty, we'll develop those muscles. If we're genuine, sweet, and kind, we'll gravitate in that direction.

He left us all with hope. "We have infinite time," Bob said. "So we will achieve nirvana if it takes us fifty lifetimes."

Jimmy, Patty, and I drifted down the stairs of Tibet House, out onto the street, trying to absorb Bob's teachings. "Did he remind you of my mother and her adventures?" I asked Jimmy.

"And how," Jimmy said, rolling his eyes. He had grown up in a much more conventional household than mine. The first time he met my mother, he told me he had no idea what to say to her. "Her conversations are not linear," he complained.

"Just pretend you're stoned," was my advice to my future husband.

"That worked!" he told me after their next meeting.

Patty had never met any of my relatives. "But it seems to me that you were born into a dharma family," she told me. "You had a lot of lessons to learn, and you chose your family wisely, because they had a lot to teach you."

I thought about Bob's teachings for days after his last lecture. I had been a bit stoned in his presence, though I'd never been a pot smoker. I thought about dying differently afterward, although my fear of death did not totally disappear. When I heard police sirens, I still worried that one of my sons had been involved in a car accident, even though they'd grown up and left home.

Usually, however, when I thought about my own family—Jimmy, Max, and Jack, and Mickey—I felt enormously grateful, blessed, and happy.

Perhaps the Tibetans were right, that I had chosen the life I was now living in very deliberately. That my soul had flown around the world, looking for the family I "chose" to be born into.

Maybe I was attracted to both the pain and the joy I saw in the people of Fall River, Massachusetts, and Hollywood, California. Maybe I circled my parents like a moth to a flame, taking a good hard look at the handsome young naval officer and the pretty artist he'd fallen in love with.

How could my father not love my mother? She had a spark, a flash of California sunshine in her soul, which obscured some of the sadness she would carry around with her for so many years, underneath all the color and drama. And my father? Louise Good-friend had reported that my mother fell for him swiftly, that he was handsome and charming.

Maybe, when I was a soul seeking a body, I even took a good look at my uncle Nathan and cousin Priscilla, the people I found most challenging in my childhood. Maybe I felt I could be of some use to them, perhaps shedding some light and joy. Maybe I thought I'd connect with them in a healing way. My father grew up in a dark family, became burdened and exhausted, but relished having a daughter to talk to. My mother liked to laugh, shock, and bewilder people, and she drew them into her wacky world, entertaining and distracting everyone—including herself—from the pain that is part of life.

Maybe my soul, too, had been drawn to the "inexpressibly far-out." Maybe I was born into exactly the right family. A dharma family, a place where lessons might not have been taught, but a place where they were certainly learned.

I had not learned those lessons too late, I realized. How much time I had left was a mystery. But the quality of that time was something I might be able to influence.

30

My Religion Is Compassion

Cҩ૭

For instruction in how to live every single day, it was time to consult a man who had made the most of every day for many lifetimes, indeed, someone who had been reincarnated fourteen times: His Holiness, the Dalai Lama.

When he walked onto the stage of Radio City Music Hall in New York City, accompanied by Secret Service men, his translator, and Richard Gere, the Dalai Lama approached the dozens of monks gathered on the stage to receive his teachings, clasped their outstretched hands, and smiled. Then he turned to the audience of several thousand, put his palms together, raised them to his face, and bowed ever so slightly.

Hollywood celebrities, yoga teachers, and their students have been using that same gesture for years, but when the Dalai Lama held his hands together and bowed to thousands, I felt a connection. It was as simple as that. Nobody does it better.

Bob Thurman had said that in all the time he'd spent with His Holiness, he'd never seen him in anyone's presence where he wasn't there 100 percent. As he walked to the front of the stage and peered out at the people in the first few rows, grinning and greeting them with enthusiasm, the Dalai Lama was most definitely present.

He walked over to a red cloth on the stage, directly in front of a gigantic thangka painting, and prostrated himself three times, in the presence of the Buddha. Then he took off his shoes and climbed a set of wooden stairs leading up to a small platform. The Dalai Lama fluffed up a giant brocade cushion, and sat down. He picked up an orange sun visor, like the ones sold in souvenir shops all over the world, and placed it on his head, to shield himself from the harsh stage lights. And he looked absolutely adorable.

At any gathering of people in New York City, I feel the energy of everyone around me, whether on a subway platform or at a Broadway show. But the only energy in this huge venue seemed to be coming directly from the Dalai Lama to the people seated in front of him. The monks onstage chanted Tibetan prayers, and His Holiness proceeded to speak.

"All human beings have sadness and anxiety," he said. "Because we have these feelings, we have a fundamental right to work on them. We have a sophisticated intelligence and we must use it to bring happiness. It's a pity it brings unhappiness. It's like self-torture."

Indeed.

Money, power, and fame are factors in bringing about happiness, the Dalai Lama continued. But the physical comforts we surround ourselves with cannot heal mental or physical pain. However, cultivating mental strength can lead to calmness, reduce fear, and bring happiness.

Staring up at the two giant video screens suspended on either side of the stage, I studied the image of the Dalai Lama, whose famous face was clean and radiant, smooth and uncreased. I'd read in Victor Chan's book, *The Wisdom of Forgiveness,* that "the Dalai Lama wears his soul on his face."

According to Chan, a psychologist named Paul Ekman was struck by how young the Dalia Lama looked when he met him.

Ekman attributed that to the fact that His Holiness uses every one of his facial muscles more often than most people to express his emotions.

Exhibiting "the childlike, carefree spontaneity of Tibetans," wrote Chan, "there is a precision in the way the Dalai Lama expresses himself. When he is happy, he is 100 percent happy. No other sentiments creep in to adulterate the experience." But, according to Chan, "he doesn't get too attached to things, including his emotions."

Meanwhile, I was extremely attached to everything the Dalai Lama was saying and took careful notes. People of all religions and no religious affiliation need to develop mutual respect and understanding, he said. "I always make it clear that it's important for you Westerners to keep your own religion. It's not like fashion, where you keep changing your dress."

I felt a sense of relief, although I hadn't seriously contemplated becoming Buddhist. I was perfectly happy with the spiritual practice I'd developed as a Jew and to have experienced the extended interfaith experiences of *The Faith Club*, as I'd traveled across America speaking to people of all faiths in synagogues, mosques, and churches.

His Holiness warned us that non-Buddhist texts would not be mentioned in the words we'd be studying. "But don't worry about that." He explained modestly how he'd received oral transmissions from "a very, very good monk," so that the teachings of his lineage would be protected. He'd chosen texts for this audience that were written by "a very great Indian master" named Nagarjuna, and urged us to read his *Commentary on Bodhicitta*, a text about achieving an awakened mind, again and again on our own. "If you read it nine times, you'll have nine different understandings."

I did my best to follow along while he read Nagarjuna's words aloud and elaborated on them, in Tibetan, waiting for his translator to interpret his teachings. I read the book we'd been given as His Holiness explained bodhicitta, "the awakening of the mind."

I took notes like "*Mind is devoid of mind because the nature of mind is clear light.*" But a few minutes later, all I could write was "Hunh?"

I looked over at my friend Liz, who had accompanied me to these teachings. She was typing away on her iPad, clearly understanding what she was hearing. Liz uses elements of Buddhist teachings in her psychoanalytic practice. She knew all about self and no-self, while I knew absolutely nothing. I'd never taken a single course in psychology because I'd always been afraid that I was crazy.

As Liz grasped concepts that were flying over my head, I decided to flip through the text, looking for passages that spoke to me, and I found a beauty:

A happy mind is tranquil indeed;
A tranquil mind is not confused;
To have no confusion is to understand the truth;
By understanding the truth one attains freedom.

I was far from understanding the truth, but my mind was feeling quite tranquil, in the presence of the Dalai Lama. I even managed to scribble down something he said that I could grasp: "*Even if you search for emptiness, you will find the emptiness of emptiness.*"

Then I sat back in my comfortable red velvet seat and basked in the spaciousness of Radio City. The lights had been dimmed; the hundred or so monks and nuns sitting onstage were clad in crimson and saffron robes. I felt like I was nestled in a Tibetan womb.

The next day, Liz and I waited in line to go through the two security checkpoints, and were given a copy of another text: *A Guide to the Bodhisattva's Way of Life* by Shantideva.

The Dalai Lama entered again and began teaching. I tried my

best to understand what he was saying. *At all times, I should be the pupil of everyone,* I read in the text.

That, I could understand. I'd been learning new lessons from everyone I'd met over the last year.

I sat back in my chair and zoned out, pleasantly, until I heard the Dalai Lama's translator say, "The four noble truths really form the framework of all else."

"Phew!" I thought. "When I get home, I can just read the four noble truths!" Of course, they're not so easy to understand or to put our understanding into practice: *Life is suffering; Suffering comes from attachments* (to earthly things, emotions, ideas, misconceptions, and false beliefs); *We can resolve our suffering;* and *There is a path out of suffering.*

I flipped through the text again and found more beautiful writing that spoke to me, including lines that seemed to justify my decision to study dharma, or the Buddha's teachings, on my own: *In the same way as a bee takes honey from a flower, I should take merely (what is necessary) for the practice of dharma.*

"This is like studying Talmud," Liz whispered to me, referring to the dense, intellectual commentary that accompanies and interprets Jewish scripture.

"Actually, it's Dharmud, a combination of the Talmud and dharma," I smiled.

When I returned home that night, Jimmy asked me what it was like to study with the Dalai Lama. I was reminded of when Jimmy had inquired, in the midst of my labor with our first child, "Can you describe to me what the pain is like?"

"Some things are just too big to describe," I told my husband.

The next afternoon, the Dalai Lama gave us all some advice on meditation. "The ability to maintain stable attention is something we possess naturally," he assured us. He suggested we take nine cleansing breaths with each practice, and that the best time to meditate was early morning, since it shapes the mind and influences the course of the rest of the day.

"It's better for a beginner to do five to ten minutes a day of good meditation," the Dalai Lama told us. "Otherwise, you spend one hour, but you're half asleep! You might cultivate a bad habit!" Generally speaking, he said, within six to nine months of meditating, one is able to reach a sense of "tranquil abiding."

Daily challenges in life are inevitable and they help us develop strength, patience, and resilience, along with a healthy ego and self confidence. He quoted the text:

Whatever joy there is in the world
All comes from desiring others to be happy.
And whatever suffering there is in the world
All comes from desiring myself to be happy.

If I do not actually exchange my happiness
For the suffering of others,
I shall not attain the state of Buddhahood . . .

A tidal wave of understanding hit me. Exchange my happiness for the suffering of others? That sounded like what I had done as a young child. Had I been training to be a bodhisattva, an earthly practitioner of compassion? Perhaps. Because I had also gone on to experience, as the text promised, a "magnificent life."

Once upon a time, I suddenly realized, I was indeed a bodhisattva-in-training. I suffered for others. And, according to these teachings, that response was a noble one.

As a child, practicing compassion for all the adults who were suffering in my family had seemed overwhelmingly difficult. But now, because of all the work I'd done, perhaps I could practice compassion for others without causing pain to myself, in the form of panic.

The Dalai Lama has often been quoted as saying, "My religion is kindness." I vowed right then and there to live my life with as much compassion as I could muster. And the last thing the Dalai Lama did in his visit to New York was read aloud—along with the thousands of people who had studied with him—"The Vow of the Bodhisattva," a magnificent piece of writing and a guide to becoming enlightened. As tears streamed down my cheeks, I recited the vow, including these verses, which I'd transcribed in my notebook. This is the Golden Rule of Buddhism, and it would become my daily guide:

May I be the doctor, the medicine
And may I be the nurse
For all sick beings in the world
Until everyone is healed.

May I be a protector for those without one,
A guide for all travellers on the way.
May I be a bridge, a boat and a ship
For all who wish to cross (the water).

May I be an island for those who seek one,
And a lamp for those desiring light,
May I be a bed for all who wish to rest
And a slave for all who want a slave.

May I be a wishing jewel, a magic vase,
Powerful mantras and great medicine,
May I become a wish-fulfilling tree
And a cow of plenty for the world.

31

A Lesson in Impermanence

Sixty blocks uptown from where the Dalai Lama was speaking to thousands of people at Radio City Music Hall, a small group of Tibetan monks had begun building an intricate sand mandala, in a chapel at the magnificent Cathedral of St. John the Divine.

I stopped by one morning just in time to see them finishing up the colorful circle in the center of the mandala, a geometric depiction of Buddhist deities. They filled hollow steel tubes with brightly colored sand, meticulously dropping each grain onto the surface of a large table. A photograph of His Holiness sat on a nearby altar, filled with flowers, tapestries, and candles.

I'd heard about the construction of this sand mandala on Twitter, which was appropriate, since tweets vanish quickly, and this mandala was being created in order to be purposefully destroyed ten days later, as an illustration of the impermanence of life.

St. John the Divine, a towering combination of Romanesque, Byzantine, and Gothic architectural elements, looks out over the campus of Columbia University, on the Upper West Side of Manhattan. Its soaring arches and stained glass windows are as spectacular as those found anywhere in the world, and the interfaith programs that take place inside the majestic space are a tribute to the diversity of New York City.

Over a decade earlier, I had admired the cathedral and its message so much that I'd convinced my mother to buy a crypt for herself there, in a rose-colored marble columbarium, not far from where the monks were working. My mother had talked about having her ashes stored at a monastery in Carmel, New York, near the house Jimmy and I had rented when my father was dying. She used to visit that monastery regularly; the monks had been enormously comforting and supportive. But when I raised the possibility of purchasing a crypt at St. John the Divine, she had agreed that it would be nice to "live" in New York. She had, after all, planned to move into the 92nd Street Y after graduating from college until she had met my father and they became engaged.

My mother's plans continued changing throughout her life. Just before she was diagnosed with Alzheimer's, she wondered if her final resting place should be next to my father, in the Jewish cemetery where he was buried. So I'd sold the crypt. But then I discovered that the rules of the cemetery prohibited women from being buried next to men. Once again, my mother was a free agent. My parents just couldn't seem to get their act together as a couple.

"Do whatever you want to do with me," my mother finally told me, in our last conversation on the topic, a few years earlier.

Maybe she should come back to St. John the Divine, I thought as I visited the sand mandala. My mother would have loved watching the monks construct their delicate masterpiece. The instruments they used made a sharp, buzzing sound as they released each grain of sand, one at a time, onto the table. Aside from an occasional whispered exchange between the monks, the marble-lined room housing the mandala was silent. I sat down on a wooden pew to meditate, with my hands in my lap and my eyes closed.

I felt like I was building a cathedral inside of myself. I imagined a tiny construction site right next to my heart, where tiny steel girders were being lifted, miniature walls and columns erected. A holy space was taking shape inside me; beautiful stained glass windows were illuminating me from the inside out.

A few days later, when I returned to St. John the Divine, the mandala had expanded outward, from a circle to a larger square, full of detailed embellishments. And when the Dalai Lama's teachings in New York City were over, the magnificent mandala was finished as well.

It was gorgeous. Every color was brilliant, every tiny detail clear and precise. A group of people watched as several monks lifted the heavy wooden table and carried it out of the chapel. I shuffled behind them, along with everyone else, in a quiet procession. Eventually they set the table down in the huge nave of the cathedral. Miraculously, the mandala was still intact.

While more than a hundred people watched, the monks began their closing ceremony. Dressed in their crimson and saffron robes, wearing huge, bright yellow hats, they chanted, in the very deep, distinctive style of the Gyuto monks. Then they played traditional Tibetan instruments—cymbals, trumpets, a bright green drum, and two gigantic brass horns, about four feet long.

A monk approached the table, and as the others chanted behind him, he bowed his head for a moment. Slowly and deliberately, he placed his hand on the outer edge of the mandala, and pushed the colorful sand into the center. He did that on all four sides, while everyone watched silently.

Another monk approached, carrying a wide brush. Slowly, he circled the table, brushing the sands of the mandala into a small pile, which grew larger and larger as slowly and steadily he erased the artwork that had been constructed so carefully. I watched in amazement. I had never seen anyone so deliberately erase something so magnificent.

When he was done, all that remained was a pile of sand in the center of the table. While two monks swept the sand into containers, the Tibetan man in charge of the proceedings announced that everyone could come up to the table and be given a packet of sand. Then a procession would form, and the monks would scatter the remaining sand into the water of a nearby park.

I waited in line, received my tiny plastic bag of a gray sand, which was actually composed of twenty different colors, and stood behind the rest of the audience members, who were beginning to form a procession.

The monks carrying the containers of sand exited the church. Other monks followed behind them, playing instruments. And the crowd followed after that, slowly and quietly.

We marched through the courtyard of St. John the Divine, past the nursery school on the premises, and a peacock whose tail was fanned out in a flashy display of color. We walked down dozens of stone steps into Morningside Park, and then over to a murky body of still, green water.

I had been taking pictures and recording this event, along with many other people. A man in front of me had remarked to his female companion about the irony of taking pictures of something that was meant to be impermanent.

Self-conscious, I tucked my little camera into my pocket, taking a surreptitious shot here and there of the monks walking ahead of me. I walked along the water's edge, trying to find the perfect spot from which to photograph the final stage of the ceremony, where the sands of the mandala would be poured into the murky pond, sending healing energy out into the world.

The golden, late afternoon light was perfect. I positioned myself in a place with an unobstructed view of the monks. And at just the right moment, I turned on my camera, adjusting it to take a video instead of a still photo. A monk in a huge yellow hat stretched his arm over the waters majestically and poured the sand into the pond.

I was elated! The camera, with a flashing red light indicating that it was recording, shook in my hands just a tiny bit, but I carefully captured this moment in time, hanging on to it for dear life. I would own, forever, a short little film of the monk throwing the sands into the waters of New York City. I would have just what I wanted to hold on to. For eternity.

I was so delighted with myself that I needed to play back the video immediately.

But I couldn't. It had disappeared.

I was absolutely positive that I had filmed a video of the monk throwing the sands into the water. I had seen it all through the viewfinder. I'd also seen a red light flashing, indicating that this was being recorded. But in a short video that I did manage to find and play back, the camera appeared to fall from my hands, taking shaky footage of the ground. Then it had shut itself off.

This blew me away. I'd taken dozens of short films with this same camera over the past year, and this had never happened.

Maybe I was supposed to learn a lesson. Apparently I was not meant to take a permanent picture of a moment that was meant to be impermanent. Paparazzi were not welcome at such events.

I looked back at the monks just in time to see one of them throw a bouquet of roses out into the pond. I watched as the sand swirled through the green water in and around the stems, flowers, and thorns.

And then it was gone.

32

One More Happy Person
on the Planet

❧

Friends began commenting on how calm I seemed. Some said I even looked different, that my face was relaxed. That my voice was smoother. That I walked without slumping forward. That I seemed very mellow.

"Do you think Priscilla is mellow?" one of our friends asked Jimmy one night at dinner.

He paused for a moment, thinking. "She's ninety-nine percent mellow," he said with a smile.

In a move that shocked me, I stopped taking Klonopin every day, with my therapist's permission. I was sleeping better.

"I've become one more happy person on the planet," I told Gina, when I returned to see her one more time.

"That's pretty huge." She smiled.

"Yes it is."

We sat quietly opposite each other for a few moments. I could hear car horns and police sirens out on the street, a neighbor playing scales on a musical instrument in a nearby apartment.

Suddenly, I noticed that Gina's dog Pilot, the yellow lab, was lying on the floor next to her.

"Has he been here all along?" I asked.

"For the last couple of sessions," Gina told me.

"He never used to come into this office when I was here," I remembered. "He used to lie out in the waiting room."

"He picks up on people's vibes," Gina told me. "He comes in and out of this space depending on what he senses."

And he must have sensed something different in me. Something joyful.

"I always thought it was selfish to be happy," I said. "That if I was happy, I was taking that joy away from somebody else. Probably someone I was related to. I thought there was a limited amount of happiness in the world and that if I got too much of it, I was being greedy."

I sat on the couch where I had grounded myself so many times, and cried and laughed and sighed. "In a funny way, I was sort of addicted to my panic," I said. "It was my identity. I was very, very connected to it and now I'm not.

"It's weird. I can barely remember what the panic felt like, because I can't replicate the symptoms in my body." I shook my head. "There are people walking around the planet right now who feel the same way I used to feel. And they don't know how to feel better."

"You can help them," Gina said. "You can educate them."

I agreed. That's how I would exercise my compassion every day. That's what I would do with my new self.

"So what should we do next?" Gina asked.

"I don't know. I'm afraid that I might be done with you."

"Let's talk about what you just said." Gina smiled. " 'I'm afraid I'm done with you'?"

I laughed. "It makes me sad to think that I'm done. I accomplished so much here—everything I always wanted, everything I always dreamed about. I'm sorry this therapy wasn't available to me when I was young. But somehow I held myself together until it was."

"So let's talk about some other stuff," Gina said. "In your present-day life, is there anything that causes you anxiety?"

I shook my head no. "I'm looking forward to happiness," I said. "I'm looking forward to some kind of tranquility. But do people really get that?"

"Yes," Gina said. "They do. People have feelings—happiness, sadness, anger, disappointment. But what's important is what we *do* with those feelings. How we live with them and release them. Because whatever we feel—happy or sad—this too shall pass. Something else will happen."

I understood that feelings come and go. I knew that mine would come and go as well. But I felt calm in that moment.

"I've never had this feeling of sustained calm before. I never knew what this felt like," I told Gina. "I've been ecstatically happy and joyful. I've got the greatest husband and the greatest kids and the greatest life. I'm very fortunate. But I've never been at peace before. And I'm so at peace that I'm not even questioning what that means, or what it's going to turn into, or what to do with this feeling. I'm not even forcing myself to enjoy it. None of that applies. It just is what it is."

I smiled at Gina. "I hope this happens every time someone walks into your office."

"It happens to a lot of people," she told me.

"I still think it's a miracle," I said. "If you define a miracle as something that you never felt could happen, something beyond your wildest dreams. You helped me to access emotions I'd been too scared to access. Thank you."

I stood up to leave. "I really appreciate everything you did to help me heal," I said. "Can I give you a hug?"

"Sure," Gina said, smiling.

I bent down and wrapped my arms around her. "You're so tiny!"

"Most people say that," Gina laughed.

"But you're so powerful," I said, turning to leave.

Gina chuckled. "People think I'm six feet tall."

I looked back and smiled at her one more time. "I would have said twenty-five feet. You're like a giant Buddha."

33

Neurotic, Heal Thyself

❦

My brain was too calm.

I lay in bed wondering if I was sick. Or depressed. Or whatever it was that people called this feeling of . . . nothingness. Who ever thought being happy would be this hard?

Had I turned into what I'd wanted to be at the start of this experiment—a serious monk, for God's sake?

I missed my panic. Cured of it, I'd become just like every other person on the planet, trying to figure out what to do next, how to live, what to care about, how to be happy.

I'm nobody special, I thought. With no exotic excuse for being unhappy.

A slightly overweight woman whose hair was turning gray, with a fairly regular craving for chocolate, I was a dime a dozen. A lady who'd hit menopause and had no idea where to go next. I was peaceful, but somehow I was also sad.

It didn't help that I wasn't eating dairy, wheat, or sugar, or drinking caffeine or alcohol. "I'm an air plant," I joked to friends.

A holistic physician had told me, "Everything you put into your body is information." So I tried changing the information I was giving my body. I started a detox with shakes and vitamins, but that lasted for one day, until I got a disturbing call from my mother's nursing home, where she was having graphic hallucinations. Although I stopped cleansing, to my credit I did not reach for ginger snaps.

"You're living in your head too much," the holistic doctor told me kindly. "A lot of people do. But you need to come back into your body."

It was still there, waiting for me—every single pound of it. Although I was feeling so much lighter overall, I hadn't lost an ounce on a scale.

So I tried to watch what I was eating and let this doctor stab a dozen acupuncture needles into me from head to toe. The needles didn't hurt a bit.

I floated out of his office and felt calm.

Which made me nervous.

I was so damn relaxed, I couldn't stand it.

And then I did begin to get depressed.

On some days I felt like I was watching my old self, my childhood, all that pain, float away, like a giant iceberg that had broken off from who I was now. I waved goodbye as my past disappeared into chilly waters, headed for parts unknown.

My panic, my constant companion, the shadow that used to follow me everywhere, had now abandoned me. I still meditated every day, taking nine cleansing breaths, as the Dalai Lama had recommended. Then I sat still, and wondered who I was.

The little girl I used to be had been frozen with sadness, erupted in flames, had been healed and revealed and then disappeared.

I'd become just another unhappy person on the planet, to misquote Gina, leading a life of quiet desperation.

Now that my adrenals weren't working overtime, pumping fear through my veins, I missed that high. I began drinking a strong decaf coffee that used to give me a buzz. Now it did nothing. Even a cookie here and there didn't make me less sad.

Fortunately, a man named Robert Sachs, trained in Buddhist studies and Asian healing arts, including Ayurvedic and Tibetan medicine, paid a visit to New York from California.

Sachs had written a beautiful book about the short life of his daughter Shamara, and the profound effect her death from sudden infant death syndrome had on him and his wife, Melanie. In a remarkable ceremony Shamara's soul had been ejected from her body and released into Pure Land. *"In that time the world changed for us,"* Bob wrote. *"And trying to get back into the box of a smaller, more well-defined world—which was impossible—became irrelevant."*

A mutual friend had thought I should meet with Bob, to talk about post-traumatic recovery. We met at a quiet restaurant in Manhattan.

I told Bob about my early childhood trauma, my tracheotomy. "My parents loved to tell me the story of how I almost died," I said.

"When people hear about trauma, over and over again, they get numb," Bob told me. "And then they develop an abnormal response to crises. But maybe telling you that story was your parents' way of celebrating your survival."

"Absolutely!" I agreed. "They were telling me how much they loved me."

"The post-traumatic response is often to put yourself back into the zone of trauma, so that you feel more alive," Bob said.

"I did feel more alive with my panic," I realized. "Even though it always made me think I was dying."

"In some ways," Bob said, "what will come now is a symbolic death."

"Should I have a symbolic funeral for my old self?" I wondered.

Bob had worked in hospices and mental hospitals, facing situations that terrified many people. He told me to trust my intuition.

"When you realize that what's most important to you doesn't die, then everything else kind of works itself out." Bob referred to the great Buddhist teacher Chögyam Trungpa, who used to compare being alive to riding on a razor banister. "You can't veer off to one side or another in life, because either way you'll get hurt," Bob said. "So how do you stay right there in the middle, on that razor's edge?"

I tried to imagine riding that banister.

"I think when you're riding it properly," Bob continued, "life is neither pleasure nor pain. If you stay in touch with that, you'll make choices that will take you through life while you stay on that edge."

"Your panic is interesting to examine in an Ayurvedic sense," Bob continued. He explained some of the basics of the ancient Indian medical system. "We start out with more *kapha* in our bodies. We're round and pudgy, snotty and blubbery, and then we go into a more *pitta* stage of life, until around the age of fifty. Anxiety is associated with pitta. Heat builds up, our critical minds race, we compare and contrast everything . . . and we panic. In the *vata* stage—where you are now—we begin to cool down and dry up."

"That feels so right!" I said.

"You hear stories about people who were raging alcoholics all their lives," Bob continued. "Wreaking havoc on their families. And suddenly at the age of fifty, they stop drinking. Why then? That pitta intensity just finally drops off. We become more vata, drier. And we're looking at the bigger picture."

Bob suggested that Ayurvedic oil treatments would help to make me feel grounded. He recommended that I use his website to find a practitioner whom he and his wife had trained,

I told Bob how much I'd enjoyed meeting him, that he'd shown up at just the right time. "People have come into my life in a profoundly perfect way over the past year," I said.

"We live with a conventional sense of time," Bob said. "But one of my teachers taught me that time is vertical, which means that we experience things in a certain succession, but it's possible that they are all occurring at the same moment."

"So everything is happening at the same time?" I asked. "And our brains just put a past, present, or future to them?"

This was getting trippy.

"We put a story to things," Bob said. "Don't question what's been going on for you. Stuff happens when it happens. Nothing makes it happen."

Timothy Leary (or my mother) couldn't have said it better.

Apparently, life was a mikvah, where past, present, and future all merge in the holy waters. I thought about all my teachers, who had been appearing at just the right times over the past year, then setting me on my own path.

Yongey Mingyur Rinpoche, who had survived panic attacks as a child, was now on a three-year retreat in Nepal. I would have missed him entirely if I hadn't met him on the day after my birthday.

I told Bob about my conversation with Rabbi Jacobson, and my desire to do something symbolic for my next birthday.

"There's a system that forms the core of Oriental astrology," Bob told me. "It's called Nine House Astrology in China, Nine Star Ki in Japanese, and the System of Birthmarks in the Tibetan tradition. It's very easy to calculate, but it works in an extremely deep way.

"The year you were born, 1953, was what is called a two-earth year, which means you have the primal mother number. That accounts for why you took on such a strong mothering role in your family. You carried the primal mother energy, so the family almost abdicated that role."

And how.

"The secondary number that relates to your year is seven metal," Bob continued. He talked about the year we were in now, and did some calculations. "Your primary number in the month of June is in the house of fire," he said finally. "So I think you should do something in relation to fire. Something like a bonfire would be terrific."

"A bonfire?" I smiled. "I'll see what I can do about that." I hated to throw cold water onto Bob's suggestion, but I couldn't imagine where I'd ever come across a bonfire, just in time for my birthday.

I pulled out my car keys and prepared to drive home. "Jimmy has been so amazing through all this," I said. "He never questioned my panic or made light of it. He knew that in time I'd figure things out, and he supported me until that time came. He was my caretaker during the years that I couldn't take care of myself."

I grew too emotional to speak. "I'm not sure what his role is now, what our dynamic is."

"Your job is to just show him boundless gratitude," Bob said. "What I'm sensing from you is this profound sense of gratitude. You and your husband should celebrate that together."

Jimmy had just returned from a ten-day bike trip with friends. He kept saying, "Thank you for letting me go!" And I'd wanted to say, "Thank you for letting me live, thank you for letting me panic, thank you for letting me feel broken and sad for so long, thank you for being so patient."

I drove home to Jimmy and told him how much I loved him.

34

Dawn

Inside a quiet, candlelit spa outside Boston, a woman named Dawn Tardif, trained in Ayurvedic healing by Bob Sachs, is tending to me.

My feet are smiling. They are soaking in warm water mixed with ginger and eucalyptus bath salts.

My eyes are closed.

I am wearing the lightest, softest robe.

Flutes and Tibetan singing bowls are playing in the background. I am about to undergo Abhyanga massage, which means that Dawn and another woman will be working on my body in tandem, giving me a rhythmic massage. Once they're done, Dawn will pour a continuous, slow stream of warm oil onto my forehead, over and over again, treating me to an ancient Ayurvedic treatment called *shirodhara*.

Do I really deserve this?

I stop asking myself that question.

Dawn passes three different vials of scented oils under my nose, and I choose one.

I lie on a padded massage table, and she and Francesca place their hands on me.

I stop trying to figure out who is doing what to me.

I am being relaxed.

I am being grounded.

I am being healed.

I am shaken and tossed and prodded.

I roll over.

The two women are a perfect team. No words are exchanged, and yet they know exactly what to do with me and when to do it.

I feel like I did as a child, when I had a fever, and my mother put washcloths dipped in rubbing alcohol onto my hot skin.

I'm relieved.

Oil is everywhere. The smell of it is thick. The sheets above and below me are drenched.

My fever breaks.

I submit.

By the end of the massage, I feel like one of the giant bluefin tuna my father used to catch and haul onto the deck of his boat. Sleek and oily and powerful and big. Slippery and wild. Ultimately tamed.

Dawn is the captain of the boat I'm on. I do whatever she tells me. But she only tells me what I need to know.

She leaves the room and I slip away.

I can't think. I don't try to.

I am without thought.

What a relief!

Dawn comes back into the room and she stands by my head.

Slowly, a thin stream of warm, scented oil begins to trickle onto my forehead.

Dawn is holding something, filled with this warm oil. She moves it back and forth across my forehead, and the oil moves with her. It falls onto my third eye, that sweet spot between my eyes, just above the brow, moving in concentric, lazy circles. It traces my hairline, races into my hair, my scalp, my ears.

Dawn drizzles the oil to one side of my forehead, and then the other, keeping it away from my eyes.

Then Dawn places some stones on my feet and wraps some soft fabric around my ankles, to keep the stones in place.

She leaves the room and I lie there, thinking about feet.

Jesus comes to mind along with a young man I have known since the day he was born, James, a divinity school student, studying to become a minister. I heard him preach for the first time a few weeks earlier. He spoke about an alabaster vase filled with the most precious oil, about how Mary had poured that jasmine-scented oil onto Jesus's feet, in an extravagant, loving manner.

I feel lucky.

I lie under the soft sheet that Dawn has wrapped under and over me.

When she is done, she whispers instructions for when I can gather myself together and leave.

I get dressed and join her in a lounge. She pours me some tea. I sit and sip. I ask her, Why all the oil?

I'm like a plant, Dawn tells me, with roots that are dangling. I have nowhere to put them. I need to be grounded. I am vata today, Dawn tells me, air. That's my *dosha,* or Ayurvedic body type. That's the oil I chose. We are different on different days. Some days I might be more pitta, or fire. Or kapha, or earth.

Dawn shares an old Ayurvedic saying with me: *You can take poison and turn it into nectar with a healthy mind and you can take nectar and turn it into poison with an ill mind.*

"Eat with the right intention," she tells me. "Live with the right intention."

On my last day at Dawn's spa, I choose a different oil, kapha, or earth. As the oil runs all over my temples, Dawn uses colored lights to balance my chakras, or energy centers. She's been using them all along, apparently. The lights correspond to the energy of the chakras—red, orange, yellow, green, blue, indigo, and violet—and she focuses them on the base of my spine, abdomen, heart, throat, third eye, and crown of the head.

Dawn massages my back, neck, shoulders, head, collarbones, hands, and feet.

She places one finger on the small of my back, holds it there, and my breathing slows way, way down, until I am barely breathing.

As she works on my feet, and attaches the stones to my soles once more, Tibetan music carries me across some sort of divide.

My father appears at the foot of my table.

My eyes are closed.

"You were loved," he says to me.

I hear it again and again.

"You were loved."

I break down and cry.

I want him to stick around. I want to hear more.

I can feel him leaving.

I don't want him to go.

But, finally I'm ready to return to my life.

I was loved.

I open my eyes.

35

Happy Birthing Day

c∞⁓

"Your mother wants to do something for you."

My hair was still drenched in oil, when Betty, my mother's caregiver, called me at the bed-and-breakfast where I was staying in Massachusetts, in between heavenly treatments with Dawn. Betty had an urgent tone to her voice that I hadn't heard before.

"Your mother didn't know who I was today," she said. "But as soon as I walked into her room, she cornered me. 'You see, I have this daughter, and I'd like to do something for her.' She kept repeating that, over and over again. 'I need to do something for my daughter. The older one.'"

What on earth could my mother do for me at this point in her life? She was fumbling to recall who she was, where she was, and who I was. She was at peace, but she was living in a dementia ward. In fact, the last time I saw her, she had no memory of ever meeting my father. She'd stared blankly when I mentioned his name. So much for Alzheimer's patients living in the past; I wasn't sure where my mother was living these days.

For the first time ever, I was annoyed with Betty, my mother's wonderful caregiver for the last nine years. It seemed somehow cruel to take Riva's intentions so seriously. My mother couldn't possibly do anything for me, I thought. Not in the way I'd always longed for her to do something.

I thanked Betty for calling, then didn't give our conversation a second thought.

A few days later, a comment showed up on the blog I'd been writing. An interfaith minister from New Hampshire, Terry O'Dell, wrote: *"I met your delightful, dynamic and funny Wise Woman Mother at a Retreat in Manchester Center Vt. many years ago . . . lots of funny warm memories I would love to share some time with you . . . of your wonderful Mother . . . who modeled 'Following your Bliss' long before it was so fashionable!!!"*

Like Louise Goodfriend, this woman had popped into my life to tell me stories about my mother, who was unable to tell them to me anymore.

I emailed Terry, overwhelmed by the notion that my mother had somehow brought us together. She sent me her phone number and I called her as I lay on the bed in the Bead Room, in the same spot where Louise Goodfriend had found me. In the room where my mother had spent so many nights.

Terry felt my mother's hand in this as well. "It's the strangest thing," she said. "I've been doing some purging around my house, going through old papers and things. I came across your mother's business card in my nightstand, and something made me hold on to it. Then I had the most powerful urge to find out where Riva was. I found the website you built of her art and traced that to your blog." She paused. "I didn't expect to discover that Riva was alive."

"She's definitely alive," I said. "And apparently she wants us to connect."

Terry recalled how she and my mother had met, at a Jesuit retreat. "Riva walked in late," Terry said. "She tromped in with these big winter boots and a long, heavy sweater. She spoke her mind and wasn't shy. I thought, There's an interesting woman. I'd like to get to know her."

Terry had been a member of the Roman Catholic Church for her entire life, but at the time, she was going through a personal and spiritual crisis that was moving her away from Catholicism. She and my mother had numerous, lengthy conversations about the suffering this was causing her. "We only met that one time," Terry told me, "but your mother had such a powerful effect on me. I talked about coming down to see her, and I'd pulled out her card on several occasions, but we never connected again."

"Until now," I said.

"I can't believe you're an interfaith minister," I continued. "I coauthored this book called *The Faith Club* . . . "

"It's right here on my bookshelf," Terry said. "That's you?"

"Where were you ordained?" I asked.

"At St. John the Divine," Terry told me.

It was my turn to be surprised. "My mother used to have a crypt there, but now I'm wondering where her final resting place should be," I said. "This stuff isn't easy to figure out."

"I know," Terry replied. "I do a lot of work with the dying."

"Wow." My mother's favorite word popped out of my mouth. "Maybe you can help me," I said. "I've been wrestling with how the final phase of my mother's life is going to go, and who will accompany us through that phase."

We agreed to talk again later that night.

Terry had told me about the two Jesuit brothers who ran the retreat where she and Riva met. I googled "The Linn Brothers" and discovered that they'd written eight books on healing life's hurts. They were still conducting retreats and workshops all over the country.

Their message, which I read in an article online, blew me away.

Dennis Linn is convinced that we have all been loved and cared for or we wouldn't be alive. His goal is to help people allow those loving experiences to sink into our daily lives.

My father had shown up at Dawn's spa to tell me that I was loved. The Linn brothers wanted me to focus on how much I was loved as well. So did my mother, apparently.

"If we let the light of the realization that we are loved shine through the darkness of our hurts, we can begin to let go of the hurts," Dennis was quoted as saying. *"God values us 'more than many sparrows,'"* he continued, quoting scripture, *"and carries us as an eagle carries its young . . . As we let this awareness in, we allow new healing to form around life's wounds. As we open our eyes to the many ways God's love is manifested in the life-giving beauty and events of our lives, and in the love that others have for us, we begin to risk living in a present awareness of love instead of with past hurts."*

My mother had jumped into my journey of healing, turning me on to the message of the Linn brothers, through Terry.

That night, Terry and I spoke again.

"Maybe I should drive up to see you in New Hampshire." I said. We tried to figure out when that would work, comparing our schedules. "What are you doing this next week?" I asked. "It's my birthday on Thursday."

"I have a lot of organizing and planning to do this weekend," Terry said, "because I'm conducting a special summer solstice ceremony on Monday."

"What's that going to be like?" I asked.

"I'm having a bonfire," Terry told me.

A bonfire.

Just before my birthday.

Exactly what Bob Sachs had suggested I do in order to celebrate, to cleanse, to heal, to move forward.

"Would you like to come?" Terry asked.

I hung up the phone, then called my friend Barbara and invited her to join me on a trip to New Hampshire.

We drove up three days later. The directions Terry had sent me said she lived on Packard Street. My mother had grown up on Packard Street in Los Angeles.

"You and Barbara were just looking for signs," my wise son Jack told me later. "And that's why you found them."

Maybe he was right.

We pulled up to Terry's house and she introduced us to the women assembled in her backyard. Her ceremony would combine elements of all the world's religions. The late afternoon light was golden. Birds chirped loudly.

I'd attended many interfaith services over the last four years, while I traveled across the country speaking about *The Faith Club*. Before every talk I gave, I'd tucked into my notecards a photograph of my mother, standing in her backyard next to a giant sunflower, and at the end of every speaking engagement, I looked down at her face and smiled.

I had never felt her presence during any of the events until I looked at that picture, but now it felt like she was truly with me. I was so moved that I was speechless.

In her invitation for this event, Terry had written, "I believe that we show up, we gather, and Divinity does what Divinity does."

Divinity did quite a bit that night.

The summer solstice is the longest day of the year, a powerful time within nature, after which the light begins to diminish. "As we mark this turning point," Terry said, "we might ask, What do we need to relinquish in order to embrace a hidden dream or desire?"

She invited us to write our thoughts down, and I made a list of what I still felt lingering in my mind—the doubts, fears, and worries I had still not been able to relinquish.

Terry lit a bonfire in her backyard, I read my words one last time, and then released my sheet of paper into the flames, where I watched it curl up and burn.

Barbara and I lit memorial candles for her brother and my father. We sat by the fire for an hour or so, talking quietly with Terry and her guests. The first time she'd been summoned to the bed of someone who was near death, Terry told us, she'd prepared diligently, with books and CDs and scripture. But when she got to the home of the young mother who needed spiritual sustenance, she knew immediately that what she needed to do was listen.

Maybe that's what my mother had been trying to teach me. Maybe I didn't need to do all of the frantic planning I'd been trying to do in anticipation of her death. Maybe worrying about where she'd end up was unnecessary.

I returned home to New York in time for my birthday. Jimmy was away on a business trip, but I'd planned to have dinner with Max and Jack in the city. As I drove through the streets of New York, I called my mother.

"Happy Birthing Day!" I said, pulling over to the curb so that I could talk.

My mother had come up with the idea that my siblings and I should thank her on our birthdays, since she'd brought us into the world, and childbirth wasn't easy. She'd invented the greeting "Happy Birthing Day!" We'd laughed and rolled our eyes. Even on our birthdays, our mother had figured out how to inject herself into the spotlight.

But now I wanted her in that spotlight.

"Do you remember my birthday?" I asked.

"No," my mother said.

My heart sank a little. But then I remembered that Rabbi Jacobson had said that my birthday was not about me. That the most magical moments in life happen quietly, in cribs and bedrooms. And nursing homes.

I gave my mother a birthday present on my birthday. I told her the wonderful story about the day I was born. She'd told it to me over and over again in the course of my life.

My mother, nine months pregnant, had decided to take a trip to Tijuana. My father was in the navy, off in the Pacific somewhere. His aunt Anne was keeping my mother company in San Diego, and proved to be a fun traveling companion. The two women drove to Tijuana, and stopped for lunch at the famous Caesar's restaurant. When Riva dug into her Caesar salad, she went right into labor. "It must have been the garlic," she always said.

Aunt Anne and my mother had rushed back to the States, but when they got to the border crossing, a guard delayed them, demanding to examine all the turquoise jewelry they'd bought. "You and I finally did get through," I told my mother now. "You were admitted to the Navy Hospital in San Diego with plenty of time to spare. And then you had me."

"That's a very exciting story!" my mother said as I prepared to get off the phone and head for dinner with my two sons. "Thank you so much for celebrating your birthday with me!"

Rabbi Jacobson was absolutely right. There's no better way to celebrate your birthday than to give someone else a gift.

36

Letting Go

When I was an anxious teenager, I used to lie in bed wondering how I'd ever be able to walk down the aisle as a bride, without having a panic attack. I never worried about where I'd find a groom; I was scared that I'd hyperventilate in front of hundreds of people.

I never dreamed about being a mother. How could a girl who couldn't drive over a bridge comfortably ever think about being responsible for a minivan full of kids? I never thought a golden retriever would help me do that. But I'd never met a dog like Mickey Warner.

When he was nine years old, Max made a declaration: "We're getting a dog between my next birthday and Jack's." That gave Jimmy and me about a month.

On a whim, I answered an ad in the *New York Times* placed by a man in New Jersey, with three-month-old golden retriever puppies, and Jimmy drove us all down to his house in our green minivan. Seeing so many beautiful, silky dogs in one place was thrilling. Max threw a stick, a light yellow puppy with dark brown eyes picked it up, and she was declared "the one."

Max held the puppy in his lap as we drove home, because I was terrified she'd choke on the popcorn scattered all over the floor. I pleaded with the kids not to let her grab one of their french fries when we stopped for Happy Meals. I was afraid she'd choke and die before we even got her home.

I was a nervous dog mother.

We named her Mickey in the car that day, since Mickey Mantle was my husband's favorite Yankee. "We can get a dog," he'd said, caving to Max's pressure a month earlier, "but I'm going to have nothing to do with it." Clearly his mind was changing, since he'd offered up the name Mickey as we approached the George Washington Bridge.

I slept with her on the floor of our living room the first night. I'd wrapped a towel around a plastic alarm clock with a loud ticking mechanism, so that Mickey could hear a heartbeat resembling that of her mother.

But of course the clock sounded nothing like her mother. Mickey whimpered all night, even as I lay next to her on the floor. Everybody else in the house slept soundly, and woke up to enjoy her before leaving for school and work.

Mickey and I were the only women in the house, and we couldn't have been more different.

I was anxious, and Mickey was oblivious to the existential angst of life. Mickey was a cheerful blonde and I was a brooding brunette. I was sedentary, and Mickey loved to exercise. She didn't even mind it when Jimmy put a choke collar around her neck, as he'd been instructed to do by a dog trainer. "He always wished he could put a choke collar on me!" I joked to friends. With every step he took beside his obedient, prancing puppy, my husband fell more and more in love.

My children were smitten from the start. They rolled on the floor with Mickey, kissing her face, tugging at her soft, velvety ears, rubbing their noses against hers, massaging her tummy. They dressed her up in hats and sunglasses. They threw her sticks and didn't mind when she refused to fetch.

A family with such a sweet, pretty dog had no choice but to be happy. Mickey, as Max observed wisely, defined the phrase "happy-go-lucky." I was so happy to be her mother.

But on the beaches of Nantucket and Martha's Vineyard, where we took family vacations, Mickey played the role of mother as well as I did. While I stood vigil on the shoreline, since there was no lifeguard, hollering for Max and Jack to come out of the waves, Mickey dashed into the water and bodysurfed with them.

I never saw another dog do that. She rode the waves with them. Of course Jimmy or another adult was always in the water, too, but Mickey took my place in the swimming department.

And Mickey adored the ocean. Gradually, she taught me lessons on how to be calm on dry land as well.

It started with all the yellow fur that she deposited on every surface of our house. She shed like crazy. Big clumps of pale fluff attached themselves to carpets, couches, and clothes. And nobody minded. Mickey loved us all so much that getting angry at her for dog behavior was not an option. So when she chewed on our shoes it was mildly frustrating. When she rolled in goose poop, we groaned. But most of the time we just loved her.

I once hosted a yoga group at my house for a few months. I'd light a candle, put on some music, and Mickey would try to get as many pats as she could from the four or five friends assembled, by nudging us repeatedly. Eventually she'd flop down on the floor and fall into deep, restorative yoga breathing. At the end of our practice, as we all lay in savasana, corpse pose, covered with blankets, Mickey would approach us, one by one, and give each of us a quick, purposeful lick on the lips. A kiss to remember.

Mickey continued doing yoga with me all her life, but she stopped bodysurfing when she turned eleven. She still loved going to the beach, however. And a week before her fourteenth birthday, when our whole family drove up to the Vineyard to stay with our cousins, Mickey trotted onto the beach, happy to see the waves once more. She lay on the cool, packed sand, writhing and scratching her back with delight. She followed the boys into the water, alert as ever, although she stayed pretty close to the shoreline.

She was fascinated with a group of people on the beach who'd brought a golden retriever, and a little blue tent, where the dog escaped from the hot sun. Mickey plopped herself down by these people as though she belonged to them, and she wouldn't leave. Max and I took turns coaxing her back to our beach towels. The people couldn't have been nicer about Mickey's intrusion. Their own golden retriever was fourteen years old, too. She'd recently had a cancerous tumor removed and was getting chemotherapy. "She's tolerating it well, and it gives us a few more months with her," a lovely woman told me.

I took a long walk in the woods a few days later, and Mickey was thrilled to trot by my side. It was, by far, the longest walk she'd taken in a couple of years, because we got lost on all the dirt paths. But she kept up with me.

Two days later, a heat wave hit the island. Mickey seemed wiped out, but so was everybody else in the house. By the time we packed up the car to leave, she could barely stand up, although we prodded her to do that. She limped out the door but her hind legs gave out and she collapsed on the front lawn.

By the time we pulled up to our house six hours later, Mickey couldn't move. Jack tried to carry her into the house, but she was so spent that he couldn't lift her. I called our vet. A recording directed us to an emergency animal hospital, where an attendant transferred her to a gurney and rolled her in to be examined.

She was bleeding internally from a cancerous tumor. As the whole family lay by her side on the floor of the examining room, we made the decision to try surgery, although we knew there was a chance that the cancer had metastasized.

Mickey made it through surgery, but the cancer had spread to her liver. She stayed in the hospital for two days, and when we brought her home, she could barely climb the steps.

But Mickey was thrilled to be home. She stood in our front hallway, sniffed some familiar smells, and turned her head around slowly, taking in all she could see through the cataracts that covered her eyes. She wagged her tail ferociously. Then she fell asleep on her bed in the dining room, while we ate dinner and tried to believe she'd be okay.

The next day, Mickey could barely walk out to the front porch. Jimmy and I helped her down the steps to our yard, and she lay on the prickly, cool grass while I sat next to her in a lawn chair. My friend Monica came over to visit and she sang into Mickey's ears. After she left, I sat with Mickey for another hour.

I have never felt so present in my life. Time passed very slowly that Sunday. "I'm at a retreat with Mickey," I thought to myself, as I sat beside her, silent, appreciating who she was. I looked at her sleeping, and then I looked out at our lush, green yard. My mother has Alzheimer's, my dog is dying, and I am happy, I thought to myself. Life is wonderful.

When it got too warm in the yard, Jack carried Mickey up to the front porch, where she slept in her bed. I put my nose to hers, and I could tell she had a fever. Angry red patches had appeared on her shaved stomach. My friend Sarah, the "mother" of five dogs, came for a visit and agreed that Mickey needed to be seen by the vet.

Jack carried her into the minivan and Jimmy and I drove her to the animal hospital again. Mickey had an infection, and spent the night there getting antibiotics and fluids. But the news the next morning was not good. "I'm so sorry," the vet told me. "I really wanted to get her home for you guys." She urged us to come soon, so that we could put Mickey to sleep before she suffered too much longer.

I hung up the phone and cried. "We need to schedule a time to put Mickey to sleep," I told Jimmy.

"I can't make that call," he told me. "You need to do that."

So I did. Then I walked around our yard, picking flowers and branches from all of Mickey's favorite bushes and trees. I sprinkled grass from our yard into the water. I wanted her to be able to smell home one last time.

Everyone took the day off from work and made the sad trip to the animal hospital. Sonia, who had been our babysitter forever, met us there. When Mickey was wheeled into the examining room, our sweet dog looked exhausted.

I thought that Mickey's attachment to the golden retriever on the beach at Martha's Vineyard had been a sign. Another miraculous message sent to me this year—that she, like the dog on the beach, would be given more time on earth. With us.

But it was time to say goodbye. One by one, we pressed our faces up to Mickey's face, kissing her, petting her, telling her how much we loved her. She began to breathe heavily, and I held my hand on her trembling shoulder, pressing it there, trying to comfort her, the way Adrienne had comforted me so many months earlier.

Mickey's breathing calmed down. I kissed the soft spot between her eyes, hoping that somehow, someday, I would meet her again, soul to soul, and kiss that sweet spot once more.

Maybe there was a chance that she'd become a human being in another lifetime, and eventually become enlightened. "You might be our Buddha," I said to her.

Or maybe she was headed for the Bardo, the in-between state where souls go between incarnations. I planned to read the Jewish Kaddish, or memorial prayer, after she died, but first I read to her from *The Tibetan Book of the Dead*, to fortify her soul for the journey ahead.

"*Hey noble one!*" I looked into Mickey's pretty brown eyes, locked with mine. "*At this time when your mind and body are parting ways, pure reality manifests itself in subtle, dazzling visions, vividly experienced, naturally frightening and worrisome, shimmering like a mirage on the plains in autumn. Do not fear them.*"

"*Do not be terrified!*" I told Mickey. "*Do not panic!*"

I could tell Mickey not to be afraid, because I wasn't afraid. I was not running away from this deathbed.

"*Whatever sounds, lights and rays may come at you, they cannot hurt you,*" I told her, "*you cannot die.*"

One by one, we approached Mickey, bent down, hugged her, and said our final goodbyes. Then we shifted her into a comfortable position and the veterinarian put her to sleep.

She lay in savasana, or corpse pose, covered in our kisses.

37

Roshi

A woman with a shaved head stared out at me from an issue of *Shambhala Sun* magazine, Roshi Pat Enkyo O'Hara.

She looked familiar.

I stared at her photo.

Had we met?

No.

But where had I seen her before?

Suddenly I realized that she was the woman who'd conducted the memorial service for my beloved former therapist Nettie, a year earlier. She was affiliated with Village Zendo, "a zen community in the heart of New York City."

Just as I was beginning to recover from Mickey's death, I learned that I still had some lessons in dying to learn. O'Hara would be giving a lecture called "How to Die" at the Rubin Museum of Art in Manhattan.

I drove into the city to see her.

A roshi is an abbot, and O'Hara is a Soto Zen priest and a certified Zen teacher. She sat on the stage of the intimate theater and got down to the business of death immediately. "When this day is over," she said quietly, "our days of life will be decreased by one."

"How we live is how we die," Roshi said simply.

Every week, people at her zendo face their mortality by chanting these words:

Let me respectfully remind you,
Life and death are of supreme importance,
Time swiftly passes by, and opportunity is lost.
Each of us should strive to awaken,
Awaken! Do not squander your life!

Roshi urged us to draw up advance directives—legal documents that detail the choices we want to make for end-of-life care. And then she introduced us to Japanese death poems.

The first day of the year, she explained, is a perfect time to write a death poem, "just in case . . ." But they can be written at any time. She writes one every year, and read us her most recent one:

Doing too many things, no discipline whatsoever,
All these sixty-eight years,
Now, letting, letting it all stand as is.
This, not-this, returns to the sky, the clouds, the sea.

She urged us to write our own death poems, and explained the structure to us. The first line should describe your life, and what you've done. Next you should address how long you've lived. The third line should describe your feelings as you approach death. The poem ends with your understanding of Zen.

She described the beautiful burial rituals of Zen Buddhism. The dead body is washed and dressed in light robes, placed in a cardboard casket, and then covered with flowers. Finally, the casket, body, and flowers are cremated. There is no focus on rebirth in Zen Buddhism, Roshi explained. "It's about life right now."

At the end of the lecture, I approached Roshi and told her

how much I'd enjoyed the memorial service she'd conducted for my late therapist. She invited me to visit Village Zendo the next weekend.

I arrived that Sunday morning, took off my shoes, and entered the large, spare meditation space, where dozens of people sat on black cushions, along three walls. Roshi sat on her own cushion at the front of the room, facing us, with a simple altar and Buddha statue behind her.

A gong was struck, and the group chanted, while I followed along, reading from a pamphlet I'd been given. The words of the chant were simple and the purposefulness of the group was powerful.

But then came the hard part.

The room became very still. People sat on their cushions, in zazen, or silent meditation. Nobody moved.

After a break, everyone turned around to face the white walls in front of them and meditate.

My ear itched like crazy, but I didn't want to scratch it. All around me, people sat perfectly still. I managed to focus on the clean plaster surface in front of me, and eventually the itching passed. But when my leg started bothering me, I took action. Nevertheless, I was quite proud of myself for gazing at a white wall with such relaxed purposefulness. That would never have been possible without my daily practice over the last year.

I stood up and began walking meditation, following others in a line that coiled around the room very slowly.

After two more periods of sitting and walking meditation, it was time for Roshi's dharma talk.

"I know that you came here for something new," she said. "But I'm going to offer you something old."

She told a story from the Zen tradition, about a teacher who paid a visit to a king at his palace in India. The story involved three princes, a lavish feast, and lessons about the true value of a rare, precious jewel.

We tend to look at life in a transactional way, Roshi said. We select people for their usefulness rather than their quality of being. Rather than thinking about the creature in front of us, we ask, "How can this person suit our needs?" We miss the awe of an unconventional person when we look at life that way. We lose the recognition of what is truly valuable. If we live transactional lives, Roshi told us, nothing will ever touch our core.

At the end of the dharma talk, I stayed behind to meet privately with Roshi, following her into a small alcove behind the altar.

Roshi suggested that my frequent tears, which had shown up again suddenly, simply meant that I was touched by life, like the Romantic poets. "Wordsworth and Keats would cry at the drop of a hat!" she said, smiling. "They'd see a golden daffodil and weep."

I was a sucker for Romantic poetry. And I'd begun to carry tissues with me lately. Reaching into my backpack, I fumbled through several half-eaten chocolate bars, and found one.

I asked Roshi to elaborate on something she'd mentioned in her talk—the significance of cherry blossoms in Asian culture.

"The Japanese see cherry blossoms as a symbol of our lives," Roshi explained. "They come at the very early part of the spring, when it's cold. Their beauty makes you want to cry."

I thought of how I'd meditated in my front yard, under thousands of cherry blossoms.

"One of the reasons why we cry is that these blossoms are so ephemeral," Roshi continued. "They will fall," she said simply. "And to watch the cherry blossoms fall is like watching ourselves die. We start off young and beautiful. Then we become middle-aged and beautiful in a different way. Eventually we're old and beautiful, and finally we're dead and beautiful.

"One of the things Zen teaches us in its austerity is that we can tolerate much more than we think we can. We can be sitting, with the room very quiet, and suddenly we want to scratch our nose, but we can't, because we're not supposed to move. So we sit and we abide in the itching. And if we sit there long enough, our nose won't itch. Something else will, and we begin to see the impermanence of our suffering."

In the Village Zendo service, each meditation period lasts only for half an hour. "No matter how uncomfortable we are, we know we're going to get up," Roshi said. "So we learn to abide."

Through her work with the New York Zen Center for Contemplative Care, Roshi provides compassionate care to people who are sick or terminally ill. She sits with people in a great deal of pain. She doesn't run away from deathbeds. When we were done speaking, Roshi escorted me out of the zendo, past the altar and Buddha statue. A group of framed photos sat nearby.

"Here's Nettie!" Roshi picked up a small black-and-white picture.

I gasped.

I recognized my dear, departed therapist, but she was so young! The photograph had been taken at a party decades earlier, when she had been in her forties. Nettie was leaning back in a chair, clearly enjoying herself in a chic dark cocktail dress, holding a cigarette!

Life is a surprising adventure, I thought.

And when I got home, I took a stab at writing my own death poem.

Dread lurked in my bloodstream while I waited for fear to pounce.
In my fifty-seventh year, raging fires became flickering flames.
Now I dread leaving this warmth.
I want to feel every single spark.

38

My Safety Net

⌒∞⌒

I'd been reborn in so many ways over the last year that I thought I'd learned to face death with a certain amount of grace.

But I still had more lessons to learn.

My friend Barbara and I have laughed a lot in the forty-five years we've been friends. She's known for giggling uncontrollably, but she's also survived rare cancer and the premature death of her brother. She was by my side when I had my very first panic attack. So when Barbara asked if she could write a paper about me for a graduate school class she was taking, The Psychology of Trauma and Loss, I agreed to be interviewed.

We sat in the Bead Room, and she asked about events from my past, which I'd spent so many years working through: my father's illness, death, and bankruptcy, my panic attacks, and my family dynamics growing up. Midway through our conversation, I had to lie down. "When this interview is over," I said quietly, "I will lock away these stories and memories. I will never talk about them again."

Barbara emailed me when she finished her paper. "You really are a miracle!" she wrote. "You are remarkably resilient."

She invited me to sit in on her class, so I drove in to meet her at

Columbia University's Teachers College, on the Upper West Side of Manhattan.

At the beginning of the class, students described the papers they were writing. One young man had interviewed his mother, whose sister committed suicide right around the time he'd been diagnosed with lymphoma. Another person was interviewing a woman who'd been gang-raped. Someone else was writing about sexual abuse at a young age. The room was quiet; the professor, Dr. George Bonanno, answered questions in a straightforward, thoughtful manner.

Then he began teaching. "Why isn't everybody resilient?" asked a slide projected on the giant screen in front of the classroom. Bonanno discussed personality factors in those who healed from trauma. He showed slides of the World Trade Center attacks on September 11, 2001.

The room was silent. Graphs and charts filled the screen next, replacing doomed people suspended in midair.

I have it easy, I thought, as the professor shared the results of numerous studies on trauma and loss.

After class, I walked out into the hallway and waited for Barbara to fill out some paperwork.

I decided to call Dr. Jaeger to find out how she was feeling. A week earlier I'd received a troubling response to an email I had sent her, requesting an appointment. Someone had sent me an email saying that my therapist had been in an accident and would not be available until "next year." It was early December. Next year seemed a long way off.

I dialed Dr. Jaeger's number. An unfamiliar male voice came on the line, and I listened to a recorded message. "This is for the patients of Dr. Jaeger. We are sorry to say that she passed away . . ."

My heart flopped around in my chest. I burst into tears.

"Dr. Jaeger had a bad accident," the voice continued slowly and clearly. "We had hoped that she would recover . . ."

Hearing my sobs, a woman from a nearby classroom dashed out to see if I was all right. Students passing me in the hallway tried to be respectful, averting their eyes.

Barbara approached and I managed to tell her the news. She had an appointment, so we agreed to meet at my car in ten minutes, and parted ways.

I walked very slowly, down corridors and steps, out onto the street, where I stopped to get my bearings. My lungs began to convulse, in the old pattern I knew all too well. Soon they would force too much air into my system, and then they'd shut down, locked tight. My throat would close up, my head would start spinning . . .

But none of that happened.

Slow down, I told myself. Breathe slowly . . . Tiny breaths . . . One little breath at a time . . .

My lungs obeyed my commands. I walked shakily back to my car, sat down in the driver's seat, and wept.

Barbara arrived and sat next to me, stunned. I focused on breathing slowly with my oldest friend sitting beside me.

Jimmy was on a business trip in California. I texted him before pulling away from the curb, to let him know that Dr. Jaeger had died.

I dropped Barbara off at her apartment and drove home, slowly and carefully, taking the same route I'd taken for ten years, driving in and out of the city to see my beloved therapist. When I reached home, I lit a candle, and sat still in a chair in my front hallway, breathing slowly, thinking about Dr. Jaeger.

The first time I ever went to see her, I'd recited my personal and panic history, hamming it up a bit, hiding my pain behind glib, colorful stories.

"You've got some stuff," Dr. Jaeger told me. "But what was your safety net?"

"Hunh?"

"What was your safety net growing up?" Dr. Jaeger asked. "It sounds like you didn't have a lot of people you could rely on."

I had woven my own sort of safety net, I realized. Barbara's stable parents showed me how healthy families could function. I made wonderful friends. I created art, and found a career that gave me great pleasure. And then I met Jimmy.

Dr. Jaeger became part of my safety net as well.

She said things in the most succinct way. "Your parents didn't raise you, but they let you grow up." Or, "You had a mother but she wasn't very maternal."

I wished I could remember more Jaegerisms.

Sometimes I would stop her mid-sentence. "Hold that thought and give me your pen!" I'd say.

Dr. Jaeger would laugh and hand me a plump, shiny blue enamel pen she kept on her desk. I'd write down what she'd just said, slowly and carefully, on a crumpled scrap of paper fished out of my backpack. But I'd never filed those scraps properly once I returned home.

Jimmy flew back a day early from California and accompanied me to Dr. Jaeger's funeral. We sat in the last row of the chapel and cried together.

I couldn't believe that my panic-to-peace experiment had begun and ended with the deaths of my two beloved therapists. I would need to practice healing for the rest of my life, with the tools they'd given me, and everything I'd been taught over the last year.

The next morning, I woke up early, feeling pain I hadn't felt since my father died. "Do you think Tibetan monks cry when someone they love dies?" I whispered to Jimmy.

"Sure," my husband said. And then he went back to sleep.

Later that day, I fished around in my backpack for any of the scraps of paper on which I'd jotted down Dr. Jaeger's words of wisdom. I came across the notes I'd taken in Barbara's class, The Psychology of Loss and Trauma.

"There is no single way to be resilient," I'd written.

And suddenly I remembered what I'd talked about with Dr. Jaeger in our last session together, on the day before her tragic accident.

I'd been feeling a bit blue while writing my account of the past year, and Dr. Jaeger had asked if I felt guilty. I had been and I knew just why.

Although I wished it were otherwise, my mother and father were never really at peace until they were dying or demented. "But I am at peace right here and right now," I told my therapist, moving my hands through the air fluidly, in small waves, as Gina and Rabbi Jacobson had taught me to do. "Life will go up and down," I said. "And I just have to stay the course."

I learned from Dr. Jaeger's obituary and funeral that she was sixty-nine, although she looked much younger. She was loved deeply by her children and they expressed that love to her regularly. She was adored by her companion, with whom she shared laughs and a peaceful kind of joy. She left behind two beautiful granddaughters, whom she cherished. She was an esteemed teacher and valued clinician, beloved by her colleagues and patients. She was known for her "charm, wit, and ageless beauty."

Sometimes a broken heart needs medication and not just meditation. I developed heart palpitations that just wouldn't stop, so I made an appointment with my internist. An EKG turned up an extra heartbeat, probably due to stress. My doctor prescribed Klonopin as needed and a daily beta blocker.

I tried to channel Dr. Jaeger's wonderful sense of humor and be lighthearted with myself, friends, and family. But tears sprang to my eyes even more than usual. I was John Boehner minus the tan.

Gradually, however, like the Buddha, I began to feel awake. I could feel bits and pieces of myself coming to life. Little threads of emotions like joy, excitement, and hope began percolating and pulsing through me, coexisting with fear, anger, and doubt.

In other words, I felt alive.

I moved through feelings as though I were walking through rain. I felt them, but they didn't drench me, flood me, or pound me until I hurt.

One night, I met a soft-spoken surgeon at a dinner party. I mentioned my history of panic attacks and told him the story of the night I almost died, the story my parents had told me so many times.

The doctor looked shaken when I pointed to the tracheotomy scar in the hollow of my throat. "I noticed that," he said. "And I can guarantee you one thing. The resident who did that surgery never forgot that night. He's probably told that story hundreds of times."

"Really?" I touched my throat reflexively.

"Absolutely! That's a doctor's worst nightmare. An airway blockage in someone that young? An emergency tracheotomy? He probably walked out of your room incontinent! I bet *he* could hardly breathe!"

The surgeon standing in front of me had been a trauma operative specialist who saw combat with the Marine Corps during Desert Storm. He teaches advanced trauma life support to other doctors at Massachusetts General Hospital in Boston.

"I'm glad I've never had to do that procedure," he told me now. "An unresponsive child not breathing?" He shook his head. "That's about as traumatic as it gets. A trachea in someone that young is tiny." He put his fingers together, nearly touching. "There's no room for error. You are very, very lucky to be alive."

I did feel that way. I remembered Thich Nhat Hanh's words: the greatest miracle is that you are alive. And one breath can show you that.

39

Just Breathe

After Mickey died, Jimmy came up with the idea of taking a ceremonial walk in our neighborhood, the same walk he'd taken with Mickey perhaps a thousand times, down to our favorite park, overlooking Long Island Sound. In all kinds of weather, we continued taking that walk over and over again, talking to each other.

"This is how it's done," I imagined Mickey saying to me. "You let Jimmy take you for a walk, even though he walks faster than you do. If you slow down, he'll let you sniff something, or take in the view. When you get home, you hang out with him around the house. Got that? It's easy. Just don't move too fast."

So I slowed down. I didn't race to get anywhere, although that caused me to feel things more acutely than I used to.

"We can't make life flatten out so that there are no ups and downs," Sharon Salzberg said when I saw her speak at Tibet House one evening. "The ups aren't worth clinging to because they will never last, and the downs won't last either. Equanimity is the peacefulness that comes with this understanding. Don't be jealous of other people's joy, because it will pass, as will your own."

I had armored myself in the course of my life, but I had shed some of that armor. I was learning to let go a bit more with each passing day.

Sometimes that was scary. I tried to reassure my body parts, telling them, as Gina had suggested I do, "We're safe. Everything's going to be okay. I'm in charge, I can handle this."

I began to spend a lot of time in the Bead Room, where I'd meditated with Mickey for so many hours—me on my black cushion, she on her green plaid bed. I imagined her sitting beside me as I meditated now.

Friends from out of town came to visit, and they slept in the Bead Room, remarking on the gorgeous golden light that crept in every morning. I made jewelry there, and read.

One day, I suddenly remembered a pretty, peaceful room in my parents' house that we all called the Sun Room. At all hours of the day, light streamed in through old casement windows.

I began to connect with my parents in new ways. When I laughed, I remembered the sound of my mother's giggle and my father's masterful way of telling funny stories and jokes. My parents made up life as they went along, never looking to others to tell them what to do or think. I inherited their creativity, spontaneity, and enthusiasm for unusual, quirky adventures.

Happy childhood memories came back to me, replacing the painful ones. I remembered wandering the vacant lot next to our suburban house when I was seven, picking plump, ripe blackberries from a hedge of wild bushes that wound around the edges of the property. I remembered "the magic rock" in the middle of that same lot—a huge expanse of flat, gray stone where neighborhood kids gathered and taught me how to tap-dance. I remembered being crowned Miss Blossom Way when I was seven years old one summer on vacation, in a wholesome, childish beauty pageant where I recited a poem. I was given a sash made of toilet paper, which I proudly wore across my bathing suit.

My sister visited from California, and we found ourselves talking about the day my father died, when I'd run away and she'd stayed by his side. "Uncle Nathan was there, too," she told me.

I was stunned at Nathan's strength. He had been brave and strong enough to be present at his twin brother's deathbed. This new piece of information was proof that I had interpreted what went on in my family in my own way, which might not have corresponded with anyone else's reality. The depth of love that had clearly existed between my uncle and my father moved me.

"The convention of panic was just a thin veil for you," Bob Sachs wrote to me in an email one day. "It cloaked the stillness and compassion that is you. It takes great courage to let it all go and to display the unbearableness of so much love."

When I drive into New York, there's a spot on Bruckner Boulevard where the skyline appears, filling my entire windshield. I almost gasp every time I see it. There's so much possibility out there.

I like to drive into New York early in the morning and walk the streets, hearing the clatter of shopkeepers lifting their metal gratings, smelling the bagels toasting and the coffee brewing, watching kids headed off to school, dog walkers on their first round of the day, leashes stretched taut, mutts and pups of all stripes trotting in controlled chaos. Teenagers flirt with each other loudly at that hour of the day, waking each other up as their voices bounce off the pavement.

I was once one of them. A teenager with my life ahead of me, before my panic set in. Before I got so scared.

But I'm not scared anymore. I haven't had a full-blown panic attack in a couple of years. Granted, my body is not always an ocean of tranquility. I still feel loneliness, fear, and what I call the black-and-blues—the sadness I finally allow myself to feel, the sadness that panic covered up for so many years.

Sometimes I wonder if it was self-indulgent for me to spend so such time over the last year trying to understand how and why I'd panicked all my life. But then I remember something I once heard Thich Nhat Hanh say: *"Understand your own suffering. Then understand the suffering of another person and you can have compassion."*

I hope I've enhanced my ability to be compassionate. Wherever I go, I carry an emotional tool kit of the techniques I've learned over the last year, as I try to gain access to the golden Buddha inside me, the one I first caught a glimpse of when Tara Brach first described it.

My crash course in relaxing is over. I am living my life now, without recording every little moment. I just experience the ups and downs that everyone else in the world experiences.

Sometimes, in the early morning, I bring my meditation cushion down to my kitchen and place it on the floor by the table where my family has shared thousands of meals. I meditate in the spot where my loved ones still gather, and I try to receive that love.

Sometimes I pull out my yoga bolster in the Bead Room and assume the restorative positions Amy taught me. They might turn into a longer practice or they might be all I need.

Sometimes I pull out Lama Tsondru's drawing of the Buddha and follow his lead, carefully measuring out a grid, and then drawing the Buddha's ears, nose, lips, and eyes.

Sometimes I remember Sylvia Boorstein saying that if we spent our lives simply practicing lovingkindness toward ourselves, that would be a perfect practice. "May I be safe," I whisper to myself. "May I be happy, be healthy; may I live with ease."

Sometimes life causes unpleasant feelings to swell up into my chest or throat or gut, and I go back to Gina's office to process them while lights flash before my eyes.

Sometimes I meditate in my den by candlelight and Dr. Jaeger comes to visit. I imagine her opening the door to her office and smiling. I hear her voice, with its slight Brooklyn twang.

Sometimes I take a Klonopin, glad that she prescribed it for me and not ashamed to need it occasionally.

Sometimes I pore through my collection of beads, pull out my Tibetan mala cord, and make long, intricate prayer necklaces.

Sometimes I cry in bed at night, remembering how King David meditated in tears upon his pillow.

Sometimes I soak my feet in the special Ayurvedic bath salts Dawn used, immersing myself in the scent of ginger and eucalyptus.

Sometimes I recite the Shema, or the Twenty-Third Psalm, or read from a collection by the Sufi poet Hafiz. His titles alone comfort me: "When the Sun Conceived a Man," "Every City Is a Dulcimer," and "Let Thought Become Your Beautiful Lover."

Sometimes I use the trick Pema Chödrön taught at her retreat, which she learned from Thich Nhat Hanh. I turn the corners of my mouth up ever so slightly, forming a smile, and I begin to feel lighter. I imagine Mickey looking down on me with approval and her wonderful, loopy grin.

And sometimes when I wake up in the middle of the night with a stab of fear in my heart, or a buzzing, anxious feeling, I lie in the dark, place my hands on my belly, and breathe.

That's the best thing to come out of my year of living meditatively, as I sometimes refer to my panic-to-peace project.

I can breathe.

Every person I met this year taught me the importance of following my breath. But I had to learn on my own how to trust that breath. It had terrified me for so many years that I grew up disassociated from the feeling of breathing. My pediatrician used to remind me to breathe whenever I trembled in his office.

Over the years, I breathed too much and too little. Too quickly and too irregularly.

But my breath has become my biggest source of comfort, something I trust more than anything else about myself. It is the cornerstone of my middle-aged peace plan. It is holy. In Hebrew it is *ruach,* the wind that God breathes into every living being.

After my father died, when I was pregnant with Jack and constantly battling panic, my mother used to come stay with me and Max, since Jimmy was often away on business. She slept on the pullout couch in our New York apartment's living room. When I woke up in the middle of the night, scared and anxious, she'd hear me making a cup of herbal tea in the kitchen, and call out my name. I'd take a seat opposite her in a chair and gulp down the hot tea, trying to force warmth into my terrified lungs so quickly that I often burned my tongue and throat.

"Just breathe," my mother would say to me. Those words used to make me crazy. Why would someone tell a girl who hyperventilated to "just breathe"? Couldn't she see that I was breathing too damn much? As usual, I felt that my mother had very little to teach me, that I was on my own in this world, parenting myself.

But my mother was right. Sometimes all we have to do is breathe.

Every breath is a gift, every breath a lesson.

It's said that the Buddha came into the world to teach eighty-four thousand lessons. Maybe I was meant to learn those lessons, through my breath. Maybe we're all here to learn eighty-four thousand lessons over the course of our lifetimes, some easy, some hard.

As a child, I used to wince when I rode the waves at Narragansett Beach and the fresh salt air made my lungs sting. I felt too alive. These days, however, I'm thrilled to be breathing on the beach and everywhere else in the world. I'm breathing up a storm. And a life. Every once in a while, I take a deep, delicious breath that is truly glorious.

But most of the time, I just breathe.

40

Proof

After all of my extraordinary adventures, I knew I'd been enormously healed. I had no doubts.

But I did have one last piece of business to attend to.

I drove down to Philadelphia to visit my brain and Andy Newberg, "my neuroscientist."

Andy had left the University of Pennsylvania to become the director of research at the Myrna Brind Center of Integrative Medicine at Thomas Jefferson University Hospital in Philadelphia. He was helping other strung-out people to become blissed out, giving them the support they needed, while encouraging them to find their own unique paths to healing, just as I had done over this past year.

We were still on the same wavelength.

Andy gave me a tour of the large, serene center. Then we sat down in his office, surrounded by all the boxes he was still unpacking.

My brain had graduated from Penn and moved out into the real world. Its scans would not be published in medical journals, pored over, or celebrated for centuries, but that was fine with me.

I pulled out my laptop and the detailed email Andy had sent me before he left Penn, with pixilated images of my brain and an analysis of my scans. I pulled up the images and Andy reviewed them for me.

He gave me a quick, comprehensive report of what my MRI revealed, rattling off terms like *posterior parietal lobe* and *thalamus*. "We saw decreased activity in your anterior singulate," I heard him say.

Decreased activity? Apparently, in my case, that was a good thing. Andy also said something about my increased ability to suppress my emotional extremes, and my ears perked up. As did my mood.

Apparently the scans showed I had greater regulation of my emotions.

That sounded wonderful.

"Mission accomplished," I said, smiling.

"By doing lovingkindness meditation for eight weeks, you've altered the way your brain responds when you do the practice," Andy told me. "You show changes particularly in areas like the frontal lobe and the thalamus," he continued. "And we've seen that happen in other meditation practices as well . . ."

So how did I stack up against the monks?

Andy pointed to images that showed increased cerebral blood flow to certain places, during my first scan and in a much more pronounced way during my second scan, eight weeks later.

All my practice had paid off!

I'd wanted the brain of a monk and everything that went along with that brain—peace, compassion, kindness, wisdom, patience, happiness, and love.

I had felt that I'd made progress on those fronts, and now these scans seemed to prove that in a concrete way.

My brain was glowing! At least in my mind.

"I started off this whole experiment wanting the brain of a

monk," I said, describing the studies I'd read about meditators whose prefrontal lobes lit up on MRI scans.

"If you want the brain of a monk, you're headed in the right direction," Andy said with a smile.

I beamed. "How can you tell?"

"In our other studies we've seen changes in the thalamus and frontal lobe, which you are now showing," he told me.

I had taught my old brain some new tricks.

"So I'm monkish?"

"Yes," my brilliant, compassionate, well-respected authority on spirituality and the brain told me. "You are monkish. At least based on our data."

I was thrilled.

I'd spent a year turning inward, and now it was time to go out into the world with confidence instead of fear, boundless gratitude instead of panic, and a heart full of compassion that I hoped to share.

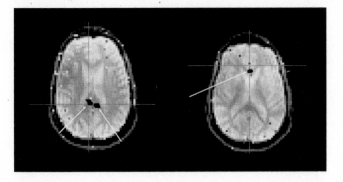

These fMRIs (functional magnetic resonance imaging) compare the initial attempt at performing lovingkindness meditation with a period of rest. During lovingkindness meditation, the scans show increased cerebral blood flow (CBF) in the posterior cingulate (area with two short arrows) and decreased CBF in the anterior cingulate (area with long arrow.) Studies on romantic and unconditional love have revealed changes in these areas, which have been shown to be involved in the emotion of love and appear to be involved in lovingkindness meditation. With results from only one person doing this practice, we cannot say whether these findings are really valid, but they are interesting.

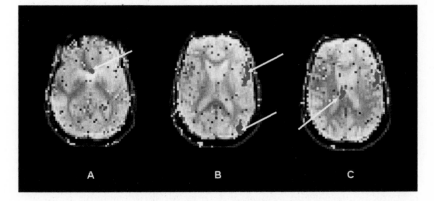

The scans done after eight weeks of practicing lovingkindness meditation show decreased CBF in the anterior cingulate (arrow in A). There is also greater activity in the left posterior parietal (lower arrow in B), in the left inferior frontal (upper arrow in B), and in the right thalamus (arrow in C). These findings illustrate how the brain is activated differently after eight weeks of meditation training compared with the initial brain activity during the first meditation practice. There appears to be a training effect such that more areas are affected after eight weeks of meditation training.

Source: *Dr. Andrew Newberg, Myrna Brind Center of Integrative Medicine, Thomas Jefferson University.*

Acknowledgments

Thank you to all of my wise, generous teachers and healers.

Thank you to all of my outstanding friends, who have been my teachers and healers for decades. Some of you are mentioned in this book; all of you have a place in my heart.

Thank you to my terrific agent, Elizabeth Kaplan, for your support, wise counsel, and Kleenex.

Thank you to Leslie Meredith, my brilliant editor. I gave you my heart and you took magnificent care of it.

Thank you to all the very talented people at Free Press.

Thank you to Linda and Jules for providing me with the perfect safe house, love, and Toblerone chocolate cake.

Thank you to Uncle Nathan and Cousin Priscilla, who showed me only love.

Thank you to Nettie, my second mother.

Thank you to the irreplaceable Dr. Roberta Jaeger, who lives on in me forever.

Thank you to Gina, my twenty-five-foot-tall Buddha.

Thank you to Mamie, Louise, and Terry, for shedding light.

Thank you to Betty. You have cared for my mother with so much compassion and dignity.

Thank you to my Warner and Lipsett families. Thanks to Mike and Annie, Courtney, Keri and Molly. Thanks to Dr. Andrew Newberg, M.D., Bobby and the students of Lama Tsondru, James DeBoer, Sam Ryder, Tamah and Mike, Tina Gombar, Linda Kurtz, Alana Kornfeld, Dr. Shari Medonick, M.D., Dr. Richard Koehler, M.D., Dr. Frank Lipman, M.D., Lisa Ravetto, Karen Brown, Sheryl

Moller, Yves Darif, Lee Kravitz, Lisa Stoffer, Jim Hardy, and all the good people at Steere House and Hallworth House.

Thank you to Stephen Batchelor for your beautiful translation of *A Guide to the Bodhisattva's Way of Life,* and to M. Elaine Dillhunt, O.S.B., for your excellent article on the Linn brothers, "Healing Your Painful Memories."

Thank you to Ranya and Suzanne for our amazing adventure, which took me to Tulsa and beyond!

I am grateful to Therese Borchard, who paved the way for me to speak honestly about mental illness.

Thank you to Sonia for helping me to make a family.

Thank you to Judy, who's always up for an adventure, with or without Dolma.

Thank you to Anna for being my Tibetan mother, rowdy roommate, and inspiration. Always, a big hug.

Thank you to Patty for bringing me lightness, love, and a glimpse of nirvana.

Thank you, Anne and Monica, my road trip buddies and dear friends.

Thank you to Meg, who joyfully reappeared in my life at just the right time, with just the right resources.

Thank you to Peggy, who read this book and inspired me at such a crucial time.

Thank you to Liz, for your companionship and insights on the road to enlightenment.

Thank you to my brother and sister, for walking the walk with me.

Thank you to Barbara, the best reader I could have asked for. You were with me the first time around, forty-five years ago, and the second time, as I relived that life for this book. I hope we'll be with each other the next time around, wherever that is.

Thank you to Jimmy, who saved my soul.

Thank you to Max and Jack, who made it soar.

Thank you to Mickey, wherever you are.

Thank you to Paul and Riva. I love you.

And thank you to everyone who ever asked me, "How is your mother?" Or for that matter, "How are you?"

Appendix: Priscilla's Plan

1. **Start off slowly.** His Holiness the Dalai Lama advises people to start a practice by meditating 5–10 minutes a day. I found that 20 minutes a day was a manageable, realistic goal. Attending a retreat is a wonderful experience, but there are many ways to create mini-retreats in our daily lives, moments of calm in all kinds of circumstances.

2. **Find a way in.** Belleruth Naparstek's guided imagery took me to a safe place I never dreamed I could access on my own. I learned what it feels like to be still and at peace, if only for a moment. Then I knew where I wanted to go, again and again.

   There are many ways to become immersed in an experience that doesn't require or encourage thought. Doing this will ease you into a meditative state. The stillness of nature always nudges me in the right direction. Taking pictures and videos makes me focus intensely on tall grass swaying and rain falling; everything else seems to fall away.

   Yongey Mingyur Rinpoche taught me to meditate with my eyes open. Try that, resting your attention on anything from a vase full of flowers to the floor of a bus you're stuck on. Don't be hard on yourself when your grocery list or angry boss pops into your head. As Sharon Salzberg teaches, "We can always begin again." And if you really want to gaze at something far-out, check out Robert Sachs's Mandala DVD (available online).

3. **Cue the music.** I started off my adventure in meditation by listening to Dustin O'Halloran's rich, meditative piano solos. Whenever I popped his CD in my car, traffic flowed, and horns were silenced. At least in my mind. And then, of course, there's Krishna Das, my joy therapist.

4. **Find a teacher.** Surf the Web and check out meditation CDs or downloads that can guide you through a practice when you need a helping hand. For my study with Dr. Newberg, I listened to the lovingkindness meditation from Sharon Salzberg's *Guided Meditations for Love and Wisdom—14 Essential Practices*. Having someone whisper in your ear is a very intimate experience. Choose your partner with care.

5. **Listen to dharma talks.** My favorite free website is www .dharmaseed.org, which features many different teachers, with many different styles of teaching. And please make a donation. The teachers I studied with all have websites, books, and videos.

6. **Slow down and be quiet.** Find a space and time somewhere in your life where you can retreat, recharge, and rejoice. I meditate all over the place, whenever I can find the time. Some people find it helpful to stick to a certain routine. Build a shrine if you like. But if you keep your eyes and heart open, you'll be amazed at the holy places and moments that will suddenly appear in everyday life.

7. **Try to be kind.** To yourself first, and then to others.

Please visit my website and Facebook page to share your favorite tools for meditation and healing.

Note: Trager therapy, Somatic Experience therapy, and EMDR were all essential tools for me as my practice deepened. Their websites are in the resources sections.

Bibliography

Batchelor, Stephen (trans.). *A Guide to the Bodhisattva's Way of Life.* Dharmasala, India: Library of Tibetan Works and Archives, 1979.

Begley, Sharon. *Train Your Mind, Change Your Brain: How a New Science Reveals Our Extraordinary Potential to Transform Ourselves.* New York: Ballantine Books, 2007.

Bonanno, George. *The Other Side of Sadness: What the New Science of Bereavement Tells Us About Life After Loss.* New York: Basic Books, 2009.

Boorstein, Sylvia. *Happiness Is an Inside Job: Practicing for a Joyful Life.* New York: Ballantine Books, 2008.

————. *That's Funny, You Don't Look Buddhist: On Being a Faithful Jew and a Passionate Buddhist.* New York: HarperOne, 1998.

Brach, Tara. *Radical Acceptance: Embracing Your Life with the Heart of a Buddha.* New York: Bantam, 2004.

Carlebach, Shlomo. *Lamed Vav: A Collection of the Favorite Stories of Rabbi Shlomo Carlebach.* Brookline, MA: Israel Book Shop, 2004.

Chödrön, Pema. *The Places That Scare You: A Guide to Fearlessness in Difficult Times.* Boston: Shambhala, 2005.

————. *When Things Fall Apart: Heart Advice for Difficult Times.* Boston: Shambhala, 2002.

Dalai Lama, and Victor Chan. *The Wisdom of Forgiveness.* New York: Riverhead Trade, 2005.

Dalai Lama, and Nicholas Vreeland. *An Open Heart: Practicing Compassion in Everyday Life.* Boston: Back Bay Books, 2002.

Das, Krishna. *Chants of a Lifetime: Searching for a Heart of Gold.* Carlsbad, CA: Hay House, 2011.

Forrest, Margot Silk, and Francine Shapiro. *EMDR: The Breakthrough Therapy for Overcoming Anxiety, Stress and Trauma.* New York: Basic Books, 1997.

Frederick, Ann, and Peter Levine. *Waking the Tiger: Healing Trauma—The Innate Capacity to Transform Overwhelming Experiences.* Berkeley, CA: North Atlantic Books, 1997.

Gerstein, Mordicai. *The Mountains of Tibet.* New York: HarperCollins, 1989.

Hafiz, and Daniel Ladinsky. *The Gift—Poems by Hafiz, the Great Sufi Master.* New York: Penguin Compass, 1999.

Hanh, Thich Nhat. *Taming the Tiger Within: Meditations on Transforming Difficult Emotions.* New York: Riverhead Trade, 2005.

———. *No Death, No Fear: Comforting Wisdom for Life.* New York: Riverhead, 2003.

Hoffman, Yoel. *Japanese Death Poems: Written by Zen Monks and Haiku Poets on the Verge of Death.* Rutland, VT: Tuttle, 1998.

Jacobson, Simon. *Toward a Meaningful Life, New Edition: The Wisdom of the Rebbe Menachem Mendel Schneerson.* New York: Harper Paperbacks, 2004.

Kaplan, Aryeh. *Jewish Meditation: A Practical Guide.* New York: Schocken, 1995.

———. *Outpouring of the Soul: Rabbi Nachman's Path in Meditation.* Jerusalem: Breslov Research Institute, 1980.

Kornfield, Jack. *Meditation for Beginners.* Louisville, CO: Sounds True, 2008.

———. *A Path with Heart: A Guide Through the Perils and Promises of a Spiritual Life.* New York: Bantam, 1993.

Liskin, Jack. *Moving Medicine: The Life and Work of Milton Trager, M.D.* Barrytown, NY: Station Hill Press, 1996.

Naparstek, Belleruth. *Invisible Heroes: Survivors of Trauma and How They Heal.* New York: Bantam, 2005.

Newberg, Andrew, and Mark Waldman. *How God Changes Your Brain: Breakthrough Findings from a Leading Neuroscientist.* New York: Ballantine Books, 2010.

———. *Born to Believe: God, Science, and the Origin of Ordinary and Extraordinary Beliefs.* New York: Free Press, 2007.

———. *Why We Believe What We Believe: Uncovering Our Biological Need for Meaning, Spirituality and Truth.* New York: Free Press, 2006.

Parnell. Laurel. *Transforming Trauma: EMDR: The Revolutionary New Therapy for Freeing the Mind, Clearing the Body, and Opening the Heart.* New York: Norton, 1998.

Ricard, Matthieu. *Why Meditate: Working with Thoughts and Emotions.* Translated by Sherab Chodzin Kohn. Carlsbad, CA: Hay House, 2010.

Rinpoche, Yongey Mingyur, and Eric Swanson. *Joyful Wisdom: Embracing Change and Finding Freedom.* New York: Three Rivers Press, 2010.

———. *The Joy of Living: Unlocking the Secret and Science of Happiness.* New York: Three Rivers Press, 2008.

Salzberg, Sharon. *Real Happiness.* New York: Workman Publishing, 2011.

———. *Faith: Trusting Your Own Deepest Experience.* New York: Riverhead, 2003.

Sambhava, Padma, and Robert Thurman. *The Tibetan Book of the Dead (The Great Book of Natural Liberation Through Understanding in the Between).* New York: Bantam Books, 1993.

Scaer, Robert. *The Body Bears the Burden: Trauma, Dissociation, and Disease.* New York: Haworth Medical Press, 2007.

———. *The Trauma Spectrum: Hidden Wounds and Human Resiliency.* New York: Norton, 2005.

Thompson, Margaret. *Rebirth into Pure Land: A True Story of Birth, Death and Transformation.* Edited by Robert Sachs. San Luis Obispo, CA: Diamond Way Ayurveda, 1994.

Trungpa, Chögyam. *Smile at Fear: Awakening the True Heart of Bravery.* Boston: Shambhala, 2010.

Resources

Visit these websites to learn more and to find a practitioner near you:

"**EMDR** is an integrative psychotherapy approach based on the theory that much of psychopathology is due to traumatic experience or disturbing life events, resulting in the impairment of one's innate ability to process and integrate such experiences within the central nervous system." —**www.emdria.org**.

"Utilizing gentle, non-invasive, natural movements, the **Trager** Approach helps clients release deep-seated physical and mental patterns and facilitates deep relaxation, increased physical mobility, and mental clarity."—**www.trager.com.**

"**Somatic Experience Therapy** restores self-regulation, and returns a sense of aliveness, relaxation and wholeness to traumatized individuals who have had these precious gifts taken away."—**www.traumahealing.com**

About the Author

Priscilla Warner grew up in Providence, Rhode Island, and raised her two sons with her husband in Westchester County, New York. After working for many years as an advertising art director, she coauthored a *New York Times* bestseller, *The Faith Club*. Visit her at PriscillaWarnerBooks.com.

98633